CRUISE SHIP TALES AND NOTES, HAWAII, AND OTHER STORIES

THIS BOOK
HAS BEEN PRESENTED TO
THE
GOFF-NELSON MEMORIAL
LIBRARY
BY

MADELINE ROCKCASTLE

CRUISE SHIP TALES AND NOTES, HAWAII, AND OTHER STORIES

Gordon H. Hills

Copyright © 2002 by Gordon H. Hills.

Library of Congress Number:		2002090876
ISBN :	Hardcover	1-4010-4931-1
	Softcover	1-4010-4930-3

All rights reserved. No part of this book may be reproduced or transmitted in any form or by any means, electronic or mechanical, including photocopying, recording, or by any information storage and retrieval system, without permission in writing from the copyright owner.

This book was printed in the United States of America.

To order additional copies of this book, contact:
Xlibris Corporation
1-888-795-4274
www.Xlibris.com
Orders@Xlibris.com

CONTENTS

Acknowledgments 11

CRUISE SHIP TALES

Mrs. Hochstein's Cabin 15
(Mrs.) Janice Younger, Widow 19
Mystery Lady 24
The Realm of "Pockets" 27
The "JESSICA" 30
Mr and Mrs. Andor Monkowski (Betty) 36
The Chilean Archipelago, ... 40
The American Spirit of Tango 45
Clyde Ryder 51
1600 Teddy Bears 55

CRUISE SHIP NOTES

Reunion 61
Deadly Table for Eleven 65
Dining while Cruising 69
A Cove in Jamaica 75
Isla de San Andres 79
Chan-Chan and the Professor 81
The Cuzco Hot Pack 86
Punta Tombo Bus Breakdown 90
The Great Man 95
Ye Olde Ship Eastern Star 100

HAWAII

Welcome! 107
The Grumpy Lady of Mud Lane 110
Angry Bees 117
Jaimee's Eden 122
A Museum Manque 127
Waikoloa Heaven 132
The Errant Heir 141

OTHER STORIES

The Jaeger Place
   Part 1 145
The Jaeger Place
   Part 2 159
The Jaeger Place
   Part 3 168
The Genealogical Researcher 179
A Difficult Time 183
The Irrationale of Things 193
Hazard Evenson 202
Loessen Hall 208
Pickering's Journal 215
The Mystical Life 221
My Immortal Friend 228
The Truth may make You Angry 231
The Registry 268
Two Characters from the novel "The Crooked Way Home"
   1. Arthur 274
   2. The Captain 280
Any Regrets? 288
Good Works 295
Donna 302
The Ultimate Click 309
The Portrait 311
"Octave Lansing's Childhood Home" 318

Professor and Mrs. Thomas Bandy	325
On Speaking Up	331
Aunt Elsie Done Wrong	335
By "Gus" Van Ness	335
The Chasm, That Primordial Mud	344

For my son Aaron
and Mary Stuart, my sister

ACKNOWLEDGMENTS

The author is indebted to his wife, Anne, for her editorial help, and to Paul R. McCormick of Waimea, Hawaii for computer formatting of the manuscript. He also must make clear that any errors or other shortcomings in these writings are the author's responsibility alone.

CRUISE SHIP TALES

MRS. HOCHSTEIN'S CABIN

Charles Hochstein was the great, great grandson and heir to the Hochstein et Fils family jewelry business, prominently based in Basel, Switzerland. His father had established the company's American branch in New York around 1900, and it flourished. Hochstein specialized in very expensive and ostentatious jewelry designs, combining gemstones and diamonds within lavish gold settings. Charles had been able to work until a very advanced age, and had always doted on his wife, Marie Louise, all the sixty-six years of their marriage. She was fifteen years his junior. He was a loving and devoted husband, and she was more than well provided for. They had everything that money, prestige and business acumen could buy, with at least one house or luxurious apartment on every continent.

Mrs. Charles Hochstein had become outrageously spoiled, used to others waiting on her hand and foot, answering to her every need, wish and demand. This produced in her a certain peevish look, yet full of expectancy and trust, that her money could command respect and obedience from the staff of the grand hotels, the five star resorts, and exclusive golf and country clubs they visited, not to mention her own domestics in all their foreign pieds-a-terre.

Then, at age 98, the venerable Charles collapsed on the company's beautifully carpeted showroom floor in Paris. He hadn't worked in years, and this was intended as only a brief appearance to impress the staff, but it proved too much. His wife, though bereft of his constant companionship, inherited his unlimited wealth, which was said to approach two billion US dollars. A long list of special trusts and foundations had been set aside for her by Mr. Hochstein, so she had no other worries than to be served, and remain healthy. And she loved to be served, waited upon, and attended.

On the Eastern Star, her wizened 93-year-old self needed a cane and often the arm of a steward, waiter or maitre d' to move about, and even a wheelchair if the sea were acting up. Her large cabin was on the top deck, where the wealthiest and most prestigious passengers lounged before tinted picture windows that looked onto the unobstructed promenade deck. Despite her frailty she managed, with help from the crew, to attend many of the ship's functions. Unfortunately, she rarely gave tips, never seemed to be satisfied, and had a disagreeable demeanor no matter how well her demands were met. Things just never seemed to go right for her any more.

On one of our first day's at sea, it happened by chance that we shared lunch with her in the dining room. Even though we sat, the three of us, at a table for four in a far corner, it was almost impossible to understand what she said, the few times she spoke to us. My wife sat next to her and still had difficulty. She was always looking away, not at us. She seemed to be a pleasant enough grande dame, but that was before we heard all the scuttlebutt about her, of course. For my part, I had to give up any attempt at conversation, especially as the dining room began filling up and the noise level rose. Later we learned that she had the waiters, stewards and maitre d's at her beck and call. A mere nod or flick of her withered and bejeweled fingers could reel one of them in, and she'd have a complaint. Her chair needed to be moved closer to the table, her untouched glass of water needed replacing because it was no longer fresh, she wanted to see the menu a second time, or there was a draft and would they send someone to her cabin for a certain ivory, button-down sweater, laying over the back of her chair by the window?

She'd been on the Eastern Star several times, and the crew actually tried to avoid her, because at the end of each and every voyage she gave the absolutely minimum tip allowable for decorum's sake. She'd always protest that the service had been below par, and didn't warrant more. Among the passengers too, she had the reputation of being a tiresome old crone, overdressed and bent over, presumably by her jewels, always trying to catch one's eye so as to share another critical commentary on the ship's services. We didn't dine with her again, and steered clear.

* * *

But alone once again in her spacious stateroom, after the obsequious cabin steward had left and her jewelry had been put away, she'd don a lounging robe for an hour or two of sitting and watching the current movie on the ship's television. Then, before retiring, she'd take a small, lace-covered Koa wood box out of one of her boudoir drawers, sit down by the coffee table next to the great window, whose draperies had been drawn by the steward, and open the lid.

There were his letters, a lock of his hair, Mr. Hochstein's wedding ring, a large ring of keys to the Hochstein empire, and a cassette recording of his voice, left with his will. He'd been around seventy when he made the tape, and it was a joy for her to hear him again, alone with her in the cabin, taking care of her as always, and being so sweet about it.

"Hello, my dear. This is your Charles, speaking to you alone, dear Marie Louise. Wherever you are, think of me as being with you always, ma cherie. Never think of me as being gone away, because I'll always be there for you, as you know, no matter where you are..."

She looked across the room at a wall mirror as she listened, fitfully scrutinizing her still image. She could easily imagine him standing by her, and she smiled a little from the embarrassment of pretending like that.

"I want you to be happy and comfortable, and will leave every resource and convenience for you. Whatever problems you may have, contact Amos Potter at the New York branch and he'll take care of you."

Amos Potter had died six years ago, replaced by a young man she'd never met and would probably never meet. His name was Denver something, in Administration.

"Always insist on good service, my dear. We've paid for it and deserve it. We've always had the best, you and I, and you should complain straight away if it's not forthcoming."

And so on. For a half hour she sat there. She never listened to the end, when he said "Goodbye, my dear Marie Louise..." She knew just when to turn off the tape player, so as to feel him still with her, remembering him holding her close in bed even unto his very last night alive. He'd whisper little endearments as they fell asleep, both snoring lightly, their two meager figures making two narrow little mounds in the bedclothes, like shallow graves.

(MRS.)JANICE YOUNGER, WIDOW

One of our company at the table for eleven was a middle-aged woman who'd lost her husband only a year before our cruise. We learned the details about Janice later by talking with a mutual acquaintance, another passenger, an elderly lady who'd been on several cruises with her. If one cruises a lot, one will eventually meet the same people over and over. We met cruisers who'd not only been on as many as thirty or forty cruises, but who'd been a repeat passenger on the Eastern Star itself ten or fifteen times!

The Youngers, Richard and Janice, had been married twenty-five years. They lived the whole time in Seattle, where he became a successful attorney in torts. They never had any children, by choice, because they preferred the good life unencumbered. They belonged to the University Club downtown, and generously supported the arts. They were charter donors to the Seattle Repertory Theatre and the Seattle Symphony, as well as season ticket holders with the Seattle Seahawks. They loved Seattle, and took vacations locally on their 40' schooner, moored at Schilshole Bay, by exploring the inland waters from Olympia to Prince Rupert.

One morning just as he was leaving for the office, coat over one arm and bulging briefcase in the other, about to kiss Janice goodbye, Richard Younger collapsed on the floor by their unopened front door. He'd had a major stroke. When he awoke in the hospital, it was only to acknowledge Janice's presence, to look at her that way, because he was unable to speak. Then he passed into a vegetative state, and remained so for five months. He succumbed just before Thanksgiving Day.

Janice was devastated. They'd had such a wonderful life together and been inseparable. Best friends and lovers, never deviating from married bliss. They shared all their experiences together, including the legal conferences Richard attended, usually held in exotic locations like Hawaii, Lake Tahoe, or New Orleans. Their home reflected their common interests, as well as their individual avocations. The two of them had become one joined soul.

Janice was totally stunned and utterly challenged emotionally as to what to do next. They had no relatives near Seattle, so she decided to visit her favorite Aunt Claudine in Syracuse, New York. Her husband had died a generation earlier, and they'd not had any children either. They could commiserate and ruminate on such points. Both of them agreed, however, that children and especially grandchildren come in very handy in one's retirement years, and the leftover time of widowhood. And now Janice joined her aunt in that lonely way. Though Aunt Claudine had made up for her loneliness by becoming very active in civic and church affairs, she still came home to an empty house, save for two very friendly cats and an old English setter.

By the time she returned to Seattle, Janice had decided what to do. On the flight home, she skimmed through the airlines' in-flight magazine, crammed full of ads and travel promotions. One article caught her eye, however. It described a typical cruise ship experience. It sounded intriguing, not so much as a place to find romance or to travel and have fun, but to fill more basic needs. It was a way to avoid being alone at home, to be with the same people over the time of the cruise, and to be waited on hand and foot by the ship's crew. She wouldn't have to lift a finger, or hunt for company. It would all be right there on the ship.

When we first met her at table one evening, at that Deadly Table for Eleven, she seemed interested to get acquainted. We talked about life aboard the ship, our ports of call, and the shore excursions. Of average height, she was slightly overweight, and the expression on her face seemed rather fixed, if not frozen, at times. As we talked, my wife and I managed to learn that she was recently widowed, but no details about her husband or how she was managing were forthcoming. She was enthusiastic about cruise ships, however, and was anxious to explain why.

She went on cruises for the steady company, seeing the same people every day and night for the duration of the cruise. Paradoxically, she explained that it was also one way she could put down social roots; one met the same people on other cruises. She preferred the longer cruises on smaller cruise ships, like the Eastern Star. There was enough to do, and not so many people that one couldn't get to know a number of them. At the table of eleven, where, because of the five (including Janice) who refused to budge from their accustomed seating, we were discouraged from sitting at different places, or rotate in order to get to know everyone at the table better. She always sat at the same place every night, as did two other singles and a couple, thus locking the table into a gridlock of chronic boredom after a month had gone by. But for Janice it was a surety, and she could count on those four others being there, all of whom sat next to or across from her, and to be dependable, superficial and non-intrusive company. The elderly couple were old enough to be her parents, a crotchety old woman served as an aunt, and a pleasant widower gentleman never flirted with her and minded his own business. So everyone in that stick-in-the-mud clique felt comfortable and secure. When any of the rest of us mildly complained about their fixed seating attitude, Janice would later defend the situation to us, because she depended on this arrangement. That way she avoided the embarrassment of going through supper with someone new every time, as happens in open seating. No one would pry into her life, or ask her how she was feeling that day.

But as we ran into her regularly around the ship and got to know her a little more, we realized that she often referred to herself using "we," and talked as if Richard were still alive and with her. She would reminisce about things they'd done together, and what a full life they had, as if it were still going on. Not that we weren't sensitive to how profoundly the loss of her husband was affecting her, and we certainly appreciated her desire to keep his memory and love alive. No one could fault her for that. On the contrary, it made us poignantly aware how much she missed him.

So any inquiry about her deceased husband was awkward and untoward, and we stopped showing any interest or concern of that kind. But how else could we get further acquainted? We had to wait until we met her elderly woman friend. And that's one of the conundrums of socializing aboard cruise ships. One rarely finds close friendships that might continue after the cruise is finished. That's not why retired and older people go on cruises. It's to be taken care of while 'traveling' in comfort. One can forget about the hassles and boredom of a home life that has become fixed, repetitive, and uneventful, or relatives who have been too persistent and tiring.

*   *   *

Meanwhile, Janice's cabin life held close the clinging ghost of her husband, Richard. His death had been slow and relentless, and all the time he never spoke a word to her. Despite this gradual preparation for his passing, his physical leaving of her behind, she was never able to accept what fate had dealt her. She didn't understand it and couldn't face it. At the end she seemed mercifully benumbed by his death, but beneath the numbness lay a profound sadness and the beginnings of a prolonged mourning.

My wife and I wished we could give her some solace and sincere understanding (for we'd lost loved ones, too), but that's precisely what she did not want. She wanted, instead, to continue enjoying life the way she'd chosen, keeping the gnawing facts and merciless truth at bay, with her husband's psychic and emotional presence less than an arm's length away to keep her company. We resigned ourselves to being casually and superficially acquainted with her, for the little distance that takes one in any relationship, but no more than that.

MYSTERY LADY

From the shoreline cafes of Igoumenitsa on Corfou, off Greece's Adriatic Coast, to the most exciting and fashionable night clubs of Athens, Rosanna Antonopoulos was famed for her vocal artistry. Her voice was a throaty alto, with a quickened tremulo, and she sang in at least a dozen languages. Unfortunately, at age forty she contracted throat cancer, and could no longer sing. Her career literally ended overnight. One day she checked into an Athens hospital, the next morning it was over. After recovery from surgery and radiation a couple of years later, she could hardly talk, let along sing a note. Then her husband died, seemingly from the shock of finding himself having lost a diva and gained a mute for a wife.

When her fans and adoring public learned of her fate, their hearts went out to her and sales of her recordings soared. Funds were raised to erect a statue in Athens, in one of the parks, in her honor. This was done, and she was left to herself. Or so it might appear. As it happened, everywhere she went, fans recognized her and came to her. It was the same on the Eastern Star, passage on which being always at her disposal, a gift of the owner of the Regal Hellas Line.

She sat alone in the dining room for most of the two months of the cruise. Red hair puffed and frizzy, heavily made-up eyes, simple gowns, and always a gracious smile. The waiters doted on her, and the strolling musicians at the evening suppers, a violinist and accordionist, knew her and serenaded her before everyone else each night, and she loved it. She did not seem lonely at all. Eventually, later in the cruise, she was to be seen at other tables, presumably as an honored guest, but most evenings she sat alone, at a corner table in the center against a wall. When she strolled the deck, she was rarely alone, however. Someone, a gentleman or lady friend, always accompanied her. Her smile was always ready, yet she remained reserved and distinguished, a mysterious Presence, a Greek Celebrity. Later she met and mixed with other passengers more readily, usually the veteran travelers, probably for amusement. Possibly she knew some of them from other cruises on the Eastern Star. A couple of times we saw her marching grandly on the promenade deck with a brace of smiling passengers, arm in arm, as if finally in her element. We were impressed by her vitality and graciousness.

Who was, or had been her audience, long ago? And what kind of life did she have now? In fact, she'd become a national treasure, a 'legend in her own time.' Everywhere she went throughout Greece, she was welcomed, honored and feted. Men and women alike kissed her hand or her garment. Everyone played her recorded voice, though as far as singing was concerned she'd been silenced.

Without her husband, time alone in her cabin was lonely, filled only with memories and recordings. She would not marry again, though she had countless suitors. Her apartment in Athens was full of photos of him, and the two of them together, as well as many show photos of herself, either in performance, or alongside celebrities from all over the world. She had a maid, and together they'd sit on her beautiful modern furniture as Rosanna let the phonograph play on and on, its spindle loaded with as many of her recordings as could fit. Sometimes she'd lip-sync along, and on those occasions her eyes filled with tears and the maid would leave the room, because in her embarrassment and helplessness she felt that there was no way she could give sufficient solace to replace such a magnificent career and voice; it was a double-void for the Mrs. alone to endure, the loss of both Mr. Antonopoulos, her loving husband and most adoring fan, and her legendary career.

For the remaining years of her life she would travel regularly on the Eastern Star, which seemed like a private yacht for her, then come home to her silent apartment, silent until she spoke to the maid and they gathered in her sitting room to listen to her sing again. After that there would be much fan mail to answer, and photos to autograph. And after all that, at the end of each day, she'd be alone to relive everything imaginable from that rich past, clutching them with such emotion as if her husband were still with her, her voice filled the music halls, and the fans roared nightly beneath her balcony, calling out her name, and her smiling husband kept his arm around her.

THE REALM OF "POCKETS"

Who would have thought they were married, Paula and Paul Reinhardt, this huge, outgoing, fiftiesh woman in bold print dresses and this quiet, musing, sixtiesh man, slightly taller and handsomely built, with receding hair and a gray moustache, who was always greeting us and introducing one of his many finger puppets. Their life at home would seem to be absurd: he marshaling and communicating through his Lilliputian stand-ins, she the matriarchal lead for his Gulliver. He aimed his wit and humor at everyone except her, everyone save her, because she was his mother-figure. So had both their mothers been dominant, so had both their fathers been dominated. They fit each other perfectly.

Paul was a closet entertainer and natural raconteur. Paula bossed him around while he played the meek spouse, but his humor lay in the wings, ready to step out and get you laughing. He celebrated the desires and exploits of his finger puppets, especially one "Pockets," made of rough cowhide. Then Pockets became lost, and Paul started going around asking other passengers and the crew if they'd seen him. He even put a notice up on the ship's bulletin board, later concluding that Pockets must have gone out with the laundry, and spent days commiserating with everyone about it.

As the cruise continued, I began wondering about Paul's public facade of bonhomie, and his constant need to fraternize with other passengers, perfect strangers like myself, and his ease at gaining our good will. He seemed to be garnering it all in order to forestall failure, or to avoid facing a life in retirement that had little meaning for him beyond pleasantries and make-believe. He always trailed behind Paula, that large ample woman full of open confidence, fully at ease with herself, and I had visions of him being the general at the head of an army of finger puppets! If only he had forty hands instead of two! In their cabin, he had to keep them in a ditty bag, because Paula said they needed all available space, i.e. she needed it.

Paul's good will was contagious, and any time I spotted the two of them I found myself hoping he'd come speak to me, with or without his wife, though I knew he was far more likely to come by and chat if alone than with her, whose loud attire and sheer bulk immediately dominated any space she entered. In such instances, he'd be dutifully at her side or just behind, tending and abetting her, opening the doors and interjecting his Gulliver's wit.

I also wondered how they happened to meet, and how they got along in private. This union of a retired man with a much younger woman turned out to be that of a seasoned widower with a virginal spouse, and on very different grounds than those a young couple would marry. Here they were, she never having married before and he on his second, but so differently. His first marriage had been glorious. They'd been perfectly matched, as if brother and sister, a wonderful couple that everyone wanted to invite to parties. But they'd had only one child, and he was killed in the Vietnam War. Paul had known the joys and benefits of married bliss, but had lost both his wife and son. And Paula had finally decided she didn't hate men after all; in fact she came to enjoy their attentions and 'alien' ways, as long as she could keep them under control. Thus theirs was a marriage offering mutual refuge! He'd found an ample women who could give him anything either a mother or wife could, and she'd found a mature and settled gentleman who could give her anything she might want from a father or husband, and on her own terms.

Thus they'd achieved a workable balance. Whatever she lacked in finesse, wit and savoir faire, she more than made up for with womanly power and expressiveness. She was also Gulliver's wife to his finger puppets. And whatever Paul might lack in machismo or derring-do, he more than compensated for with his charm, his ease with others in whatever social milieu they might find themselves, and his unconditional affection for her.

As for "Pockets," he may never have turned up, but we suspect he eventually was found, somewhere. Wherever he could have ended up, like with one of the ship's crew, we hope he will continue to sail with the Eastern Star. On the other hand, there is a strong probability that Paul or Paula found "Pockets" when they were packing to leave the ship, or while they were unpacking at home. And Paul would have an explanation.

"Sure, I got him. He never intended . . . (smiling) Oh, no, he's not that kind! (looks around, lowers his voice) You see, "Pockets" is the kind of guy who just doesn't run out on you like that. No! Well, yes . . . (starts laughing with our smiles, then turns mock serious) I wouldn't let him leave. We'd talk it over, he'd explain why he disappeared, I'd be magnanimous about it, and that's all. End of story. That's why I always keep him here (pats his shirt pocket), so he's ready to see people any time. He loves to do that, as you know (smiles broadly). Paula keeps hiding him on me, but I always figure out where he is. That's what makes life interesting, things like that. What? No, she doesn't mind, not at all. In fact, she's glad I've got my puppets. Keeps me off the street, and gives me something to do. There's only so much she and I can talk about (smiles slyly, looking around again), and "Pockets" and the others fill in the rest. Sure! Why not?! Glad to see you! 'Bye!"

THE "JESSICA"

As an aspiring writer, or, I should say, a writer and literary person, an intellectual of the expatriate stripe, I'd agreed to go on the cruise only if I might take my old laptop and the draft of a novel I was working on. We had reserved an ample cabin, because we wanted it to be our home away from home during those two months of circumnavigating South America. My wife had interests similar to mine, reading and watching foreign films and so on, and we agreed to select one on the port side, one deck above the waterline, the better to see the coast whenever we approached a port. It had its own bath and a movie monitor or internal television, two beds, upholstered chairs, a sofa and table, plenty of closet space and three portholes.

So between meals, ports of call, shore excursions, and meals in the dining room or the café up by the swimming pool, we spent a lot of time in our cabin. With the help of a ship's electrician, I got my laptop going. Just before our departure, months before actually, I'd decided to expand the portion of the novel that has the protagonist, a son seeking out the past of his deceased and alienated biological father, leaving his family farm in Central New York and heading out to the West Coast, where he was last known to have lived. I wanted him taken by a yachtsman uncle up the Great Lakes by sailboat, using a large ketch left to the boy by his father, who had spent his remaining life in a maritime career.

Unfortunately, I knew little about sailing the Great Lakes, let alone going from one end to the other, though I've had other kinds of sailing experience. On the cruise, it occurred to me that there might be, among the 600 passengers, most of them retired, a few who had done such sailing. I put up a notice on the bulletin board outside the Main Lounge, and immediately had two replies. One had done much sailing on Lake Superior, and the other had gone from the Detroit area through Lake Huron and Superior to Isle Royale. As for Lakes Ontario and Erie, I had to use other, second-hand accounts.

It turned out that the gentleman who'd sailed Lake Superior, John Ownley, was the most informative and interesting source, because the other man had only traveled on a big power cruiser, which didn't interest me. John and Jessica Ownley had done a lot of sailing, and at least John was anxious to share what he knew. Although we met several times together, the three of us, on the forward lounging deck outside a bar, after ten minutes his wife Jessica would leave John and me alone. They were a curious pair, even at first glance. John was stocky, with a thin gray beard and balding pate. He walked slightly stooped, and appeared to be older and worn out, compared to his trim wife, who was also taller than him. She walked with a relaxed stride, and had a statuesque, upright figure. She was always stylishly dressed, quite handsome in fact, whereas John's clothes looked a little dumpy no matter what he wore. I wondered how the two of them ever got together.

John had sailed every nook and cranny, every shore-hugging and cross-lake route I could come up with. I'd brought a large scale map of the lakes along with me, and was delighted to learn that he actually had a chart and cruising guide for Superior right with him on the ship. Once Jessica left, I'd order beer for the two of us and the reminiscences began. I shouldn't dismiss her so summarily, however, because she, in her 10-15 minutes with us, always contributed some local knowledge of places, and of John navigating around them, that only a wife could come up with. Her comments, delivered deadpan through the best sunglasses and lips that were perfectly defined by lipstick the hue of sweetheart roses, served to put John in his place in their childless marriage of 37 years, in which she seemed to have flourished, possibly at his expense, literally, figuratively and psychologically. She could still have been a model in catalogs of clothing for 'mature' women of sophisticated taste.

She had been a debutante out of Grosse Pointe, he a chemist at Dow, and a prominent one. She was raised on horses, the decks of yachts, country club lawns, and at cotillion balls. As a prospective bride, she was a plum. But with no children and years of wifely socializing, she was now hollow and cool, a former debutante with no place to go. He was raised by a stern father, who was a chemical engineer, to follow in his footsteps, which he had done. Yet the upshot of their marriage was that she was superior class stuff to his working class ways. With company on shore, she was the one, he being in her shadow.

But on board their 32' sloop, the "Jessica," John told me, he was Captain and Navigator, she the second mate, galley cook and bottle washer, he added, chuckling. The glint in his eye told me he probably enjoyed getting her on the sloop every chance he could, as soon as the lake was free of ice. It may have been the only way his self-esteem could recuperate. The Ownleys were one of those couples in which one spouse seems to flourish while the other struggles to keep up normal appearances.

Jess, as he referred to her, was a good cruiser on the Eastern Star, going to movies and lectures, walking the perimeter promenade deck, playing cards, patronizing the beauty salon, and signing up for all the shore excursions. Although John went on about half the excursions with her, most of the time he holed up in their cabin, which was better than ours, taking naps or reading. I wondered if having to accompany her in so many ship activities was depressing for him. They made an incongruous couple, he showing and feeling his age, she exuding a womanly energy and attractiveness that just wouldn't stop. Every time we saw them together, my wife and I, we winced, the difference between them was so evident.

I looked forward to my bull sessions with John, relaxing and talking sailing while nursing good foreign beer under an umbrella on the sunny deck, the blue sea all around. Jessica's husband then became another person, smiling and waving his arms about, joking and leaning forward, laughing joyfully at points of humor in the stories he told, solely for my benefit. He proved to be quite a performer away from her. Actually, come to think of it, he talked more about his sloop "Jessica" than about his wife. No wonder we got on so well. He was always waiting for me, well before the appointed time of 3PM.

Though I learned a great deal about sailing on Lake Superior, that largest and coldest of the Great Lakes, it was John and his relationship to others that most intrigued me, and most attached me to our afternoon talks. These included Jess, the sloop, our fellow passengers, his old job, and the world at large, in general and in particular. He was bored by most passengers he'd encountered, his old job was a 9-5, white collar beast that almost turned him into a zombie despite several notable product discoveries, the world was a foreign land rather than any kind of 'oyster' to be plucked for eating, and his wife, he confided one day, after we'd retired to the inside bar when it became too cool and windy outside, had been eating him alive for 37 years.

So it was "Jessica," his sloop, that had kept them afloat, in more ways than one. For John Ownley, that sloop had become his be all and end all of existence. He showed me old style photo albums, black in color with black cord holding them together, full of black and white snapshots from the '40s with serrated white borders and later color photos, plus some 8x10 enlargements of their life aboard "Jessica" each summer. It was kept moored in the Apostle Islands, to the south of their home in Moose Creek, Wisconsin. There was a section for each year, and I realized that most of the photos lacked his image. I think he joined his wife and his sloop into a sort of dual personality, in order to strive for a balance in his life. He couldn't match his wife away from the boat, whenever they were on land. He really couldn't, and when he didn't feel inferior to her, he was suppressing a lot of anger. But when aboard "Jessica," he was in charge of both of them. The sloop and John equaled his wife, or better, once the mooring lines were cast off. She was at his bidding, at his mercy, and at his side, cooking his meals, keeping the galley stocked, swabbing the decks, polishing the bright work and working the lines. With this the balance sheet between them was reconciled. He could live with her yet another year.

Since his retirement, she'd begun to insist on more travel each year, but he held firm: they'd launch "Jessica" for another summer's yachting. The winters, like this one, were another matter; she got her way for that season. Thus their marriage continued; cruises and other travel winters, back to the "Jessica" summers.

"I've had to maintain that balance," he emphasized, toward the end of our last session together, "Otherwise I'd be a candidate for the looney bin, or worse."

Jess came out and strolled over to our table. "Have you learned all about sailing on the lakes yet?" she asked me. I couldn't follow her eyes, due to her sunglasses, but I assumed, from her tone of voice, that they weren't only directed at me.

"John, we have to dress for dinner. Besides, it's getting cold. How can you stay out here? Are you through?"

"We've had a good talk. John has a lot to share," I weakly added, impulsively providing cover for John. She was standing just behind him, to one side. John sat there, the hard lines in his grim smile speaking volumes, his gaze fixed on me.

"I should go too," I said, straightening up and closing my notebook. And with that move John abruptly stood up and walked away behind his wife. I couldn't wait to rejoin my own beloved, who I knew was reading or napping in our excellent cabin.

MR AND MRS. ANDOR MONKOWSKI (BETTY)

We wondered at the average age of the passengers on the Eastern Star. We were told it was over 70. Some were in their eighties and very frail, needing help at every turn, while others just as old seemed hardy, indefatigable and constantly socializing. Where did they get the energy and good health? On one shore excursion we paired up with such a couple. He was 85, yet so healthy and spirited that I, almost twenty years younger, was astonished, and, I must say, jealous as well as envious. How had they managed to stay so youthful, or been lucky enough to avoid all the afflictions, accidents, infirmities and diseases of old age? Incredible.

Another couple, an opposite version of the first, frail and doddering, tried to be just as relentlessly active, but seemed to be falling apart from the exertion to accomplish the most ordinary things, like walking into the Main Lounge after dinner, or making their way down stairs and along corridors to their cabin. It was clear they were stretching themselves to the limit in enduring all the demands of our two-month cruise, which included twenty-two shore excursions. Why did they keep at the struggle to live like the rest of us at their advanced age when they needed help so often, sometimes just to remain standing in a cathedral, or to keep up with the rest of us as we'd slowly walk cobbled streets in some colorful coastal city.

At the start of each shore excursion, when everyone was waiting in the Main Lounge, or had already made their way to the deck from which we'd debark, there they'd be, pale and gaunt, as likely to lose their balance as take a step, he leaning on his cane, she clinging to his other arm. You could tell he was a tough old guy, and would never give up. His wife, a pleasant woman, would always put on the best face she could muster, aided by cosmetics, which always made her eyes large, open and overly rounded, a human owl. They would keep going until they dropped, and often ended a city excursion early by taking a taxi back to the ship. Persevering in their hobbled walks into foreign cities, fending off the beggars and walking vendors who thrust hats and shawls and jewelry into their faces, and during which they saw little beyond the trial of keeping up with the rest, we had to wonder why they tortured themselves needlessly this way. Why didn't they stay home and quietly vegetate their Golden Years away? Perhaps they had nothing back home to return to, and nothing left in their laps with which to occupy themselves.

Then we heard the reason, as passed on to us in a moment of laxity by a male passenger who'd shared several cruises with them. One late evening I was restless, quietly dressed so as not to wake my wife, and went topside. On the main deck I found some people in the bar, and wandered in. I sat down next to an elderly gentleman. I also noticed our doddering couple seated at a corner table, sipping something that looked like a coke drink. Between sips they were holding hands as if they were holding on to life support itself, as I fancied it. I commented to my bar mate that the wife, Betty Monkowski, had collapsed or fallen at the entrance to the Main Lounge earlier that day. I wondered aloud why they kept going on the shore excursions; they never seemed to complete them, and needed constant assistance from the crew, tour guides, or other passengers.

"I'll tell you why," he said. "They're determined not to die at home. It's as simple as that. Out here they're well taken care of, and don't have to cook or do laundry or get themselves somewhere by themselves. It's all right here. One or the other is going to kick the bucket on one of these cruises, then the other can give up. They've been on over fifty of them, y'know. Father Jack (the ship's Chaplain) says that, on average, somebody dies every thirty days on cruises. And that's the average. We've had more than our share on this one."

He was right. There had been two deaths already in forty days, and another man who'd collapsed and been taken to the hospital in Punta Arenas had either died or been shipped back home with his wife. It was hard to get exact information, because naturally the ship and cruise line kept such untoward news quiet.

"It's funny,", my companion continued. "When you get over 80 or 85 you either shrink into yourself and stay home, or you'd just as soon travel abroad and buy the farm somewhere else. Of course, you've got to have the money and tolerable health, but aside from that . . . I think you reach a point, as an oldster, when you just don't give a damn any more what anybody thinks! You just go with your heart's desire. Maybe your kids are all grown up, or maybe they've started to die off before you, Lord save us from that. Maybe there aren't any grandchildren, or they're too far away, and there's just the two of you sitting home wondering what's going to happen next, what's going to go wrong . . . You know what I mean?" I nodded.

"So you have lots of money sitting around, and you find out about these cruises. So you go out on one cruise after another, and it doesn't matter any more. You don't have to worry. Whatever the roll of the dice, you're doing something. Anything is better than nothing, or just waiting." He paused, handling his empty glass and glancing over at the corner.

"I have to hand it to them,' he said flatly. "They got their priorities right. I wish them well. Whatever happens, they're going on love alone, I'm sure. I wish them well. If I'm ever around when one of them keels over, no matter where we are, it will be my honor to help comfort them and carry them away."

When we turned to look again, they were gone. It was nearly 2AM. So they were burning the candle at both ends too, and with another strenuous shore excursion scheduled first thing in the morning, after we made port and tied up at dockside in Salvador da Bahia. As I came down the stairway and reached my deck, I glanced down the corridor forward where I knew their cabin was located. There they were, tottering along, arm in arm, Mister bracing himself against the movement of the ship, she moving in step with him. It almost resembled a dance, they way they moved. I think it was a dance, and I hoped that my wife and I would be able to do it, too, at their age.

THE CHILEAN ARCHIPELAGO,
by Jeb and Carol Parker

We were finally experiencing it. Our venerable old cruise ship was circumnavigating South America, and we were ready to walk through those ancient Inca ruins, dance the tango in Buenos Aires, lie on the beaches in Rio and celebrate Mardi Gras in Trinidad! Leaving Fort Lauderdale far behind and heading south, we stopped at the Columbian island of San Andres, and were surprised at the poverty. Then we went through the complicated Panama Canal, an obvious marvel of engineering, reached the Pacific Ocean and turned south.

First we were let off in Peru, where we visited the ancient palace ruins of Chan Chan and the Gold Museum in Lima, then flew to serene Cuzco and took that breathtaking train ride down the Urubamba Valley to Machu Picchu, trekking all over that spectacular site. Next we visited Chile. Thin as a snake and barely clinging to South America's west coast; it took a week for our ship to go from the top to bottom of it, as seen on a map. We'd seen the ruins of ancient coastal civilizations on the dry deserts of the northern coast, with little fertile valleys between heavily eroded hills, Inca sites and various museums, but one detail intrigued us in Chile: all through the country stray dogs were treated and cared for like pets, almost like the sacred cattle of India! Chile was like Peru in some ways, a country of a few large, crowded cities and a desolate countryside, except in the verdant little coastal valleys with farms and the almost empty mountain country, washed by moisture-laden clouds off the Pacific and its cold Humboldt current.

But below Santiago, the capital and largest city situated much farther south, our world began to change. The Eastern Star turned inside to begin following the Chilean Archipelago down, down, down south, and from Puerto Montt we slowly entered winter, yet it was the southern hemisphere's summer! It was cloudy all the time and getting cooler. As we descended the 1200 winding water miles from Puerto Montt to Ushuaia and Cape Horn, we found an unoccupied land, half drowned.

Smooth rocky hills covered with bushes were on every side, sometimes close, sometimes far off, frequently interrupted by glaciers. On the eastern horizon, we could occasionally see distant mountains brightly shining with snow. The water of the channels was calm, our passage smooth. Two or three times we were told our ship came within 10 or 12 feet of the bottom. At such times we moved ever so slowly, crawling ever so carefully, and if there'd been a window and floodlight on the bottom of the hull, we could have easily seen the rocks as well as any fish underneath, in these clear waters. We were following a narrow inside passage, twisting and turning and extremely shallow in places, where our ship's speed was 'dead slow.'

Everyone put on winter clothes, because to stay out on deck very long required it. Not exactly a sunny beach or the bright, balmy days we'd had on the Caribbean! After brief visits on deck to see the strange, inhospitable landscape around us, huddled on deck chairs and covered with blankets, we'd return to our cabin to read or listen to classical music on our portable CD player. We weren't much for the usual shipboard activities.

Then in the middle of one night, as the old ship continued its tortuous way south, I had a disturbing dream; at least I think it was a dream. I was walking the promenade deck, it was nighttime, and as usual all the decks and superstructure were illuminated by the ship's lighting. In fact I was so blinded by all the lights that I couldn't see the sullen uninhabited rock hills moving past on either side. Nothing. Just darkness. I looked over the rail; there was the water going past, and the slight bow wash of the ship turning the water a hissing white for a few moments. I had the odd sensation that we were far at sea, it was very cloudy, and no one had any idea where we were, or where we were going. Our slower cruising speed only underlined this feeling of disorientation.

I walked all the corridors and visited all the common rooms inside and below, but saw no one. I went up and down the forward and aft stairwells, stepped into the library, sat in the main lounge with its two hundred upholstered chairs oriented toward the little center dance floor and band stage, but I was alone, absolutely alone. And everywhere the lighting was on, waiting and ready. At three o'clock in the morning! I began imagining that I was alone on the ship, its only passenger, yet having no control over the ship's passage or destination, which was true, of course. I was only a passenger who'd paid thousands of dollars for this experience, being carried through the Stygian darkness toward stormy Cape Horn and Antarctica, the South Pole and the bottom of Planet Earth.

In truth, I began feeling like I was on the bottom, the bottom of a very deep stone well, and slowly sinking lower! Was the southern end of the continent subsiding into dark chaos, a watery Never-Never Land? It was a hallucination, a fear, and a virtual certainty, made more palpable by the perpetual drone of the ship's power plant below, the suffocating warmth of the ship's interior, the cold damp air surrounding me when on deck, and the black silence out there, as far as I could sense. I became afraid to return inside, to descend three decks to our dark cabin, located just above the waterline, like we were just floating above the surface of the dark sea, and the only saving thought was that I'd be with my wife, who was undoubtedly sleeping soundly as usual. I was the restless one, always waking and going topside for no reason in the middle of the night. I pushed in a heavy side door from the promenade deck and went to the elevators. I entered and pushed the letter for our deck. I was slowly lowered, lower and lower, and with terror I realized I was going down faster and faster! A sucking sound and whoosh of air deafened my ears! Had the elevator cable broken and I was hurtling down through the bottom of the ship, into the cold darkness of these low latitude waters?! I clung to the railing on the side of the elevator and closed my eyes, gritting my teeth, moaning with despair . . .

I awoke with a violent start, sitting upright.

"What on earth were you dreaming, dear? You made such a noise I thought you had a stroke or something?!"

Carol was sitting up in her bunk with her bedside light on, quietly reading. She often did that in the middle of the night, if she couldn't sleep.

"No . . . I don't know, I just imagined . . . it wasn't a pleasant dream. All I can say is . . . am I'm glad to see you!"

"Well," she said, smiling and putting down her book. "C'mon over and stay with me for a while. I've gotten chilled for some reason. We need to get more sleep because we'll be in Ushuaia tomorrow, and we're signed up for the shore excursion."

When she said she was chilled, it briefly revived the now fading memory of my dream. I eagerly joined her and we merged our warmth into a few more hours of sleep. But as I lay there, slipping away, I had difficulty ridding myself of those visions and sensations in the dream, of being forever alone, the uninhabited darkness, and the black, rockbound cold of the night out there, beyond the old ship's protective lighting, that seemed to reflect humanity's immemorial fear of the dark and the unknown.

THE AMERICAN SPIRIT OF TANGO

Lewis Leahy was a very successful regional sales manager for the manufacturer of a brand name power tools company. After several years of working for them, he believed he was worth a lot more, and put out feelers to another such firm. He received a strong invitation, with generous incentives, so he decided to switch over. He resigned his old job. And since he and his wife Jan would now have to move across the country to the East Coast, he allowed for a three months' break. This would give them time for packing and moving to the nice home the new company found for them, and for a vacation. And Jan and Lew's tenth wedding anniversary was coming up.

Lew was a tall, good-looking man with dark hair. He wasn't overweight, didn't need eyeglasses, and tried to stay fit. At the old location he played tennis with Jan three times a week at the company spa and tennis club. She was six inches shorter, and had no need to diet. She kept her long brown hair in a natural looking bouffant, which looked cute on her. She let it down every night. They both looked forward to a long, lazy South American cruise.

It was on short notice, but they were able to book an inside cabin aft, on one of the middle decks, above the crews quarters and well forward of the engine room. Still, they could feel the constant roar, especially at night. There was no porthole, and they had separate single beds; they would have to make do. Not exactly the accommodations they'd hoped for, but this cruise, circumnavigating South America, had been a long deferred dream of Jan's, and so here they were. They figured they wouldn't be spending much time in the cabin anyway, because they anticipated partying, dancing, strolling the decks, and enjoying the floor shows. Following others' lead, as soon as the crew brought their luggage down to their cabin, which took a while, they went to the dining room to reserve a table for evening meals. (Breakfasts and lunches were open seating everywhere, whether in the dining room or the café by the swimming pool.) Unfortunately, there was little choice by the time they reached the maitre d' at the end of a long line. As first time cruisers, they weren't aware that one made one's table reservations before tending to one's luggage! They ended up alone at a table for four.

They soon discovered that their cabin left much to be desired as well. The toilet had an absolutely violent flush, and scalding hot water could suddenly gush into your tub or shower. At least they didn't have the problems of others, on this old ship, which included leaky plumbing and even burst pipes up forward, and the aft elevator that broke down for a while. They didn't mind the shuddering and noise from the engines, at least not in the daytime, but at night, especially when they were restless and couldn't sleep, it could be deafening. They both remarked on it. Also, their air conditioning wasn't dependable, and would wake them some nights with a suffocating warmth; they'd endure the rest of the night while sweating and sleeping nude. They tried complaining, and asking for another cabin, but nothing was done. "Everything is full," they were told. Yet they also heard that a few cabins were always kept open.

Shore excursions were hurried and crowded, and the spiels of bus tour guides in Trujillo, Lima, Santiago and Punta Arenas, etc., became fearsomely similar and boring. The buses themselves, of course, modern and air-conditioned, with tinted windows that couldn't be opened, insulated the cruisers from the local population. And when they were able to come down onto the street, for the most part they were herded here and there and told to stay close, so as not to be left behind or robbed.

After meandering down the Chilean Archipelago and rounding Cape Horn, they entered the broad River Platte to visit Montevideo and Buenos Aires. Montevideo had beautiful and endless beaches, but there was no time to stop and enjoy them. Instead, they had a prolonged and extensive visit to the Parliament Building, of all places! On to Buenos Aires, 134 miles away. The channel across the great brown 'river,' which seemed more like a sea, was narrow and dredged, marked by buoys. A little over halfway across, the Eastern Star developed an engine problem. Anchors were immediately dropped, but she drifted a little off the channel before they held. Other ships, boats and barges had to get by her as best they could, passing perilously close, so close that the Star's bridge could holler to some, using an electronic megaphone.

The whole thing was disorienting to the Leahys. The current and tide pulled and pushed their ship this way and that, back and forth. At last a huge tugboat came and towed her into the harbor of Buenos Aires. As they were being tied up to a pier, the Captain announced to a gathering of all passengers in the main lounge that the Eastern Star would be under repair for a week in Buenos Aires. Everyone groaned and complained, and many were angry. But there was no question of continuing because crucial repairs were needed on one of the two giant turbine engines. The Greek Line would arrange free travel home and refunds for anyone having to return on time, for whatever reason, with discounts being offered for future cruises. Only about 10% of the passengers left the ship because most of them were retirees, who don't have to get back to work! And after all, to be 'stranded' in the beautiful, cosmopolitan city of Buenos Aires for a week wasn't exactly the worst of fates for a cruiser. It was certainly difficult for the Captain and cruise staff to reschedule the remaining ports of call and shore excursions for a week later, but there was plenty of time to work on it.

Lew and Jan couldn't get off the old ship fast enough. They declined immediate air travel home, because they wanted to finish the cruise. They had the time. So they went into the city and took a nice suite of rooms in a small hotel near Castro Street until the Eastern Star was ready to continue on. Castro was a long pedestrian street in the heart of a congested shopping district, situated in a quarter popular with tourists and locals alike. Exhausted, they slept in late, then started roaming the neighborhood and the pedestrian promenade, hand in hand.

The atmosphere in the city was liberating and romantic. The sun beat down, and the air one breathed was intimate with a hundred fragrances and smells. They wandered everywhere, laughing, mostly at themselves. Jan had let her hair down, and tossed it about. She'd chosen a black dress to wear, with bare shoulders, one she'd worn for dancing on formal nights on the ship. It somehow seemed suitable for a promenade in Buenos Aires. Lew wore a short-sleeved white shirt with embroidered white filigree on the front, and dark slacks. Jan had picked it out. With their slim sunglasses, they looked the epitome of cool romantics on the loose. They sauntered back and forth, up and down the Castro, their shiny black shoes pointing to this sight or that.

Loud tango music came to them from an old boom box somewhere. Then they saw the street tango dancers, two young couples dressed all in black. They were performing in the middle of a crowd of passers-by, raising money for their School of Tango. Lew and Jan came close in, and were fascinated. Lew held his wife in front of him, his arms around her. Neither could dance the tango, but they loved it, and wished they could. Then one of the professional dancers picked Jan out, inviting her to dance with him. His female partner took Lew by the hand into the center of onlookers. They were each led into the basic steps, to the applause of the crowd. It was easier than they expected, and the atmosphere was intoxicating. Each couple moved around the circle, with the crowd's encouragement and approval. They felt transformed by the music, the admiring crowd, and their teachers.

Suddenly they were released by their partners, and found themselves standing alone, in an embrace. They began slowly dancing a simple tango step or two, ones they'd just been taught. The professional couples danced around them. Lew and Jan tried another move or two, or imagined they did. They stopped, and kissed. The crowd laughed and applauded, with smiles all around. The raucous yet passionate music, their tango teachers whirling around them, and the approving circle of locals and tourists, all expressed tango aggression restrained, and covert passion. Eyes flashed, bodies pressed together and bent, ever so slightly, hands and arms held and let go, feet flicked between legs, and dresses swished while the male dancers proudly wore their dark fedoras at a rakish angle.

Back at their picturesque hotel later that evening, after visiting a couple of tango clubs a taxi driver found for them, Lew and Jan fell into bed, deeply in love. They slept in the next morning. Word came to them that the Eastern Star would be leaving the following morning, so they decided to spend the day at a beach at Ipanema. There was just a little surf, the kind that laps. While they were sunning themselves beside a beach umbrella they'd rented, they heard music. It was the tango again, this time being sung. It was coming from a beachside club a short distance away, perhaps 100 yards. All the windows were open, apparently, because for Lew and Jan it was almost like being one of their clientele. A breeze carried the music to their ears very nicely. An emotional baritone voice conveyed in articulate Spanish all the passions of the tango to whomever might be listening, as a small instrumental ensemble played, featuring a concertina, which seemed to be in a duet with the vocalist. Lew turned and raised himself on an elbow alongside Jan, then leaned over and kissed her, his hand cradling her head. The tango music and passionate male vocal joined with the lapping waves and the sun's heat to watch over the American couple, and they impulsively yet slowly, tearfully yet joyfully, embraced and kissed again and again. The spirit of American tango had overtaken them.

CLYDE RYDER

Clyde was a portly man with a florid complexion and bad legs. He walked slowly and with a cane, and spent a lot of time drinking in the bars on the ship. Yet we never saw him drunk. We met him at our table for eleven, where he said little though he was pleasant enough. One evening he sat between us and we talked about cruising. His favorite way to cruise was on rivers all over the world, because on a river boat the landings were more frequent and picturesque and he didn't necessarily have to go ashore to see the town. It was almost like having one's own private boat, and you got to know the passengers and crew better, because there were fewer of them and they were closer. A cruise ship was like a town, whereas a river boat was more like a small village. You got to know a much higher percentage of the people on board, and the atmosphere was more informal.

Clyde's cabin was far below decks, aft near the engine room and crews quarters. Sometimes when we descended four decks to see a movie or listen to a lecture in the theatre, we'd catch a glimpse of him disappearing around a corner down a narrow corridor. And it seemed every time we passed by one of the three bars on board, there he'd be sipping some drink, usually next to a drinking buddy, man or woman. Later he told us with a smile that he'd keep drinking until he was carried ashore on a stretcher. He loved to eat and drink, but especially the latter. Sometimes he missed meals with us because of this chronic habit. He readily admitted he was a devote of alcohol, and could care less what happened to him because of it. He spoke no foreign languages, not even phrases, and maintained that his willingness to take or share any alcoholic drink available had the result of making communication and friendship in any country or culture an easy matter, the most natural thing. Especially in Russia, he added.

It was on a Russian river cruise that a bizarre yet inevitable end came to Clyde. We learned about it later, from a letter he sent to us, and from mutual friends, a couple we corresponded with after our cruise on the Eastern Star. He was on the Volga, and must have gotten very drunk, because in Rybinsk he was taken ashore to see a doctor, who promptly prescribed a glass of vodka as the last remedy for his troubles and joined him in a toast. The doctor, who spoke some English, even invited him out to a local hotel, where they settled in for more daytime drinking, which extended into dusk and darkness. Miraculously, Clyde recovered normal feelings of health on that occasion, and likened the experience to a resurrection! He explained it all plus a good deal else in a letter to our mutual friends, who shared it with us. What brought us together, not incidentally, was our concern for Clyde's health. He was a good soul, but couldn't pull himself away from booze.

Apparently he was an orphan, but had been fed a birth fantasy by the elderly lady who raised him. From earliest childhood he was told that he was the illegitimate son of European royalty, probably Russian or some other Slavic kingdom. She spoke English with a heavy accent, but Clyde never knew what her native tongue was because she died while he was quite young. She'd raised him within her spinsterhood, answering his genealogical questions with one fairy tale after another. In fact, by the time she died she'd concocted a richly embroidered personal history for him, so that by the time he reached manhood, he believed he was related to the Romanovs of Russian Czardom, and in fact was probably the grandchild of one of Czar Nicholai's alleged pre-Revolutionary peccadillos.

In later years, after we met him on the Eastern Star, he apparently gravitated more and more to Eastern Europe and Russia for his river cruises. Over time he even picked up enough of the Russian language, by necessity as well as a kind of emotionally enhanced cultural osmosis, so that whenever his river boat tied up at one of those magical riverside towns such as Vladimir or Murom and the trip into town didn't involve a lot of stairs or uphill walking, he'd make his way with a sturdy cane into the old squares, past the little shops, fantastical cathedrals and dour monastaries, and preside over an 'obed' or dinner at a restaurant, no matter whether it was frequented by the working class or local officialdom. After a few glasses of kvass or a 'stakan' of vodka he could actually carry on a passable conversation in the language, which was certainly interesting for the locals, especially when he'd start dropping hints as to his fabled ancestry. On occasion he was more than a curiosity with such talk, and once or twice was questioned by officials.

We eventually received a long letter directly from Clyde himself, postmarked Odessa, because we'd shared with him our goal of eventually visiting Russia, and he knew we'd be interested in any of his observations and insights, not to mention how he was doing. Now and then a card had come our way, many weeks after he'd mailed it. But sadly, this one last letter finally made it to our door, postmarked Pavlovsk six weeks earlier. I was shocked on reading it, and sat staring out a window into our garden for a long time. So long ago, so far away, and he must have been so alone. And there was no way to respond, because the deed was already done.

For the letter told of his impending suicide the following day, by dropping off one of those beautiful river boats he loved, at night, whose regular itinerary included stops at Liski and Kazanskaya on the Don. He explained that he wanted his remains to become part of his Native land. No matter that his alleged place in Imperial Russia would never be recognized, he would die happy and fulfilled, home at last. Of course, his parentage was entirely unknown, and whatever he believed was the fabricated legacy of an imaginative and loving guardian. That much was true. But what did it matter now?

For me, and I can't quite explain it, his death came as a great release, almost an epiphany. I found a Russian Orthodox church in town and spent an hour at one of the services, standing in the midst of a devout congregation, intoning the hymns, which to my ear sounded so dreary, staring at the icons up front, flat faces surrounded by flat gold. Perhaps, as an adopted son myself, I identified with Clyde's life story more deeply than I'd realized, or could ever understand.

1600 TEDDY BEARS

Harriet Manley was not a widow; she was a spinster in her sixties. We met her at lunch one day, and she mentioned that she collected Teddy Bears. Since we had a number of them ourselves at home, and had brought a couple with us, we expanded on the subject. She owned 1600 Teddies, she declared, and had brought a large trunk of fifty of them with her. In fact, she had a double cabin, and the Teddy Bears occupied the other half! They were on the second bed, a large chair and half the sofa. Later, we heard from others that she talked of them as royalty and precocious children, and became transformed herself, in personality, as she waxed on and on. At first it was interesting to hear her, but since that was all she ever talked about, she became a tiresome shipboard acquaintance.

We lost track of her for a while, among the 600 passengers, and didn't dine with her again. Toward the end of the cruise, I think it was the sixth week, we heard that she'd had a noisy, argumentative scene with the maitre d'. It seems she wanted to bring her fifty Teddies, or at least a sizable number of them, to dine with her. As she was signed up for the second sitting, it was impossible, because this was the most popular one, when the Captain's table was full and the evening's entertainment followed immediately after.

Still, she persisted, and finally negociated a deal with the maitre d', which was no mean feat. The Sunday evening before the cruise ended, she came to the first sitting, which was ours, accompanied by her cabin steward carrying a large suitcase. She came late, so everyone noticed her entourage making its way to the head of the dining room, where the Captain's table, a table for twelve, was unused at that time. The suitcase was opened, and the maitre d's, dining room stewards, her own room steward and a couple of waiters helped her place the fifty Teddy Bears all around the table. Some larger ones sat on risers on the chairs, but most sat or stood on the edge of the table, some being propped up by pitchers of water placed behind them. Then she took her place at the head of the table, in the middle of one long side as the Captain would, against the wall and facing the rest of the dining room. As her waiter stood by, she proceeded to introduce him to every one of her charges, assuming a special and unique voice and personality for each. Some spoke loudly, others softly, a few even in a foreign language, and it was obvious and fascinating to all that Ms. Manley was utterly changed by this situation, her prominence that evening, and all the attention.

For as soon as she began, oblivious of the rest of us, the dining room conversation level dropped to a murmur, which was a miracle in itself. Anyone who has dined on cruise ships knows about the noisy main dining room when it's full. You can hardly understand those at your own table. But now we beheld a fascinating sight, fifty Teddy Bears being asked quite seriously for their orders by the perspiring waiter, dressed in a black bow tie, red jacket and black pants! Of course, we all know that Teddies 'don't eat or poop,' as my grandchildren would say, because they're immune from all that, so none of them placed an order. The waiter dutifully took his notes, and Harriet Manley herself ordered the Greek Special, which was always available at dinner.

As diners emptied their wine glasses, finished their desserts and coffee and got up to leave, they made their way back to the Captain's table. One just had to see this up close. Several people returned to their cabins and brought back a camera. Flash photos looked like lightning at that end, which was more in shadows. Lights over that table had been turned off, and a row of six candles lit the amusing faces and garb of the fifty Teddies, as well as the beaming, flaccid face of Ms. Manley. A small crowd gathered, and the maitre d's had to keep the situation from interfering with the waiters' travel back and forth to the kitchen.

For the remaining days of the cruise, Harriet Manley became a celebrity. Everyone wanted to not only meet her Teddies, but to tell her about their own. Teddy Bears and dolls of every description began appearing at other tables each evening, and Harriet was eventually given a table for six in the center of the second sitting, the place on her right hand being occupied by two or three of her bears on a riser. The maitre d' took reservations for those wanting to dine with her, and the invitation became even more desirable than one to the Captain's Table, who on one or two occasions was left alone to dine with a couple of his officers. He didn't stay long at table.

The last night of the cruise, there was another one of those Captain's Receptions, every one in formal dress, in the Main Lounge. But when we went though the line, the chief guest host was Harriet Manley, right after the Captain himself. To her right had been placed three long tables covered with luxuriously thick white linen tablecloths, and there, in a long playful row, sat or stood the fifty Teddy Bears! What a splendid sight!

The evening's entertainment was not the usual singers and dancers, a noisy band and an M.C. with raunchy jokes, but Harriet herself, with her Teddies arrayed on the edge of the raised stage. And so she began, speaking into a hand-held mike before the hushed audience of her fellow passengers, telling the story of each and every Bear. The experience was quite affecting for all of us, and we shared tears as well as laughter. When she was through, to deafening applause and cheers, she invited anyone to come up to the mike and introduce their own Teddies or dolls, whatever they'd brought along on the cruise. Well, for the next two hours they paraded up front. Many had gone to their cabins to bring back their little companions, to share in this moment of 'coming out of the closet,' one might say.

For some bizarre reason, this whole unprecedented Finale seemed to cap off the cruise, as if something irrepressibly childish in all of us had, at last, been publicly acknowledged as necessary and legitimate. It was okay to admit to being disposed that way, to want to play at life with these little alter egos so willing to carry our joys and sorrows. Yes, it was okay.

CRUISE SHIP NOTES

REUNION

It was a dream, or rather a dream come true. For many years we'd wanted to sail around South America, and now we were in Florida at last, come from New England, ready with all our luggage for the two month cruise. But first we planned to visit an elderly aunt of mine, recently widowed, my favorite Aunt Lucy. After renting a car and stuffing the trunk with our four huge pieces of luggage, we headed west from Fort Lauderdale, crossing the great empty interior swampland, which resembled more the primeval plains of Kansas than the exotic Florida I knew from ads and movies.

Wonderful Aunt Lucy lived in one of those countless gated condominium developments, lushly landscaped and hidden in tropical foliage, that litter the western coast south of Fort Wayne and Sanibel Island. As to how to get there, all we had, besides her telephoned directions, was a number and street name. By the time we found the tract, I had to drive back to a mall outside the gate and phone her again, because she'd forgotten to give me the number to punch in. We entered the maze of winding roads and driveways, the paved alleys and cul de sacs, finally arriving at her own paved driveway, which served a number of condominiums. They all looked alike and we couldn't see any numbers, so we parked and both of us searched for the numbers, which were discretely set over the door of each secreted apartment and nowhere else. There didn't seem to be any order to their arrangement, so we walked up to each one in the row. There wasn't a soul in sight, so we were on our own. At last we found her number and knocked, hoping she hadn't given up and left for a lunch and golfing date she'd said she had later on. The door opened and there she stood, as pretty and well met as ever, well dressed and seemingly at ease, despite the loss of her husband of fifty years.

Sam had died a couple of years earlier. They'd met during the second world war, when he was a dashing and handsome captain in the infantry, which he'd managed to survive. His lifelong job had been with a major tool company, where he'd been a very successful regional sales manager. After he retired, they became full time golf partners right up to the time he contracted his cancer.

She invited us in, and we sat on the delicately upholstered furniture that adorned her apartment and chatted about this and that. She still had that witty, ironic and self-deprecating sense of humor I always associated with her, and which was such a contrast to the normal family humor and way of talking about things that I'd grown up with. She was always very different from her brothers, my stepfather and another brother, who were rather taciturn and slow to see humor in things. They needed thawing or shaking in order to laugh. She delighted in deflating such family pretensions and posturing, and was merciless in ribbing her brothers and father about it. Still, she was so unassuming and charming in how she went about it, that no one seemed to mind. That was simply Aunt Lucy. Of course she only carried on that way within the family circle, so her way of playing with us was private, and not exposed to public attention. Or perhaps I should add that I never saw her in her own social circles, so she may well have been that way with everyone. Once I left Cornell, I left home almost forever, and lost track of her and other peripheral family.

I was gone so much from my family's ancestral Central New York country that I lost out on the usual benefits of being near kinfolks. My mother's parents died just before and after I was born, and I never met my biological father's family, never even learned about them until recently, so my only available grandparents were my stepfather's parents, who were very good to me and my mother. Yet I wasn't around when both of them were ailing and dying. I'd have dearly wished to kiss my grandmother in her last years and assure her how much I loved and appreciated my only 'Gramma,' but I was always too far away, out of touch for so long. Favorite uncles and aunts died, cousins grew up and had children, as did my half-brother and half-sister, and I rarely saw them, perhaps for a few weeks in the summer every two or three years. I was unable to keep up with all the changes within the family, the marriages, graduations and changes of fortune, the aging of cherished parental figures and the growth of delightful children, so I was increasingly that remote, bearded uncle in Seattle whom no one really knew. Now I found myself running down a widowed aunt from long ago, trying to rebuild all the extended family relationships I'd missed. I can see now that I invested far too much in our visit of thirty minutes or so in her Florida home.

As I say, we chatted, not about how she really felt, being alone and unaccompanied, but lightheartedly about how life was in this retirement community for widows, widowers and old couples, with usually one or both spouses holding off some dire condition or disease. She asked only the most superficial questions of us. I was disappointed, of course, because I'd had the notion that I might have an adult relationship with her, now that she was alone. But it was an unrealistic expectation, and I shouldn't have looked for it. So we exchanged pleasantries and some humor and left her elegant place.

Later I wrote her a letter of commiseration and affection, bringing her up to date on our life and doings. Not that it mattered, because we hadn't seen each other in decades, and her life, as the companionable wife of a successful businessman, had been uniquely her own and their own, summering in upstate New York and wintering near an exclusive golf and country club in Florida. So they had distanced themselves from us, too, in choosing such a lifestyle. When her husband was working, they had moved a lot, and we lost touch with them. In retirement they had their own friends, and we knew little of what they were really doing and thinking. But in my boyhood she was one of my best aunts, a parental figure and older woman I delighted in seeing, as much for her educated interests in the arts as for her ready, warm wit, which constantly needled the family's blemish-free and boring smugness like there was no tomorrow. I wished her well, and we drove back to Fort Lauderdale straight away, to drop off the car and make our way to the pier where the Eastern Star awaited us.

DEADLY TABLE FOR ELEVEN

The Eastern Star of the Greek Line was over 35 years old, yet very seaworthy and queenly. She carried 600 passengers and 300 crew, a floating village, busy from bow to stern and bridge to bilge. On her cruises she never rested, even in the ports or at anchorage, such as that stormy one in the delta of the Amazon, with the wind blowing one way and the current another, and the tide changing directions too. She never rested. Her white superstructure and dark blue hull, her classic lines beneath a single stack forward, made her distinctly compact and handsome. In rough seas she ran steady, without yawing. The pitching was minimal, but enough to let you know she must love the porpoises that occasionally ran alongside on the open sea.

We were new to cruise ships, and ignorant of the fact that the first thing one does on coming aboard, even before making sure your luggage is in your cabin, is go to the dining room and sign up for a desirable table with the maitre d'. What is a desirable table? A round table for eight away from the noisy center, to one side. Well, we were late as well as being virginal to cruising, and got what was left: a table for four right in the middle of things, and without table mates! It took a month before we were able to make a change, and that was to a rectangular table for eleven. It was right in the center as well, with noise all around, not so much from its own conversation, but from happy diners all around it. For various reasons it turned out to be an incredibly boring table.

As I've indicated, its location and shape were poor. And in contrast to the custom at a large table, where diners are encouraged to sit wherever they want each night, one couple and three singles insisted on having the same seats every night, all at one end and down one side. That left six of us to try to liven things up, with limited seating opportunities. It was deadly. Conversation with the Stagnant Five was limited to what one had seen on shore excursions, or other cruises. With certain of the other four we were able, with much prying (and they made it seem like prying), to learn something more about them, their families, their past lives, and their other activities and interests in retirement. But not much, and then the subject would be dropped for good. Political and religious subjects were verboten. Thus the whole table often sat immobile, silent, not knowing or daring what to say, toying with silverware or clothing, waiting interminably for the next course, which, at a table for eleven with one waiter, seemed to take forever. Carol and I were bored beyond forbearance. Our hardworking waiter was always in a sweat, and often needed help from the stewards and even the maitre d' on occasion. But still we were one of the last tables to finish the first sitting. Is 1½ to 2 hours too long for dining, under the circumstances? You better believe it!

The only dominant personality we had was a single man (one of our Gang of Six) who talked loudly about his own convictions. After some weeks of exposure to him every night, most everyone gave up and nursed their wine. And so he'd hold forth untrammeled, as the mood moved him. He sat in the center of the upside, toward the bow, and so appeared to be our host. We all sat helplessly as he'd fill in the void of boredom of that long table, at which only the ends could carry on an intimate conversation. We'd sip our ice water or ask for more wine, anxious to break away once the last course was done and cleared, then return to our cabin to put on leisure clothes and go for a promenade on the perimeter deck. Others of our retirement generation went into the main lounge and sat in the overstuffed furniture, to fall asleep with the help of ubiquitous cocktail waitresses in miniskirts, or be entertained by the M.C.'s coarse humor and his girly shows, or loud, romantic singing and dancing of foreign entertainers, mostly attractive young people from Eastern Europe with thick accents. They must have prepared about thirty stage shows for our two month voyage around South America.

But the Deadly Table of Eleven continued to dog us, and we regularly buttonholed the maitre d' for a change. This seemed to take forever, so we began staying away from the dining room evenings. We had supper brought to our cabin a few times, or would wait until the café up by the swimming pool opened for late night snacks. We saved sandwiches, pastry, and fruit from breakfast and lunch (which had open seating), as well as four o'clock tea, and used the ice in our ice bucket to keep it preserved until the evening, when we'd dine in our cabin. At some ports of call we could buy soda pop much cheaper than on the ship, so we kept a drawer full of these for our cabin use. We tried everything we could think of to avoid sitting at that table of eleven. When we didn't appear for one and even two nights, however, our table mates and even the maitre d' and our waiter would become worried, and ask how we were. What could we say? How could we explain? The maitre d' already knew we were thoroughly dissatisfied where we were seated. We did our best to be tactful and discrete with our table partners. A couple of times our steward brought messages from the dining room, asking if we were coming to supper. And so it went. The pressure to conform was uncomfortable and annoying.

Another aspect of the evening supper that eventually became a bother was the custom of rotating formal, informal and casual nights, sometimes livened up by a Greek Night, Caribbean Night or whatever. Being told how to dress, too, can eventually become tiresome. We took along a garment bag full of appropriate wear for all these occasions. I even learned how to tie a bow tie again, which I hadn't done since college days. But after a while, this nightly requirement to dress a certain way becomes burdensome. Were we there to meet and know people, to have conversation and enjoy life, or simply to make a good show? Perhaps, to be candid, we weren't good cruise ship passengers. Not yet. Things got so turgid at the table for eleven that one night, for distraction and to stir up the table's somnolent decorum, one of our Gang of Six brought a little battered Teddy Bear to supper. He was introduced all around, complete with a squeaky falsetto voice. The Teddy was dressed in a Hawaiian shirt, denim shorts and cool sunglasses, and stole the show, throwing the whole table into disarray. Suddenly everyone confessed to having Teddy Bears or dolls, and promised to bring them. But they never did. When the strolling musicians came by, a violinist and accordionist, they first glared at the Teddy, then broke into broad smiles. It was an unusually stimulating evening, thanks to a bedraggled little Teddy Bear.

But at last the maitre d' came to see us one noon. "I have a table for you. We've had an unexpected vacancy, and there are now two places at this table." He pointed at a round table for eight off to one side on his table chart. (It turned out that a gentleman had died, and he and his wife were taken off the ship at the last port of call.)

We were overjoyed. At last we could, hopefully, rejoin the living again. And our new table proved to be more stimulating, exciting, and challenging than we ever expected. Our new table mates knew how to have conversation, and enjoyed sharing their life experiences, and life itself. Altogether, it was an urbane, sophisticated, and cultured group. So for two weeks, just before the end of the cruise, our evening meals were quite eventful. On our next cruise, if there ever is a next time for us, we will disregard the fate of our luggage and head straight away to the desk of the maitre d' outside the dining room, and secure places at a round table for eight!

DINING WHILE CRUISING

While on a cruise, one is encouraged to forget about dieting, or keeping to a fat-free regime, but if you prefer lean meals or vegetarian fare, or have any other special dietary requirements, the cruise ship galley will oblige you. As a lover of good food and drink, however, I looked forward to partaking of a wide variety of wonderful cuisine on board the Eastern Star. I wasn't disappointed, but after a month our menu took on a certain sameness and degree of repetition, which is inevitable. Relief would come in the form of dining in restaurants ashore, or in simply avoiding the dining room for a night or two. That alone freshened one's appetite and appreciation of the ship's rich and varied cuisine. Of course, we're talking about a two month cruise, which isn't at all like the 5-7 day vacation holidays on the Carribean. The ship's routine, her crew and regime of dining becomes your home and your life for the duration.

Being a Greek ship, roast lamb was on the menu pretty regularly, about once a week, as were many other meats and seafood. She had several levels of huge freezer rooms, which were served by their own elevator. These were filled in Fort Lauderdale and fed us and the crew for the entire trip. Apparently a few dinners were victualed with local fish freshly bought, and almost all fruits and vegetables were purchased in ports as we traveled. Great quantities of these were needed to take care of the nearly one thousand mouths on board.

Beverages of all types were always available, and wine was encouraged at every evening dinner. It was paid for when consumed. At all meetings and social functions in our main lounge, young cocktail waitresses in short skirts constantly circulated, with little round tray and pad in hand. We were an older breed of cruiser on this long cruise, so all the crew serving passengers were much younger, especially the entertainment troupe. Cocktails before and after dinner and at all social functions seemed to be the thing to do, but this was neither our custom nor our desire. Once in a great while, perhaps, but not all the time. Once or twice I sampled the ubiquitous whiskey sours served at our lunches ashore in nice restaurants, but never finished one. That's not why we went on the cruise, and besides, I much prefer a nice wine, and often had a glass at dinner on the ship. We had so much food available that, if one added wine all the time, not to mention cocktails, one felt and looked corpulent, not to say bloated. Toward the end of our cruise, it was announced that we passengers had set a record on the ship, having consumed the lowest amount of alcohol of any comparable cruise. We weren't sure if the deliverer of that message was pleased or disappointed with us. Although exercise, walks and a smallish swimming pool were available, and a significant percentage of the passengers used them, we didn't go on the cruise to keep fit. We wanted to see all of South America we could, and between ports relax and enjoy life at sea.

The ship's menu was almost limitless, practically speaking. Breakfasts could be a slim continental type or a feast. We tended to have the same breakfast that we do at home. Many had breakfast luxuriously served in their cabin. Lunch was similarly dealt with, but inevitably we tried new and additional items of the fare available. And one could always order anything on demand at any time. The staff did everything except eat the food they served us. If you felt like you didn't receive enough of a particular vegetable at dinner, a whole plateful would be brought right away. Meat not cooked to your pleasure? Send it back and get it right. You like certain a la carte items with your meal? Fine, here you are. There was always a selection of wines, including Greek wines (but not retsina), some drawn from countries we visited, and a roaming wine steward was there if some gentleman decided to order a bottle for all at his table. Strolling musicians, a violinist and accordionist, created a convivial and genteel atmosphere at every evening dinner, playing songs on demand and leading birthday and anniversary singing. Both had good voices, and the accordionist could belt out the final note like an opera star, eliciting much applause.

Here's how the menu went: Bread always. Then an appetizer of your choice, soup or salad, fruit, or something exotic. Next the "Farinaceous" course, a dish made of flour or pasta. Now the main course, centered around a meat or seafood. As alternatives, there was a vegetarian dish, and always the Greek Specialty. That's where one found the lamb. Dessert involved a choice among three or four items. And finally coffee or tea, and a liqueur if desired. Rise all from the table, and exeunt to the main lounge, where cocktails would be served, as they were before dinner at an official Happy Hour. And so it went, day after day, night after night. Cabin service was available too, of course, and there were three bars, one with a disco in the bowels of the ship, that were open at various times.

Seating at breakfast and lunch was 'open' in the main dining room, and there was a café on the top deck by the swimming pool. We usually ate lunch there, out in the open air or inside if it was cool and windy. One noon at a deep south latitude it was so squally and cold that we were about the only ones eating outside, and bundled up in parkas and warm hats. A tea time at 4PM in the forward lounge provided sandwiches and pastries, and sometimes we took away some of these wrapped in napkins so we could stow them in our ice bucket. They later served as dinner if we decided to skip going to the dining room. From time to time we needed a break like that, and besides, we weren't comfortable feeling helpless all the time, and chose to dine by ourselves now and then. Cabin food service was always available, and we did use it a few times, though inevitably the maitre d' or our table mates would make inquiries to see if we were well! So we felt a certain pressure to go to the dining room for our supper.

Each evening in the dining room had a prescribed dress code, and one of our four huge suitcases included a bulging garment bag, so we could adhere to it. The dress code was: Casual, Informal and Formal, in that rotation, with occasionally a Carribean, Greek or Carnaval night. We wore more formal dress (tux, or white jacket and cummerbund for the men), during this cruise than we probably ever will for the rest of our lives. I re-learned how to tie a bow tie, something I hadn't done since college, forty years before. Informal meant coat and tie for men, though a nice sport shirt under the coat was also acceptable. Women could wear non-formal dresses or skirts, or pant suits, as informal. Casual was anything except shorts, bare shoulders or midriffs, or sandals. We were an older crowd, used to more traditional dress, so this code seemed reasonable to us, except that after several weeks it becomes a chore to dress up or dress down every night, according to a schedule. Our formal clothes were all new, and the first times we wore them, we had to check to make sure all the tags and labels had been removed. One evening we were about to take our seats in the dining room when we noticed I had a very prominent price tag hanging from one cuff of my dinner jacket! With much amusement it was quickly removed.

Our onshore dining took on quite a variety, featuring the food of the country and unlimited cocktails and wine. Sometimes there was a great view, and always the local ambience, and as cruise ship visitors we received excellent service, which makes one feel really special, though it can become boring, too. After all, it was only our money that made it so, not any celebrity status! In Costa Rica we ate next to a rain forest, in Chile at a wonderful seafood restaurant at the end of a pier in Miraflores, surrounded by surf and excellent food and drink. Sometimes while visiting a city we'd try the local 'fast food.' In Rio, in the Ipanema district, we stopped at "Bob's Burgers," for lunch. As we munched on their version of 'take-out,' or 'eat here,' which was delicious, a man our age came in and sat down alone at one of the Formica tables. He was gaunt and not well dressed. The manager, a young man, immediately came out to ask him what he wanted. A coke, he said. As the manager stood over him, the old man spread a quantity of little coins over the tabletop, and proceeded to count them. He had enough for a small coke. This display was too much for us well-heeled cruisers, dallying for a few days in Rio with relatively unlimited food and drink at our beck and call. As we left, we slipped him the equivalent of around five dollars, hopefully for food. After we left, we regretted not giving him more. He wasn't beggarly, and seemed genuinely grateful.

From Buenos Aires we took a day excursion to a "gaucho picnic." This was on a former ranch, which had been totally converted for entertaining large numbers of tourists and cruisers, like ourselves. There was a huge dining hall, complete with stage and full banquet facilities. Adjoining this sprawling complex were paddocks for three small groups of horses numbering about ten or fifteen each, and in three colors, white, black and dark brown. Several gauchos showed off their riding skills, and guests were invited to take a short ride on a horse. The day we were there, no less than ten or twelve full busloads were parked in the driveway, all invited for the daily lunch feast. I think there were two different kinds of big sausage, chicken, and beefsteak, plus the trimmings, and all the wine and beer or cocktails you could drink. A tango demonstration took place on the stage, and the photos we took of the dining hall show about 400 guests gorging themselves. It was fun, but not exactly a gaucho feed out on the pampas. The whole show was a great show of Argentine tourism.

During all our city tours around the continent, by the way, we were never shown where most poor people live, in the slums and 'Bidonvilles,' or Shanty-towns, though some of us wanted that education. It was explained that it might be dangerous to do so, or there wasn't enough time, and 'Aren't you enjoying this luxury neighborhood we're showing you, and our stops at posh jewelry stores, gemstone dealers and fancy gift shops?' The closest we came to it was in Belem, Brazil, on the Amazon River delta. Our buses had to cut cross one side of this city of over a million (the size of coastal cities all around South American was an eye opener for us), which took us through some lower class neighborhoods.

Each morning when we returned to our cabin after breakfast, our beds were perfectly made up, and each evening our beds were turned down and a small chocolate mint left lying on our pillows. The final day at sea, our excellent cabin steward personally gave each of us a half dozen of these little chocolates, which gesture summed up for us the multitude of gifts this circumnavigation of South America had given us. We loved those mints.

A COVE IN JAMAICA

We hadn't been on the little beach five minutes when suddenly we were afraid. The catamaran, with black Captain and crew, had motored us older white folks about 45 minutes from the port and turned into this cove, mooring across the rocky entrance for snorkeling. Those of us who weren't good swimmers were taken to the beach in a skiff and left. It was a three minute ride.

We had left our carry-all bags against a tree trunk back from the beach and were heading for the water, when we noticed a couple of men emerge from the trees. One was our age, the other younger. They came to the back of the beach and just stood there, watching us, saying and doing nothing. One wore only shorts, the older man shorts and an old shirt. We had the feeling we might be using his beach, and he'd allowed the catamaran Captain to bring cruise ship passengers to it. Was he given a cut by the Captain, or did this offer the opportunity for theft?! Obviously one factor that elicited apprehension on our part, along with some guilt, was their poor blackness and our wealthy whiteness. And the fact that they just stood there, saying nothing and watching us. Everyone on the island whom we saw, which wasn't very many, was black, Afro-Americans brought to the Carribean as slaves hundreds of years ago, before our own ancestors arrived on the East Coast of the U.S.

Why did they just stand there, without greeting us and doing nothing? The older man didn't move, an unsmiling statue, his arms at his sides; the younger one soon disappeared. The effect of all this on us tourists was unsettling. We agreed among ourselves that one of us would sit by our bags while the rest went in the water. I tied our bag to a protruding root of a tree. Why we were so apprehensive is hard to explain, and I can only ascribe it to the unknown, and the fear of strangers in a strange land. Ridiculous as it may seem, the older man who watched us seemed ominous. But to imagine that he or his younger companion might grab some of our bags and run off was surely to overreact? If that happened just once, the cruise lines would never authorize this shore excursion again, and the catamaran Captain would be out of business. Short term gain for long term loss.

We went in the water. From the beach we explored the rocky sides of the cove, without finding much. The water was unusually warm. All I saw was a small eel and a fierce looking fish about 18 inches long. That made me get out of the water. There was no one there to ask about what we were seeing, so we were left to wonder. We sat under the tree and watched the others, as the catamaran remained framed in the cove entrance. It was mid—afternoon of a brilliant day. I tried reading but was unnerved by that man, now almost a statue, who continued to watch us. I couldn't figure it out. Had he never seen people like us before? Was he simply curious, or possibly a little dim-witted or senile? Then I heard music somewhere, coming from a radio or tape player. It was back in the trees. At last the older man turned and walked toward the music. I got up to follow him, and what I saw made me feel easier. It was a homely snack bar, and open for business. A couple from our beach group came and sat down, ordering a kind of punch or lemonade or fruit cocktail, I couldn't tell which. The men we'd seen were there, visiting and laughing with the couple who ran the place. Not being thirsty, I returned to the beach and waited. We wanted to return to the catamaran because we'd been there two hours and it was getting cool. We were dressed for midday on the shores of the Carribean.

The skiff was beginning to shuttle back and forth, taking our little group back to the boat. We were among the last to leave. When all were aboard, the Captain's crew untied the anchor lines to the shore on each side of the narrow cove entrance and we motored away. The mainsail was up, but only for stability. It had cooled down considerably, and we hunkered down in the cockpit. The cabin was for the crew, who proceeded to serve us snacks and drinks all the way in. (We could have used some on the beach; Actually they'd been available all afternoon on the catamaran.) Smiling faces all round, and questions being asked and answered. Up ahead, as we approached the port, we could see our cruise ship silhouetted against the Voyager of the Seas, the largest cruise ship afloat, making ours look like its little brother. The Eastern Star had traditional classic lines and contrasting colors, sea blue hull and white superstructure, whereas the Voyager was humongous and all white. It looked like it might capsize in a storm; ours looked safer for all weather.

It had been a minimally satisfactory outing, but was marred somewhat by the situation on the beach, if you can understand the position we felt we were in. If only the people we found there had been introduced to us, it would have gone much better. The tension, fear and suspicion would have dissipated. Then I thought: Why should we Americans, or any foreign visitor, be made to feel safe and comfortable by Third World residents, every time our money brings us into their midst? Are we to be treated like children, pampered in our delusions of innocence and excess of affluence? Is it reasonable to expect our wealth and privilege to be respected and served by the locals, everywhere we go on this cruise? My own views were liberal, if not radical. They owed us nothing, and we were intruders, even if we did 'help the local economy.' I wondered how we materially benefitted those pleasant snack bar owners and their friends under the trees by their beautiful cove, secluded and quiet. We had been brought there, and apparently been found wanting. Should we have walked up to the two men and made friends? Why not? Our response was to be afraid, and to isolate ourselves. There was very little cross-cultural communication in that little cove in Jamaica that day.

ISLA DE SAN ANDRES

This was our second shore excursion, and though I was familiar with poverty and destitution, having worked on Indian reservations and in the ghettos, and traveled and lived all over Europe as a poor student, I somehow expected this Carribean island to be a tropical paradise, like so many are described in the travel magazines. Isla de San Andres is part of Columbia, yet far away, just to the north of the Panama Canal entrance. Its dimensions are 1 ½ by 7 miles. We tendered in, using our own lifeboats as always, and were greeted by a rag tag row of old taxis. We commandeered one, and asked for a tour of the island, which is easily done in an hour or two, at the most.

The island's buildings and homes resembled a war zone, where refugees were trying to survive. First we noticed the estates of former drug lords, confiscated by the government and for the most part closed and abandoned to nature. These took up a lot of land. When we went through little villages and hamlets, the housing was substandard and crowded, with many small concrete buildings unfinished and empty, occupied by squatters. Unfunctional pillars and walls and rusty re-bar stuck out everywhere. When had the money stopped for all these structures? Then we reached the largest town, and it looked more prosperous, but not much. Driving through to the other end, we understood why. There, out on a narrow peninsula, sat several large luxury hotels. Access was apparently through a guarded gate, and we didn't turn down that way. We continued to drive around, through uninhabited areas and over the crest of the island, then back to the landing.

I couldn't get over my reaction to the poverty. It was the wholesale and populous, Third World kind, and the first I'd ever seen. As an old civil rights worker, it made me angry. Here were all these grand estates of criminals, but no one could live on them except here and there a rich buyer had moved in. Here was an infrastructure crippled and unfinished, for the common people, and luxury hotels for wealthy Americans and other foreigners Where was the justice and fairness in this? I was chided for reacting so strongly to these disturbing sights and contrasts, as sophisticated as I've considered myself to be, but I couldn't help it. Years ago, when I was playing soccer year round in Seattle, ending up in an 'over 40' league, some of my fellow players organized a soccer vacation to Rio de Janiero. We'd stay at five star hotels and play soccer with our Brazilian counterparts. It sounded great to my soccer heart, but I couldn't do it: go down there on a lark just to play soccer while hundreds of thousands of the poor were surviving in slums up on the hillsides outside the city, and swarming over the dumps for whatever they could find to reuse? I couldn't see it, and my friends left on the trip without me.

So Isla de San Andres was an eye opener. Thenceforth I would develop a more 'tolerant' attitude toward poverty, but I still retained a resentment and embarrassment that we were so rich we could look at slums and destitution as a tourist attraction, while powerless to do anything to remedy it. I had to accept the conditions of each country and each neighborhood around me, regardless. There was nothing I could do to change things, except to hope that perhaps my American dollars might filter down here and there, to help improve economic conditions overall. But this, too, was really beyond my control.

CHAN-CHAN AND THE PROFESSOR

We visited several South American countries during the cruise. Prior to each shore excursion, which lasted from one to four days each, there were informational lectures given by guest experts aboard, usually in the ship's auditorium on the lowest passenger deck. They were well attended.

One lecturer in particular was outstanding. We were about to go ashore in Peru, on an excursion lasting four days, visiting sites near Trujillo, Lima and Cuzco. He was a professor of archeology who was thoroughly familiar with all the sites, having initiated and conducted all types of excavations, written or edited several books and many scientific papers, and continued to teach classes. In fact, he was one of several world authorities on the archeology of Peru and Chile.

He appeared as an older man of average height and build, with thinning hair, a short beard, and eyeglasses that were hardly visible because of their pencil-thin frames and a weak prescription. One site especially was featured in his lectures, after he gave us an overview and spot survey of all early civilizations along the coast, including the Inca Realm. And that was Chan-Chan. We had done some background reading on the places we knew we'd be visiting, the countries and sites of our shore excursions, but nothing prepared us for the presentations of our Professor. In a few words, he was riveting. He had maps, charts, slides and aerial photo enlargements from various angles to show, and for all three of his one-hour lectures he had us in the palm of his hand, probably three hundred retired folks, talking about this, for us, strange new discovery called Chan-Chan!

Chan-Chan is a complex of several ancient royal palaces near Trujillo, or perhaps I should say Trujillo was near the incredible site of Chan-Chan, within sight of the Pacific and spread over the wide coastal Moche Valley bottom. To our ears, the palaces had almost occult names, sounding like an incantation when one put them together: Squier, Gran Chimu, Bandelier, Uhle, Chayhuac, Tschudi, Rivero, Laberinto and Velarde. They had been built at different times in the immemorial past, because when a new ruler arose, he ignored any previous palaces and built a new one, sometimes partially on the ruined site of an old one.

At one point our Professor projected a slide of a line map of the entire coastline, that showed the coastal valleys with their namesake rivers: Lambayeque, Jequetepeque, Chicama, Moche and Viru. Explaining how these verdant valleys supported agriculture through irrigation, fed by rivers with origins in the high Andes, he somehow caught us up in the thrall of his lifelong, arcane research. We felt like we were already becoming his proteges, and might have assisted him in his work, given time and opportunity.

When we finally arrived at the site of Chan-Chan, and entered the Tschudi (pronounced CHOO-dee) Palace, we felt like we'd been there before, the Professor's explanations, descriptions, graphics and orientations had been so clear and well organized, so dynamic and colorful, garnished with anecdotes and stories. Everything was laid out exactly as we'd been told. We could identify every section, structure and room, every pit and wall, even prompting and enlarging on the spiel of our site guide. We'd been there already! There were the several pits that led down to wells, the burial mound, the grain storage, the offices of the provincial chiefs of the empire. It was one of the most illuminating site visits of the entire cruise.

Looking back on Chan-Chan, what most impressed us, first of all, had to be our ignorance of these early coastal civilizations, and second, how much we learned in such a short time, thanks to the Professor. And he did devote a lot of time and effort to making sure that, once we stepped onto the site of Chan-Chan, we'd have very good background, and a clear conception of the historical antecedents and use made of the palaces, as well as the details on the ground.

By way of contrast, and to emphasize the point, I can imagine being plunked down in Chan-Chan without a clue as to what this mounded and walled dry desert was, surrounding me on every side. Sure, a site guide, if I were willing to pay for one, could have pointed out the salient structures and interesting features of these ancient palaces, but the larger, deeper history and all the details would have been missing. It would have seemed like a desert ruin with little interest beyond obvious and superficial tourist considerations. As it turned out, some of us felt we could have stepped into ongoing archeological work and made an intelligent contribution. There was so much to learn, and the Professor gave us every opportunity to allay our ignorance and make us "Friends of Chan-Chan," so to speak.

So it was an astounding experience, with an impact that fixes forever in my memory the early civilizations of South America's west coast, all the way from southern Bolivia through Peru and down into Chile, 1800 miles of some of the most barren coastline in the world. Yet the Andean rivers and creeks flowing through to the Pacific through valley cuts made eons ago were utilized in complex irrigation systems that turned these valley bottoms, as they reached the coast and broadened, into rich agricultural lands. But these same irrigation systems were also the Achille's heel of, for example, the Chimu Civilization of the Moche (MO-chay) River Valley. Once their rivers and creeks were cut off by the Incas, they were doomed to succumb.

He lectured on the Inca Empire too, describing the Incas and their controversial origins, the vast network of trails that joined every corner and outpost to the center, its excellent military organization, its rigid bureaucracy and society, its culture and art. When the Inca Empire in the highlands eventually expanded north and south and crept down the coastal valleys, they forced the Chimu to capitulate simply be redirecting their irrigation canals back into the river. So where irrigation ceased, all crops failed. The Chimu were subjugated, to become itself another province of the Incan Empire, with an office in the capitol of Cuzco, high up in the Andes. At its peak, the Inca Empire, more properly called the Tahuatinsuyu, or Four Quarters United, lasted from about 1200 AD to the Spanish Conquest in 1572. Its lands included all of Peru west of the Andean Range, southwest Columbia, Ecuador, most of Chile, and parts of Bolivia and Argentina. It was the largest civilization, in extent, in the Americas. Inca was the title given to the rulers themselves.

So we learned all this from the good Professor, and have followed up with more reading and study of our own. The upshot of our cruise was that we became students of South American life, history and problems, and henceforth have followed every news item about the continent. It brought South America into our living rooms, and its troubles became our concern: the ouster of Premier Fujimori from Peru, the return of the dictator Auguste Pinochet to Argentina, and earlier, the death and martyrdom of Evita Peron, whose family mausoleum in the Cemetiere de Recoleta in Buenos Aires always shows a fresh red rose behind the door. But these were only the most public and sensational events. It was the life and history on the ground and in the streets, among the people, that most impressed and moved us, the lives of the millions of peasants and workers in all the coastal cities and countryside of the American southern hemisphere.

THE CUZCO HOT PACK

For us, Peru was the essence of South America, at least until we reached Buenos Aires and Brazil! Its shape is a long north-south rectangle that backs up against the foothills and high peaks of the Andes, where towns and cities are as high as 8-10,000' in elevation. This was Inca country, but there were also less ambitious civilizations along the coast, from Ecuador down to Trujillo and south to Santiago. But before the Spanish came in the 16th century, the Incas ruled, and it was some semblance of their legacy that we most wanted to see and feel.

We flew to Cuzco with the group from the ship, after a few rushed and restless hours spent in a luxury hotel in Lima. (Due to a late flight from Trujillo, we staggered in after midnight in Lima, never touched the gourmet foods that had waited so long for us, and arose very early in order to catch our morning flight.) We arrived in 11,000' high Cuzco exhausted, and Jasmine had a bad case of the flu in addition to her chronic neck pains that had flared up again. Unfortunately, as soon as we were settled in our nice, fancy tourist hotel in Cuzco, her neck pain reached a peak. Not only that, we both began feeling the altitude, which at times was like being suffocated. We were struggling to breathe normally. The next step in this prolonged yet rushed "shore excursion" was to catch the picturesque and beautiful train ride to Machu Picchu the following morning, which would take us down to a much more comfortable 7,000' or so. But due to Jasmine's flu, there was no chance of our going. We would stay behind in the hotel, and so miss that pilgrimage. We were both very disappointed, and as for myself, I wanted to stay with her. There was no question in my mind about that. Jasmine said I should go with the group, but I firmly declined.

Life in the wonderful, old luxury hotel was actually good. Looking out the windows on our floor, we could gaze over miles of clay tile roofs, which was a uniquely pleasant landscape, the backdrop of which was the green hills all around. It was peaceful and undisturbed, and the jet runway was at the other end of the valley. Our room was comfortable, and we could relax and read. However, I spent much of my time making hot packs for Jasmine's neck, as hot as I could stand it in the bathroom sink, using a carefully folded hand towel that was just the right size. Then I'd slip it into the sleeve of her rain parka to keep her from getting wet, and she'd gratefully wrap it around her neck and try to rest and sleep. That night I had difficulty sleeping myself, due to feelings of claustrophobia from the thin air. She was having trouble breathing too, so we had an oxygen tank brought to our room. She tried inhaling with a mask, but it didn't seem to make any difference. So the tank was taken away by the hotel attendant who'd brought it and stayed, seated at the foot of Jasmine's bed, to make sure we used it correctly.

We'd missed going to Machu Picchu, but we were together, and I was caring for my wife as best I could. Everything considered, we were happy and content. For me, each hot pack I made for her, using their devilishly hot water (it seemed close to scalding), was a kind of love gift I gave my wife. Each time she wrapped it around her neck, she smiled and felt better. I was glad and fulfilled in making her more comfortable that way. We would keep up this treatment all through the next day and night.

Later the second day we decided to go out. We went downstairs, across the spacious lobby with its floor of dark tile, then out through a gauntlet of street vendors, and slowly walked up narrow streets toward the main square, Plaza de Armas. It was exhausting work. Up until then we'd been having meals brought to our room, but the last evening we felt acclimated and well enough to eat in the dining room with the rest of our group. The entertainment was an excellent local group playing the Native instruments we always associate with the Andes. As soon as we sat down, they began playing a very slow and majestic version of El Condor Pasa, a really beautiful version, and both Jasmine and I found ourselves full of emotion, wiping tears from our eyes. In a sense, it was the culmination of our visit to Cuzco.

Before we left on the bus for the airport the next morning, our driver took us up to a high vista next to a huge white statue of Christ, with arms outstretched (a copy of the larger Corcovado in Rio de Janiero, we were told), from where we could see the city overall as well as the surrounding green hills. We liked Cuzco very much, and were glad we could spend a couple of nights together there. But it was the hot packs that made it special for us. It made Jasmine feel better, and kept her in good spirits. Down in the lobby I bought her an alpaca scarf, and it is now the main souvenir of our visit to the Andes, after our memories of the hot packs, of course. We still use them at home, now and then, when Jasmine's neck bothers her more than usual, referring to them affectionately as our 'Cuzco Hot Packs.'

We never made it to Machu Picchu, which was supposed to be the goal of this lengthy and arduous side trip, but we made a home for ourselves in our hotel room, and took care of each other. There we were, in the heart of Cuzco, the ancient capitol of the Incan Empire, privileged guests of Peru. It was another dream come true for the two of us, a dream that had little to do with the fabled Machu Picchu fastness, where the other cruisers in our group had spent their time, climbing all over those remarkable ruins in the rain for a day, with fog and clouds obscuring the surrounding peaks and valleys, they told us later. It was our love for each other that we'd quietly celebrated in the Hotel Libertador, and there we found our own personal "Machu Picchu," which in our eyes was quite the equal of the original.

PUNTA TOMBO BUS BREAKDOWN

We'd spent hours driving down the coast in a tour bus, listening again to a female guide's spiel in heavily accented English with intonations from the Spanish. Our cruise ship had been left behind at Puerto Madryn, Argentina. It wasn't long before we simply heard her, without paying much attention to what she was saying because it was work to do so. We'd heard so many of these local guides, whose two-pronged approach was to do their job as expeditiously as possible and elicit higher tips.

The weather was clear; the coastal pampas and low hills were dry and sparsely vegetated with grasses and low bushes. And yes, we saw the great rookeries of Magellanic Penguins along those vast and isolated, beautiful beaches, devoid of humans, and took many photos. It was really an incredible sight, and one we'd paid dearly for in going on our cruise. But it was definitely worth it, and the weather cooperated fully. Another shore excursion completed, and we started the long drive back to the ship, cooped up in our air conditioned bus. People settled down to nap.

Twice we stopped, then started again, then pulled over and parked on the graveled dirt road. At first we assumed someone had asked to take a picture, but no, the driver was having problems. He went back along the bus and opened the engine compartment, then returned. We continued on, winding our way up out of the hilly coastal area. Then he stopped a third time, and turned off the engine. It was quiet for once, except for some chatter from our busload of veteran cruisers, all past retirement and glad of it. At first the stop was treated as a lark, something different to talk about.

The driver hailed another tour bus, headed for the coast, apparently asking that help be sent. Something was wrong with the belts that ran the cooling system. They were slipping or something; we didn't hear all the details. Word was sent on to Punta Tombo, where there was a mechanic as part of the resident staff for the wildlife preserve.

We found ourselves alone in a little uphill valley, with scrubby hills on both sides. They weren't high, the kind an able-bodied older person could climb in twenty minutes. Many passengers got out and stood around, close to the bus, a few taking photos of each other. We went across the road and explored an arroyo, scoured a few feet deep, its bottom strewn with stones and pebbles polished by water and wind. You could see where the water currents had gone, first to one side then the other. The bus was out of sight. There was nothing particularly unusual to see; we seemed to be nowhere. As the repairs would take much longer than anticipated, once help arrived, a few of us decided to go for a little hike up a hill on the coastal side. There were three of us, a French couple and myself. It was easy terrain because there was little vegetation, and the hill was a lesser one, appearing to have trails of some kind leading us upward. The French pair took another direction, off to one side, tentative and dallying; I went straight up for a ways, then returned to the bus because we hadn't been told how long the wait would be.

My wife was just coming out, and we impulsively decided to go to the top of the hill. Most others stayed put, with a few who were handicapped remaining inside the bus, though the air conditioning was off, of course. It was much more comfortable outside. Climbing inside to get my camera, I noticed one woman apparently unable to leave the bus, who was sweating. I spoke briefly to her, then left. We started up the slope, looking for trails to make the going easier. The bus always remained visible, but became smaller and smaller as we ascended. Then nothing could be heard from below. We felt like children on an expedition, free for an hour or two, liberated to pursue nothing at all! For once we were on our own, without a guide or prescribed itinerary. We were creating our own "shore excursion."

At our feet and on all sides we noticed a myriad of shiny stones, mostly brown or gray or shiny black. They appeared to have once been under the sea, eons ago. I picked them up now and then, fingering their miniature, gem-like qualities. Something to do in this barren landscape. I tried to imagine the geology and history of this coast, so featureless and empty except for penguins and tourists. Not that I'm against leaving wilderness alone, mind you, but coming from inhabited places, 'developed' places if you will, it just seemed weird that we were suddenly alone out there, without dependable technology to take us home.

We continued on up, farther and farther, our goal being some kind of view from the top. The French couple followed, but at some distance. Maybe they wanted some quiet and solitude too, and kept separate from us. Looking down, there was our bus; if I extended my arm toward it, I could now cover it with my thumb, blotting it out. For some reason this gave me a good feeling. The trail petered out on a steeper slope, and we were looking around for another way to reach the top when the French caught up with us. I tried out my French on them, but we ended up speaking broken English. So much for my language skills between cultures. You try learning another language or two over your lifetime, of cultures and peoples you admire, but without constant use communication is still pitiful.

Then we found a distinct trail around on one side, but our French pair, who were younger, had taken off toward another, slightly higher hill about two hundred yards away. The slope before us was slippery with those little stones, but we finally made it to the top, or so we thought. Actually it was one of those nondescript and inconclusive summits that goes on, farther away yet, and we had no sense of having 'reached the summit.' Looking around a little, we found a strange structure, long out of use, a ruined thing really, just some posts with a few boards attached; then some sheep we encountered quickly skittered out of sight. We were both readying our cameras, but they were gone. What to photograph? We could now see the grayish blue Atlantic, hazy and several miles away to the east, but not a view to take home, or even talk about. "We saw the ocean," we could say. "It was on the barren Argentine coast, and we climbed up for the view, but we didn't see anything else." A featureless downslope and ocean. Not exactly an adventure!

So what was it we had found on our little sortie? It was so simple; stepping away from the big, disabled bus, still sitting cold and dead on that graveled dirt road through the low coastal hills . . . Nothing in particular, really, except that we enjoyed it, and were glad we went up there, something completely independent of our hosts, the cruise line. We'd gotten away from 'the cruise ship experience!' Maybe that's it. They wait on you hand and foot, you know, keeping you stuffed with food and entertained every night, shepherding everyone on shore excursions like this one, away from the ship and back again, and you can actually get tired of it, especially on a two month cruise around South America. I mean tired of all the luxury and care, of never lacking any necessity and surrounded by staff ready to fill your every need, a floating, traveling island of privileged luxury, immune from the cares of the world as summarized each day on the ship's internal TV system.

Then the tour bus you're on breaks down, and suddenly you're on your own. You can do what you want; where shall we go? Leave the road and walk, hiking away and up, over the wilderness and into the breeze, seeking the far views alone, the peace and quiet of the explorer, the revelation of an unknown, empty place, a place that we never would have encountered had not our technology failed us at last, and we were free, if only for a brief time. We would never forget that little hike, and what it meant to us. That simple ruined structure at the top with its old boards, the silent sheep moving away as we approached; the sight and memory of it became a pilgrimage, a visit to a reliquary or icon tended by the meek and humble in spirit. We were there to escape, to learn and bear witness, and somehow that little hike had renewed our spirits. Once our bus was running again and we were on our way, we felt we'd received something extra from Argentina, a side view of the surrounding landscape denied to most passengers on cruise ship excursions. It gave us a special, even a VIP feeling, and the lore of stories to share with our table mates at supper that evening.

THE GREAT MAN

We first saw him at what was to be, unfortunately, his last appearance in public. It was on a catamaran tour boat at a landing in the waters around Ushuaia. We cruisers from the Eastern Star had left our bus at the edge of a national park in Tierra del Fuego, amid woods and hills. There was a long trek over a boardwalk to the glass-enclosed tour boat, from which we were to see waterfowl and sea mammals on scattered islets in front of Ushuaia. It was a rather long walk. No sooner had everyone boarded the vessel, holding perhaps forty of us, when suddenly there was a commotion behind us. Someone had fallen and was lying on the floor. A few gathered around the man, who was a white-haired and bearded gentleman. A stretcher was brought from the bus, and he was carried off, his wife accompanying him. I'll always remember the little wave he gave us all as he left the cabin, feet first. We later learned, long after we'd left Ushuaia, that he died in one of the local hospitals.

Alright. That's some background for what follows. We'd been trying to get a better table in the dining room, a round one for eight away from the noise of the center, and I'd been pestering the maitre d' for the change. Our table for eleven was a bore, and there were only a few weeks left on the cruise. We were desperate for some interesting supper companions. Then, shortly after we left Cape Horn, the maitre d' caught me after breakfast. Two places had opened up at a round table for 8. We grabbed them. The way we got those places, however, was by the back door, so to speak. Only the Great Man's death and departure, with his wife, had made it possible. So we replaced them. Or rather, our live and well bodies occupied their chairs. That's more accurate, because over the remaining few weeks we learned that we could never replace this man and his wife, not after he'd so impressed and dominated his table the previous six weeks of the cruise.

We soon learned that the deceased gentleman had been so remarkable, so distinguished and witty, so accomplished a raconteur and venerable a sage, that it seemed we could only sit in his shadow. Clearly, his abrupt demise and absence was traumatic for our new table mates, all of whom were younger than the average onboard, like ourselves. Every evening the talk would eventually come around to him, and we could feel his legacy quite clearly, because we were no match for him and his beloved wife, who was Kindness itself. These were people we'd never met, and never would meet. Our one image of him was that little wave of his weak hand as he was carried off our tour boat, which was soon to fall cold and still at his side.

Thus our time with the six survivors, two couples and two singles, could be characterized as continual frustration. But we were good listeners, and would occasionally tell stories based on our own special experiences in Europe, Asia, Alaska, and Hawaii, where our home is. Or we'd confide aspects of our home and family life, as did the others. For we truly did want to get to know each other, and fill in the void created by the untimely and distressing departure of our predecessors. We listened carefully to their jokes, some of them well lubricated with alcohol and pretty crude, and to the storytelling, responding with enthusiasm because they were quite sophisticated and witty, a far cry from the silence, banalities and boredom of our former table for eleven.

A wife of one of the couples was absent for the first few days of our arrival at their table. We wondered if she'd become burned out after sitting at the same table for over six weeks, as we had, despite the much more interesting character of this one. We didn't understand why the cruise line made us sit at the same table with the same people night after night for eight weeks. Needless to add, most everyone managed a switch or two over the total time of the cruise. She eventually returned, was gone for a couple more nights, then returned again for good, dressed to the hilt. We found ourselves confronted by a wife loaded with jewels, bracelets and rings. Her facial expression was glowering and predatory, fixed with darkly shadowed eyes that said, 'Watch out! I'm out to win!' For she was a compulsive gambler, and she and her handsome husband regularly went to Vegas and Reno, some of the Indian casinos, and even Monte Carlo. And, her husband assured us, she won most of the time, and 'she never has to ask me for any money.' He had been in some kind of basic business like construction materials, which he never talked about.

It soon became apparent that the table had regional antipodes. Two couples and one man were based in the Northeast. A California woman and ourselves were from the West Coast and Hawaii. The Easterners nightly mentioned their college and cultural connections, all in the Ivy League and New York City, or Boston, and we westerners could only be vaguely expansive about our own regional bias, scattered as it was across the country and the world, which seemingly could never surmount the provincialism of our friends from the Northeast and New England. And so Oneupmanship became a feature of our table talk.

Naturally, as Americans will do, at some point each one of us would try to confide his or her life story, fractionally or in toto, or at least the current condition of it, to some one or two others at the table. These could be intense confidences, disclosed almost like confessionals, but spoken as asides to one's dinner partner. The overall impression was theatrical, as if we, the main characters, needed these feverish personal exchanges in order to maintain our individual respect and integrity among the others, who'd known the Great Man. Our disadvantage consisted in having joined in so late, during the final quarter of the cruise, so it was a nightly game of catch-up, and we never really reached any significant degree of parity.

Still, we had our moments. There was a lone single man, who was actually married yet always went on cruises alone, his wife not liking the cruise ship life. He was a retired editor and free lance writer for Time-Life back in the '50s and '60s, and I found myself talking to him like I was one of his famous interviewees. In fact, due to his friendly yet direct and closely attentive questioning, I eventually spilled my guts out to him, to the extent that eventually the whole table was listening in. Odd to admit, I wasn't in the least embarrassed. I became excited and began stammering, as I do when something really matters to me. The retired editor, whose name shall be Mark, just kept smiling engagingly, quietly putting forth one pointed question after another. At the end, when I'd given out, he exclaimed, "Well, that's your story right there! Put that in a book and it can be a bestseller!"

After that performance with Mark, I thought we might at last have 'arrived' in the group. Not at all. In fact, my caving in to Mark's impromptu yet skillful 'sensational' interview technique seemed to compromise our status. At least that was my fear. Here I was, being so honest and trusting in sharing confidences about myself, when I should have been posturing and pontificating, broadly ironic and self-deprecating. When we returned to our cabin, my wife reassured me by saying she was impressed by my extraordinary performance. To feel impelled to confess all those personal details and hidden emotions to a perfect stranger! Yet she commended my courage, and reminded me of Mark's summary remarks: 'That's it! That's your story! Put that in a book and it'll sell a million!'

But, much as I felt flattered and encouraged by this experienced editor and writer, who at one time worked for the most prestigious weekly news magazines, it troubled me that I'd bared myself so, and I even thought to ask the maitre d' to move us to another table for the remaining few days of the cruise. However, being confined on such a small cruise ship, with many people with whom we'd traveled and dined with for several weeks, we really couldn't leave the bed we'd made for ourselves. And besides, my wife wouldn't have it. So from then on we smiled longer and laughed louder, told the most bizarre stories we could think of, interrupted our attention span to flatter others, bought bottles of wine for the table, and recounted all our travels thrice over, especially if we could top the experience of others. We'd never see any of them again, so what did it matter what we said?! We just kept talking as wittily and eccentrically as time allowed, and gave up being ourselves, let alone trying to be replacements for the deceased Great Man and his good, grieving wife!

YE OLDE SHIP EASTERN STAR

The first time we saw raw sewage coming from our ship was in a port. We were tied up at a dock, and one morning I looked out our porthole. There, riding on the turbulent upwelling from an outflow pipe somewhere beneath the surface, we saw toilet paper, effluent and lumps. Our waste was being dumped directly into the water, in harbors as well as at sea. Also, all our gray water, cleaning solvents and paint was disposed of the same way.

Another revelation occurred at sea. We sometimes got up in the middle of the night to walk on the deck, look at the stars, and once joined others to watch an eclipse of the moon, when it turns a dull red. This one night we wanted to take a walk. It was 3:00AM. First we looked out our porthole. In the light from the superstructure above, we could see papers falling into the sea. Puzzled, we dressed and went topside. As soon as we opened the door onto the deck, we saw papers flying everywhere. What was going on, we wondered. Where were they coming from? We walked forward, as the debris seemed to be coming from there. We reached the railing at the bow and looked down. There, coming out from a metal canopy on the foredeck, men were dragging large plastic bags of rubbish to the side and emptying them overboard. Unfortunately, the wind caught a lot of it and sent trash scattering over all the decks above. As soon as one of the crew noticed us, however, everyone disappeared and the activity stopped. As we continued walking around the promenade deck, we met crew members running here and there, trying to pick up the papers and plastic that had lodged everywhere. When we went back inside and were walking through the foyer of the main deck, we met another passenger, an older man with a deeply lined face. He hadn't been able to sleep, and had seen the same sights. He described the Eastern Star as a "gross polluter." He also said that our ship had lots of company. Almost all ships discard waste of all types into the ocean, certainly on the high seas, and always have. Only in the ports can some controls be imposed.

We had a fire drill and evacuation the very first day of the cruise, and periodically thereafter. We noticed that our section of the ship took an unusually long time to reach the lifeboat deck. After a few drills we became more concerned and observant. The final door onto the deck only half opened; the other half stayed shut for some reason, and no one said anything. Later we examined the hand operated locks on that half. One of the little ring handles, just large enough for a finger to pull it, was broken off. It was odd no crew member had noticed, or cared. As a result, our group was coming up from below at half the speed, compared to the others. We pointed this out in a note to the Captain, and within a day the broken lock was replaced. What a difference it made in our lifeboat drills. We could almost run up the stairs! But we never received any acknowledgment or thanks from the Captain or his officers, and at a reception when I tried to thank him for having it fixed so promptly, he abruptly turned away and greeted other passengers. But we were pleased, because we'd made possible a crucial repair, one that would help save our own as well as others' lives. Otherwise the ship seemed to be very safely run. All the lifeboats were employed as tenders at one time or another, so we knew they would work if an evacuation became necessary. Also, there were many life rafts cached all over the upper decks, and the crew had its own lifeboat drills, much more often than the passengers.

But there were minor shortcomings too, of a more homely nature. The ship's laundry prices were exorbitant, so few used this service. We never did. As we passed by the open doors of other passengers' cabins, we noted laundry drying on jury rigged clotheslines everywhere, which worked quite well. At first we thought we might be the only ones so cheap and frugal as to handwash our own laundry, but it turned out to be a common practice. We often drank soda pop in our cabin, in the evenings and whenever we had food brought down, or were just relaxing and watching a movie on our cabin TV monitor. But it cost $2.00 per can on the ship! So whenever we reached a port, we headed straight for the nearest pop machine or grocery and stocked up at 50 cents a can. We used our ice bucket, which was filled every morning, for various purposes, keeping wrapped sandwiches cold and letting the ice melt to serve as our drinking water. We hoped the water used for the ice was purer than the stuff that came out of the tap for basin or shower, which was off color.

Repairs as well as maintenance were a regular part of crew activities. But on this old ship, some systems constantly needed attention and monitoring, especially the plumbing and air conditioning. We had no trouble ourselves, but pipes burst at one or two locations elsewhere, forcing passengers to be moved until the mess could be cleaned up, dried out and any needed restoration done. The hot water was scalding hot, and could change suddenly from tepid to steaming hot, so we had to learn how to govern water delivery in our showers and tub baths. The first time we flushed the toilet was a shock as well, though there was nothing wrong with it. It had an explosive flush that was a little scary. Anything down that toilet was down and gone forever! Toward the end of the cruise the aft passenger elevator broke down, and though everyone, including repair crews in ports and the Captain himself tried to fix it, we finished the cruise in Fort Lauderdale without it. Our air conditioning worked fine, which is very important, especially in tropical waters, because the portholes can't be opened for safety reasons. But others weren't so fortunate. Their cabins could become suffocatingly warm and uncomfortable, and we assume they applied for a partial refund of some kind, or pleaded with the Captain to switch to another cabin. And, we suppose the wealthier, better connected or repeat passengers could do so.

Health problems on a long cruise like this one, far from home for a long period, can add misery to one's cruise experience. We caught some kind of flu cold and cough early on, and either one or the other of us suffered from it right to the end. It didn't prevent us from doing most things, or going on shore excursions, but at Cuzco's 11,000 foot elevation it contributed to our inability to go to Macchu Picchu. That was a big disappointment. We had the feeling that, on an old ship like the Eastern Star, with all of us breathing the same air conditioned or heated air, we might catch anything. The ship's Greek doctor was okay, but the basic conditions made us vulnerable, and we were glad we brought along some medications of our own. Thousands of people from all countries live on the ship over the course of a year, and it never stops for long. Lord knows what is brought aboard and left for the rest of us to breathe!

It was a once in a lifetime experience, those two months circumnavigating South America on the Greek Lines' Eastern Star, with its excellent officers and crew. We navigated in and out of crowded ports and down narrow, sometimes shallow channels both day and night, with never a mishap. It was all very impressive, and we always felt we were in safe hands. There were two periodic tours of the bridge and the kitchen, where we could ask all the questions we wanted, and did. An old ship, but a venerable and salty one, steady and reliable, and altogether with a pleasant yet keen disposition. She loves nothing better than to sail the Seven Seas until the end of her days.

HAWAII

WELCOME!

The Hawaiian Islands are a wonderful mixture of ethnic and racial peoples. Their cultures bloom like the tropical foliage all around. The population of the "neighbor islands," away from overly populous Oahu, is rural. Each island town or hamlet or district has its array of distinctive and picturesque personalities. Especially the Big Island, where we now live. Many of these folks have lived here a lifetime, if they weren't born here. Not recent arrivals like us. In Hilo, where there is a great public market, we stopped at a nearby restaurant to eat, and that's where we first met Mildred Dillingham.

"It took 37 years, y'know, to get that award." She was nodding confidentially for our benefit, glancing from me to my wife and back again, letting us know she'd waited a long time for recognition, but at 82 she was a lively, affectionate Elder waitress at Bob's Steak House. Regular customers went there because of her motherly welcome. She'd finally been written up in the local Sunday magazine, because the city fathers had finally recognized her long time service as a waitress at Bob's, as well as other charitable works. We'd seen the photos and faded newspaper clippings behind glass in the entrance.

We were seated in a booth overlooking the parking lot and she'd come over to welcome us and bring us water, right away engaging our attention, using terms of endearment and smiling all the while, drawing us out and toward her. She came back to get our orders, and brought them to our booth expeditiously. She was a good mother to us sixty-somethings. It was a different experience, because usually we were the parents or grandparents to younger waitresses and waiters. As you get older, the whole world seems more and more populated by 'children.' On the way out, we again looked over the framed assortment of faded newspaper notices, photos and snapshots under glass, telling of this local celebrity waitress.

Elsewhere on the island are other notables, what you might call Big Fish in our Little Ponds, but no less regarded for that, by those of us who look for Welcomers in generally unfamiliar country, wherever we are. I think back to an awesome high school principal in my youth, and a legendary Jewish pharmacist in my hometown who seemed immortal, who lived and worked to such an advanced age. And even after his death, family members kept the same drugstore going. One of his children must have become a pharmacist too. And my stocky, barrel-chested high school Social Studies teacher, studying for his PhD. after World War II, always dressed in a tweedy three-piece suit, who one afternoon declared, "I don't ever want to hear any of you advocating war to solve international problems. Do you understand?" Silence. Then he put his hands on his desk and leaned forward, his face reddening, and shouted at his Home Room full of seniors: "DO YOU UNDERSTAND!?" A subdued 'yes' from most of us came back. He served as a major in the infantry, and had been describing the horrors of war that he'd personally witnessed.

As we recall such memorable incidents from our past life, we often remember the names associated with them. They've been burned into our 50-year-old memory. The principal was Raymond Van Geisen, the pharmacist was Irving Rutkoff, and the teacher was Wayne Merrick! Their strength of character or warmth or love of life became part of our own reason for living, our own response to life's challenges. I had an uncle who, after I'd said something impulsively foolish at age 16, while working in his restaurant, gave me advice during a quiet conversation in his little office. "Gus, if you remember only one thing from your summer here working for me, I want it to be this: Think before you Speak. There's too much said that's stupid and ignorant. You're a smart kid, and that's the best advice I can give you. Never forget it." Little did he or I know that this admonition would govern my conversational skills for most of my life. Especially for a stutterer, which I was as a youth, and an adult who still stammers when excited, these sage words justified my taciturn ways. In conversations I calmly waited, listening carefully until that pause arrived when I could deliver my two-cents worth, as if it were, as I hoped, a brilliant revelation for everyone within hearing!

In Bob's Steak House in Hilo, Mildred reigned as the Queen Waitress. She made you feel at home, and shared the dietary merits and delights of various offerings on the menu. The need for food had brought us together, and as our welcoming waitress she ensured that her food and friendliness cemented us to her and Bob's. No wonder the parking lot was always full, all day long. There were other waitresses, of course, and even Bob himself circulated among the tables, making sure we had all we wanted, the way we wanted it.

But Mildred had added a note of regret, after all, in that opening remark of hers. She'd been at Bob's for over 40 years, and only received her civic achievement award a few years ago. Did she somehow feel unappreciated, in her fullness? Had all the years of 'waiting' been worth it? Were those brief, fading press notices and photos to be her life's memorial? Would anyone really remember or care about her, once she was gone, to spend her last days relegated to a nursing home in Hilo, the award plaque lost on the wall above her rocker, listening to the torrential rain showers that came and went, unheeding and perennial on that windward coast so many thousands and millions of years?

THE GRUMPY LADY
OF MUD LANE

There was no reason for it, but there she was, glancing balefully at us and muttering something before she disappeared into her Sports Utility Vehicle. We'd reached the end of Mud Lane, and as she had just come through one of two locked gates, we'd asked her if the road had originally gone down through a wooded lane in front of us, and that was the response we got. A glare and a mutter.

We'd recently retired to the Big Island of Hawaii, bought a jeep, and proceeded to explore the island's back roads. First it was the redoubtable Mana Road that goes around Mauna Kea at a high elevation, then roads upcountry from Waipio, then Mud Lane, which was aptly named. Full of potholes, roots and all mucky soil, it used to join the interior highway to the coastal road, dropping down 1500' in about six miles. For the first mile or two it was overgrown and shaded by rows of old ironwood trees on both sides. Then it met two locked gates on either side of trees that used to mark the original Mud Lane. We could see more open country, sloping ranch land and patches of old woods in the distance, but the public was barred from continuing. Why were we following all these back country roads, determined to follow them all the way to the end, and to know everything about them, both historically and contemporarily? I don't really know, except as retirees we had time to do things like that, any day of the week, any time the weather was pleasant, so we enjoyed going on these adventures. We'd bought our jeep expressly with the idea of using it this way.

We looked into the Grumpy Lady's situation. She was close to our age, maybe 8-10 years younger. She was a widow, and she and her husband used to raise stock horses and offer trail rides into the densely wooded gulch country along the windward coast. Earl and Harriet Reiser were their names. In those days, Mud Lane had already been cut off near their place. The route from that point on had long since become overgrown with younger trees. Only motorcycles could follow it now, or hikers like ourselves. We had parked our jeep when confronted by the two locked gates on either side of the impassable old "Mud Lane, now a kind of secret trail and windbreak, leading straight ahead down a heavily wooded passage into . . . what, we knew not.

Our Grumpy Lady lived alone (and here I will cease calling her that), keeping a few saddle horses for herself and friends to use. Her house and a couple of outbuildings sat in the middle of open pasture. The country was eastward sloping down and slightly rolling. In the days before foreigners came to raise cattle and sugar cane, it was all woods, constantly washed by the clouds and rain brought in by the trade winds, which still prevailed.

We learned from a longtime local resident and friend that since her husband died she'd become a recluse, and hated to see strange vehicles come down Mud Lane. Her neighbors on the other side were active ranchers, but she kept to herself more and more. They—she and her husband, had taken many movies on their trail rides, showing guests enjoying the country. She had been the photographer, so was rarely seen in them. But her husband was prominently shown. He'd be explaining the history of this rough country, the old trails from the coastal valleys up to Waimea, the irrigation ditches, the way the Natives cultivated the valley bottoms, the wild pig hunters, and the old sugar cane plantations and camps for field workers, most of whom were brought from Asian countries and at first were treated like slaves and indentured servants.

It was easy to get lost on the gulch trails, especially if one strayed off them, he'd explain to his wife's camera, while answering questions about the flora and fauna. For Harriet Reiser, watching these old movies had become her favorite pastime, other than the soaps and old movies on TV. The projector and screen was permanently set up at one end of her living room, and she'd spend hours watching their old trail rides, drawing on a library of over sixty reels of film, with sound. She could listen to her husband's voice forever, that voice that used to bring her love and adoration every night. For they had togetherness in every way, at home or at work. On the overnighters, she was the quartermaster, loading the packhorses and cooking the meals, once Earl had started the fire.

Now and then he went off riding alone, usually looking for new routes to take. Sometimes she went along, but when he went alone, she worried. He'd been a bomber pilot in World War II, but had rarely talked about it. She knew the experience had bothered him, and, early in their marriage bed, she'd tried to draw him out. She wanted to know everything about him. But he'd said little.

The coastal gulches were treacherous to explore. There were drop offs hundreds of feet down, and thick, jungle vegetation between. Until a safe way was found, it could be dangerous for the unwary stranger. Earl was thoroughly familiar with these risks, and was always careful. If in doubt, he held back. But that one time, when he never returned, must have done in both him and his horse. No trace was ever found. He must have gotten into new country and the fog and rain rolled in, disorienting to both man and beast. Earl knew well how to survive, what the essentials were. But something must have happened. He always took a rifle along, in case he saw a wild pig he could bring home. So Harriet was left to wonder, and wonder. Had he really gotten lost, and fallen into one of those horrific gulches, so deep and unforgiving, lined with jagged lava rocks, or had he taken his own life and that of his favorite horse, Charlie, alone together in some remote, inaccessible place that only he knew about, and perhaps had reserved for such a time.

Even for the experienced, the gulch country was a potential killer, literally a no man's land. For the novice and amateur, to venture even twenty yards off a trail might be a death sentence. Every year or so, tourists or some daring young man would head into that rugged part of the coast, full of old, criss-crossing and dead end trails, never to return and never to be found. It was so easy to get lost, and just as easy to get hurt, or stumble through thick wet foliage onto a drop off. And nobody would have seen or heard. You'd simply vanish from the world of the living, to starve to death or die of injuries.

At first she'd discounted suicide, because they were so happily in love, and lifelong partners in the trail riding business. But since reaching his late middle age, Earl had taken to brooding more, that she knew, and it had worried her. They rarely talked about his war experiences, except to gloss over the main points, but she had to suspect that all that bombing and other wartime stress, not just over the destruction he'd meted out, but because of having lost so many close friends in his wing, almost half not surviving the raids over Europe, that his buried guilt might have risen up and called for an end to his torment, which showed more and more in the lines of depression in his face.

After he was gone, Harriet kept watching the movies, and never rode a horse again. Others went riding around her meadows, but she never allowed riders to leave her sight. And there was no question of going into the gulch country. That was forbidden. Earl and Harriet had never had children, because a war injury had made him impotent, but there were other children in the family, on the mainland, and "Uncle Earl and Aunt Harriet" were much loved. Now that she was alone, there were fewer visits by family, and Earl's local friends faded away.

Harriet's closest friend, Betty, was a local Hawaiian Native "Aunty" her same age, whose husband Jeff used to help them on the trail rides. And since he'd died from too much smoking, Harriet and Betty had become close friends; two widows remembering the old times, when their men were around every day and night.

One morning they were having coffee together in Harriet's quiet living room, which overlooked the empty meadows, peaceful and forever green on this windward side of the island. Neither had spoken for a minute or so. Finally Harriet asked one of those depressing questions that have no reassuring answer.

"What do you think drives our men so, to shorten their lives and suddenly they're gone?"

"I don't know, Betty. Earl was always so restless, always on the move, needing to be doing something. Seems like he couldn't stand just sitting around."

"Same with Jeff. 'Cept he loved his food. My, how he could put it away. No matter how much I gave him, he'd usually clean his plate."

"Seems like Earl was never quite happy, I mean with life in general. We were happy in our marriage, as far as I could see, y'know, I'm not talking about that. I mean the war; I know it really got to him as he got older, all those memories I've told you about."

"Yes, I remember. I think he must have talked with Jeff about it. Men share things like that, y'know. They don't think us women would understand. I think maybe Jeff gave up on himself too, for other reasons. He always wanted to have his own restaurant, but we were never able to swing it. Then I think he was hoping he could take over the trail riding business, but that was out of reach too, as you know."

"Yes."

"Then when Earl never came back and there wasn't any more to do here, he sort of gave up. He went into 'early retirement,' I guess you could say, which is funny, 'cause he was so much younger than Earl. He just stopped being interested in working, and we got by as best we could, as you know. We sure appreciated the help you gave us." Harriet nodded and sipped her coffee.

"But he was already coughing a lot."

"Yes, he was really bad. I kept telling him to go home, but he kept coming over."

The two widows sat still, their heads turned to look out over the meadows, as there were a great deal to see, and a great deal to feel, out there. The heavy mist obscured all detail, as water started dripping from the eaves. As happens at this latitude, the dusk came sooner than expected, and the brightest thing in the house became the TV, which had been muted for an hour. Its images were now strobing. After Betty went home, Harriet sat there in the surreal semi-darkness. Finally she turned off the TV and lay down on the sofa to nap, pulling an old blanket up over her.

She woke up at 12:30AM, and got the movie projector going. She put on one of the early reels, one that Earl especially liked. After some preliminary footage showing the horses being saddled and the packhorse loaded, there was Earl talking.

"My name's Earl Reiser, and that's my wife Harriet behind the movie camera. We've been going into these gulches for many years. It's a wonderful ride, and we'll talk about history and plants and other things, along the way. At noon we'll stop at the brink for lunch, then we'll spend the afternoon going down to the bottom, and out to the ocean beach for the night. Just remember one thing. Stay on the trail and do what I say. That way we won't have any accidents. Because if you don't pay attention, or go off alone, even on foot . . ." Earl smiled, nodding the while, looking around at the group of touristy riders. There were a few chuckles and smiles. Then the screen went dark.

She had turned off the projector at that point, for the 100th time. Each reel was edited like that, with an automatic and abrupt end before he talked much about the dangers. Just as Earl's life had been cut off somewhere, somehow, without her being aware of anything at all, to do with his passing. So it seemed fitting to watch their movies like that, over and over. There was no other way for her to fill the emptiness or remove the ache. And it would never cease being that way for her . . .

ANGRY BEES

The old man was adamant, so much lava rock wall in the face of Foster's probing question, one he'd put forward a dozen times.

"You're sure you don't want to sell? Sometime in the future, maybe? I'm a very patient man; I love this place, and it's perfect for my bees." Jon Foster had been a bee keeper for almost twenty years now, ever since he came to the Big Island and fell in love with North Kohala, and began renting the six acres of woods and meadows, lush with flowering trees and bushes, from Zeke Pohana.

"Naw, I got plans for it. My daughter's gonna get it, once she marries. She's gettin' close to it, I think." Old Zeke's weathered brown face smiled wanly. He was a heavy man, big boned with heavy arms and legs and a big torso and belly. His fattened face exuded both contentment and resignation. He had the land and seemingly would never let go of a single square foot. As for his daughter, Waiola, she was going on forty, and no one was seriously courting her. Everyone told Foster he might as well give up and buy some land of his own somewhere else. The island was big; there was good bee forage elsewhere, like over at Puako.

But he loved those six acres near Kapa'au. He'd buy those and more, if it were possible. For years he'd tried to figure Zeke out, what would bring him around to accept the idea of selling to him. After all, that little parcel was only a fraction of his holdings. What was six acres from the 400 acres of former sugar plantation land Zeke had accumulated in recent years, and was now selling in little pieces for house lots and diversified agricultural use like coffee, Macadamia nuts and papaya. The six acres in question weren't close to Kapa'au or Hawi Town; they were down near the rocky coastline at the end of a long steep road. Nobody went down there any more except pig hunters, and the occasional carload of teenagers looking for a hideaway to drink themselves silly or make out with their girls. But beyond some woods lay the six acres Foster rented from Zeke, where he had many hives and hundreds of thousands of bees, which ranged all over North Kohala. Foster lived in a house he also rented from Zeke, on the edge of town toward Kawaihae. That's where he processed the bees' production into various honey products, in his old house, which was a former plantation worker's cottage. It was a good business if worked right, and Foster had found some Mainland outlets that were taking all he could produce.

Waiola knew and liked Foster, and sometimes came over to see him at his house. She was forty, yes, but a beautiful woman. She'd never gained much weight, just the pleasing kind, and a good worker. She was intrigued with Foster's bees, and with his blonde beard and pale skin. She longed to make trips to Honolulu and the Mainland, but had never been off the island. Foster had often invited her to go with him to Oahu, where he went about once a month to supply his outlets there, but Zeke wouldn't have it. So she didn't go. It made her angry, because her father had sat on her aspirations and made her his servant ever since his wife died. She couldn't do anything away from his control. As for Foster, he had to be careful not to offend Zeke or make him angry, because he had his eyes on that six acres. Waiola knew about this plan of Foster's, and gradually the two of them came up with an idea.

Zeke wasn't well. In fact, his days were numbered. The doctors at North Hawaii Hospital gave him at most two or three years to live. And when he died, they assumed Waiola would get everything of Zeke's. So Foster and Waiola came up with a joint plan. If Waiola married Foster after her father died, could they travel together to the other islands and to the island? If so, Foster could have the use of all Zeke's lands for his bees, including the six acres down by the water.

One winter day, when the temperature had dropped almost to 60 and it had been raining hard for over a day, Zeke fell ill and began vomiting. They took him over Kohala Mountain to the hospital. Zeke fell into a coma, from which he never recovered. A week after the funeral, Foster and Waiola got married, and began making plans. Then the family lawyer called Waiola; it was time to go over Zeke's will. It was a shocker, almost diabolically so. It was learned that if Waiola married or sold any of the lands, including the six acres, they would all go to the Hawaii Nature Conservancy and she would be left with her father's rundown old house.

Foster was beside himself. Not only was he losing his six acres, but he and Waiola would have no land at all. All his patient years of waiting and hoping came crashing down that morning, as they quietly sat in the lawyer's office in Hawi. Just like that; all for nothing. In that instant Foster's composure broke, and he stared at the floor, waiting until the lawyer finished droning on. Waiola was very upset too, but held her tongue. She was hoping that Foster would stay with her anyway, he'd been so nice to her. And he was the only man she'd ever known.

As they left the office, Foster was trembling and tight-lipped. Finally he spoke. He'd stopped on the sidewalk.

"You go home. I have something to do."

"But Foster, we need to talk."

"Not now. I told you to go home! My business comes FIRST! (He shouted the last word) There's something I need to do, right now, and don't you follow me!", he warned. He hurried away, and she saw him turn down the road toward the six acres. He was about to get even with Hawi and everyone around there.

When he reached his long row of hives, the woods rang with his shouts and curses as he commenced to kick and throw the full hives in every direction. And he kept doing it, as if to beat and batter then to pieces. He would send those bees out to sting everyone in sight! But as he kept violating the bees' home and preventing them from doing what they were born to do, they began swarming around him. In exhaustion he fell against a tree, and the bees came to him; he felt helpless to leave, and no longer cared. As the end came, he stood and leaned against the tree, a human pillar being covered with so many bees from head to foot that he not only lost all recognition, but became so thick and swollen as to become an actual pillar, fashioned by a swarm of angry bees. By then he was blind and numb, and lost consciousness while dying a million tiny deaths. His own senseless anger and despair had transformed his bees from nectar-gatherers into death-dealers.

When the horror was done and they found him, a beekeeper was brought from Pauilo to gather the bees. Foster had a simple funeral and, at Waiola's insistence, was buried in Zeke's old family plot down near the rocky shore, not far from the six acres. The background for the funeral gathering that day was a view to the north over the restless whitecaps, toward Maui.

Waiola later heard from the Nature Conservancy representative, who met her in her lawyer's offices, and she tearfully related Foster's tragic end. The nicely dressed white gentleman was her same age. He leaned back in his chair; he hardly knew how to say it.

"Mrs. Foster, we would have welcomed your husband's bees. In fact, he could have expanded his beekeeping throughout all 400 of your father's acres. It's really unfortunate, and I'm so sorry, I really am. It's just the kind of benign use of the land we like to see on Conservancy land." At that disclosure, Waiola completely broke down, and he was hard pressed to console and quiet her.

At home, lying in bed late every morning, alone again, she wondered what to do. Then she had an idea, a wonderful and intriguing idea. Maybe she could find another beekeeper, perhaps that one from Pauilo. He was divorced, but very nice. He was also good looking, and they'd gotten along. She even imagined he'd given her the eye, and flirted a little. Maybe, just maybe, beekeeping could still hold a bright future for her, as well as a dark shadow in her past. She had a lot to offer. She got up from bed and stood in front of her dresser mirror, primping her hair and straightening her gown. She still looked good for her age.

"Yes, oh my yes, I've got a lot to offer!" She began sharing a sneaky, knowing smile with her own image, moving her body this way and that. "Yes, indeed!" she declared.

JAIMEE'S EDEN

He would show us all, in restoring and glorifying his corner of the ancient volcanic island of Hawaii, but for his own gain. That was Jaimee's mistake. Just as Kamehameha I had stripped the land of Sandalwood for his own profit and warring needs in the 18th century, enslaving his own people to harvest it for the special tax it represented, so Jaimee McVane would become rich by cultivating and displaying the wealth of flowers and plants along the shore just outside Hilo.

In the same way, he would argue, had modern astronomers built so many observatories on the summit of Mauna Kea, at over 13,000', to follow in the great tradition of the prehistoric Polynesian navigators who used the same stars to explore the Pacific.

He bought twenty eight acres of land in the shoreline woods, and began constructing a botanical garden. He knew the history of agriculture on that windward coast, and that the land had been created by successive lava flows and ash falls. And an occasional tsunami overwhelmed the shoreline. But that was the past, and the chances of any volcanic eruption impacting his land were certainly low, as any future lava flows must surely stay south. For he believed the geologists and volcanologists who told him he was reasonably safe. He also believed that those twenty-eight acres were his forever, and that was another big mistake.

He hired local Native Hawaiian men to help with the laborious work of clearing brush and making trails, transplanting bushes and trees, and building a visitors center, parking area and gift shop. Some of them told of living in Laupahoehoe and Hilo, where the last two tsunamis, in the '40s and '60s, did so much damage with many lives lost, and the eruption in the 1980s that threatened Hilo itself, but to Jaimee that was history, and the chances of such things happening again in his lifetime were so remote as to be academic. The 20th-century had already given its quota of natural calamities to the Big Island.

But then there was a sudden eruption of Kilauwea that bypassed Hilo, extending all the way down to the coast, slowly burying Jaimee's acreage, and even Jaimee himself, who couldn't believe what was happening, was cornered and driven into the sea by two pincer-like lava flows. He rowed away in a skiff, all the time watching his lush gardens, ponds, bridges, stairways and trails being overrun by red, fuming, steaming, serpentine lava.

When he made it to the untouched shore further north, he was a broken man. The police took him to a psychologist the next day, after holding him under restraint because he was incoherent and in a rage. He was babbling so fast that they gave him a sedative. After sleeping for 18 hours, he refused to talk altogether. From one extreme to another. So Dr. Jansen, the psychologist, injected one of those truth serums. He needed the help of a memory-relaxant drug if he were ever to get through to the actuality of Jaimee's mind. Finally Jaimee spoke. He was lying on a couch.

"Where am I?"

"You're in my office in Hilo. You've just had a tragic loss, and I'm here to help you. We all are. My name is Dr. Jansen."

"Is there anything left?"

"Well, you're here, which is the important thing. But I'm afraid the lava took the rest."

"There's nothing there, nothing at all?"

The doctor paused. "Well, you can see the land, of course, but Pele has taken it back, as they say. The lava covered everything. Actually, if you look at it that way, You've got more land than you started with."

"But the plantings, the flowers, all the buildings and equipment . . ."

"It's not there any more. Well, in a sense it is, the spirit of what you accomplished, in the minds and memory of everyone who helped you, and those of us who saw and enjoyed it all, and learned so much. But as for the existence and survival of your Botanical Garden, it's gone the way of so much else on the Big Island. It's been buried under a big warm blanket of molten rock."

"Oh God . . ."

"No, now wait. Think about it. You fulfilled your dream and many of us shared your dream. We'll never forget it."

"But I wanted it to go on forever. I wanted to leave it as a gift to Hilo and everyone who comes here."

"It is still here, Jaimee. Look at it this way. Remember the tsunamis that took all the businesses along the waterfront in Hilo, and the village the last lava flow buried, south of your place? Even Hilo itself almost got it. One lava flow came pretty close that time, in '84."

"Yes, but I took every precaution, got the best advice."

"Science doesn't know everything, Jaimee. Sometimes, as they say in California, 'shit happens.'" Dr Jansen smiled to himself, savoring his little hip witticism. "And I wonder," he added, "at the kind of advice you received, and how much you didn't want to believe. We have to take all this into account."

'Yeah, but why me, at just this time? Why couldn't it have happened fifty or a hundred years from now?"

"Because that's the way fate comes to us, Jaimee. These things come and go, and the works of man are puny by comparison. We just keep trying, despite everything." Jaimee sat there, pondering the psychologist's words, which sounded like a professional cop-out. Was he there to help him or not?

"So 'what else is new'? That's no help. C'mon, shrink, help me deal with this!"

Dr. Jansen leaned forward. "Okay, it's like the loss of a loved one in a terrible accident, a catastrophic or natural event you had no control over. Usually, if we really look at things objectively, there were decisions we made and extenuating circumstances we created that led in that direction. Mother Nature isn't malevolent or vengeful; it's we who perceive her that way. The same can be said of everything in life, good or bad. Why, I could get killed in an accident after I leave this room, and just like that my life's work would be over, my accomplishments obliterated by some stranger, or some strange, fateful happening, something I would say I had no control over whatsoever. Except that's not what happens, Jaimee. That's man's egotistical and subjective assessment. The truth is this: one, usually accidents or losses come to us because we, in some way, prepared the way for them, and two, everything you've done and been lives after you in the minds and memory of others."

Jaimee was silent. Then he slowly nodded his head. "Yeah. Okay. I can see that. But now what?"

"Pick up the pieces and move on, Jaimee. You have insurance, there is disaster relief and cheap loans available from the state and Federal government, and you could even write a book about what happened to you out there. You're not exactly destitute or without support, either. The workers you had will help you. Call them together and explain things. Tell them you still have that dream, and you want them to help you rebuild."

After Jaimee left Dr. Jansen, he felt better. He followed through in the ways suggested, and was surprised at the help, support and financial aid he found available. It would take him ten years to buy another piece of land, this time far from the current eruption of Kilauwea, on the other side of Hilo, and to design, plan and recreate his second garden of Eden. He was older, and had developed a heart condition, but in so many other ways he was wiser and stronger. He would do it, and live to see it flourish. As long as his health lasted. As long as he could breathe. Pele herself had given him another chance.

A MUSEUM MANQUE

The museum, located nearer the country than the small town, was surrounded by a high wall. The townspeople gossiped about it, and went there only once or twice in their lifetimes. It was named after the town, but was private. Admission was five dollars, less for children. The owners, curators and guides were an ancient couple, who lived in a cubby hole apartment on the premises.

At least they were an ancient couple by the time we went through the place that one time, being in their nineties. When we entered the double entrance doors, a bell rang. The interior was dark; a feeble light came on in the large foyer. An elderly gentleman, gaunt and eccentric, appeared out of the gloom. But his voice was stentorian. He announced the price per while pulling a battered cash box out of a small desk. We paid, and he ushered us toward some enormous Chinese vases, which framed the lobby and designated the main passage.

As we went along, he turned on banks of barely adequate lights in the sector just ahead of us. Then he'd slowly walk to the end and sit on a chair, waiting for us to finish looking and reading. He appeared to be napping, and never spoke. The whole place was aclutter with exhibits, relics, artifacts and oddities, every one labeled with scrawling penmanship, on cards of various sizes. They were on the walls, in glass cases, hung from the ceiling, underfoot, and on tables and shelves. The elderly man himself seemed like an exhibit, and we found ourselves discretely scrutinizing him, as if he were a mummified Native chief from the oldtime. Many of the labels were barely legible, in the archaic handwriting, or the labored text far too long to be read with interest. Usually these longer notes were historical ones, or told of the provenance of the item. There was no order to the displays, neither by subject or historical period or geographical location, or on what continent they'd been found.

For the old man, who was born around 1900, had been a collector since early manhood. And he was a diligent, not to say fanatical collector, going after anything and everything that might conceivably have curiosity value for others. Over the decades he visited Europe and the Orient, roamed Native lands, rummaged in old archeological sites, including burial grounds he'd learn of, and explored flea markets around the world, even visiting thrift shops and garage sales near home when he reached his dotage, and settled down in this town, where at last they constructed the museum that housed it all.

There was such disorder and confusion in the exhibits that one's head had a tendency to spin in a sort of nightmare vortex of past civilizations, personalities and events. The absence of windows heightened the sensation which, soon enough, made one anxious to get through there as soon as possible. The feeble lighting in each sector was doused behind us and we'd enter another shadowy realm, which began resembling nothing so much as those breached tombs underneath the Egyptian pyramids, full of stillness and gloom. The extreme age of our guide only increased this verisimilitude. When would it end? Where was the exit? We urged each other on.

Then we turned a corner, and were bathed in the light and color from a row of picture windows at the foot of some terraced steps. There sat the old man, on another chair of the same, simple style, alternately mumbling to himself and dozing off. We all walked down to the window, which held a view of a dry steam bed that ran beside the museum, and meadows and scattered woods stretching into the distance. Some cattle were visible. Life and sunlight! Fresh air and warmth! Then I asked our guide how the museum got started.

'I collected it all myself, you see. Yes, of course it took many years. I've been all over the world: Africa, Tibet, India, the Argentine and the Andes, the high Arctic, all of it. You'll see things here you won't see anywhere else! Yessir! We built this museum back in 19 and 35, to hold it all. I made all the signs myself. Well, thank you. It took a long time. 'Course some of them need to be done over, but there's no time for that now. It'd be too much trouble; we're all alone here, and don't have much help. Everything in the museum is in the order I found them. Yes, a collector's treasure house, and it's ours, nobody else's. People have come in here and offered to reorganize the place, but I want no part of it. Not on your life, I'd say! I found them myself and don't need others to tell me what I have, or how to display them. That's hogwash anyway; everything's labeled; what more do they want? That's right, many things need cleaning and restoring, but then they'd be damaged and ruined. It's not worth doing that. That's right, what you see is exactly how I found it. We keep the place ventilated and the floor as clean as we can. You won't find another museum like it anywhere around here, I can tell you. Took a lifetime to find it all. Kids come here with their parents and love it. It's the old world come alive, on every side. What? We don't keep the lights on because it's too expensive.'

Some other questions were asked and he addressed them, but he talked so fast and with such slurred speech that we gave up and moved toward the exit. We never did see his wife. As we went through the doors, he said nothing and I noticed all the lights were being turned off again.

We wondered what would happen to the museum and its contents once the old couple died. We couldn't recall ever seeing them in town, and could only imagine the kind of existence they had, holed up in their tiny apartment in this dark museum, full of artifacts and relics from their own past lives of collecting. The most recent exhibits seemed to be thirty years old already. Was this to be the legacy they'd pass on the townspeople and succeeding generations? Would first one, then the other be found someday, lying dead in their bed or sitting still and cold in one of the guide chairs? What would happen then? Or would a court have it all auctioned off, to be scattered around the world again, like the dust from a cremation.

The old couple had collected and cherished it all, protecting it from further depredation and weathering. There seemed to be no outlet for the collection, no future save dispersal and silence, an even greater silence than that in the museum's dank corridors and fetid exhibition areas, with the distinct whiff of mold here and there, through which we passed in hushed whispers. The high walls and massive gate protected the concrete walls and tile roof of the main building, and the pair of heavy doors and an alarm system prevented unwanted entry. But when these ancient curators were gone, what then? Would the unwashed public swarm in, turn on all the lights and haul everything in sight away, or would the museum become part of the public domain, its contents reordered and better displayed and lighted, following modern museum practices?

No one seemed to know, among the townspeople, and the old man never mentioned to whom their museum would be left. I'm sure if we'd asked, he'd have snapped, 'That's our business!' Perhaps, like some healthy elderly as well as the young in body, he felt they might live forever, their 'forever' being tomorrow, or at the most next week. They didn't give it a thought, I'm sure. Later we saw him riding a self-propelled mower on the lawns outside the walls, and once we saw both of them being chauffeured somewhere in a shiny, late model sedan, like celebrities. Some elderly couples have all the luck like that, living to extreme old age and still able to conduct the semblance of a normal life. Or was it? Had they actually become live exhibits in their own museum, ancient survivors of a past whose shadows inexorably receded within their dimming memories? Their final throes would surely bring greedy outsiders crashing in, taking whatever they wanted for a bargain, in ignorance of all that had gone before, in their lives. Whatever had been private would now be exposed to public view, whether remembered or forgotten, whether cherished or left to decay. The end of their unique odyssey was surely near . . .

WAIKOLOA HEAVEN

After the realtor for the Waikola Home Association showed us a couple of condominiums overlooking the golf course fairways, she said she wanted us to see a newly refurbished condo close by. That sounded better, because the first one we were shown was too small and the cabinets and cupboards in the other evidenced definite signs of termite activity. We needed to see something more promising. She said that, though this condo was occupied, the residents wouldn't mind at all showing it off. She'd known them for a year or so, and they were close friends.

She knocked on the door, and a thin elderly lady in a long, silky white gown opened the door, followed by another lady similarly clad, and a gentleman with a cane. All were white haired and without tans. The man had on white slacks and a very conservative, rather faded aloha shirt. We followed them in, and our realtor friend gave all three hugs and kisses, with oohs and aahs about the decor of their condo. On the other side we could look out floor-to-ceiling glass doors onto a fairway. A party was playing through, riding golf carts. We couldn't hear them.

The decor was indeed striking in its cleanliness and plainness. The whole place had been painted an old ivory color, the new carpet was snow white, the few small tables were of wrought iron with glass plates as tops, and the sofa and two sparsely upholstered chairs were adorned with flowery slip covers. The walls were almost bare of decoration. As we three visitors complimented the seniors on their redecorating job, I couldn't help thinking how eerily un-lived-in the place appeared. It was explained that all the household goods and personal belongings they'd hoarded and saved for three lifetimes were in storage on the island, and they'd brought themselves, their essential clothes, some kitchenware and linen, and all their family photo albums and framed photos to the condo. So we found them drifting and wafting about like wraiths and ghosts, veritable angels in this strangely antiseptic space. Their white hair, slender figures and flowing light garments further emphasized this impression. We didn't dare sit down, and at first neither did our hosts. It just wasn't a homey place, and our curiosity was piqued as to why. Finally they invited us to have tea, and extra chairs were brought in from the other rooms.

They had moved from Michigan a year previous, bringing everything with them in a forty-foot container. The couple, Jared and Rachel Elson, had their own condo side by side with that of Jared's sister, Ophelia. There was so much furniture to arrange, so many clothes to put away yet keep ventilated because of mold, too much houseware, and the extra crates, chests and hampers left little room for the countless boxes of memorabilia and mementoes from their long lives. All three were in their late seventies or early eighties, so between them they'd accumulated an enormous quantity of 'stuff.' And they found themselves at a loss as to what to do with it all. Pleasant Hawaii seemed to deny its usefulness and relevance to their new life on a volcanic island in the middle of the vast Pacific Ocean.

As they settled into their new digs, the two condominiums side by side, they didn't mind the rules of the Association that said no pets, no hanging of laundry outside, and no gardening. There was no lawn to mow either, which pleased Jared. But in time they felt hemmed in and clogged by all the things they'd brought with them, much of which remained unpacked. It all needed sorting, organizing and storage away somewhere else, not in their limited space. There was no extra storage available elsewhere in the building.

One day at lunch on their ground-level lanai overlooking the golf course they came to a decision. Everything except the barest essentials was to be packed up and returned to storage. They didn't really need much of anything they'd brought with them, after all! Sure, there was a host of souvenirs, heirlooms and family ephemera somewhere in the mass of it, but after all, it was their brimming memories that carried them from day to day, with reminiscences, stories, anecdotes, recollections of old haunts both foreign and domestic, and photos. These last they decided to keep with them. The best ones, amounting to over two hundred and fifty, were framed under glass and placed in rows at eye level all around every room of both condos. So everywhere they went or sat or turned, their gaze was met by those they'd known, loved or created, in the case of children, all their lives. Obviously the languor and lassitude of island living had gotten to them. They would vegetate, cogitate and conjure up the past vicariously.

They had no newspaper or periodical subscriptions, no radios, and after a week of sampling island cable television, had the cable canceled and the TV sent to storage too. Now it was just the three of them alone, talking about the past and gazing lovingly at the photo galleries, because quite frankly they'd tacitly recognized that they no longer had any future worth mentioning. At first they had tentatively looked into local clubs and activity groups, but after a few sessions, they dropped out. They'd seen it all before, 'been there and done that.' The expenditure of time and energy in such directions wasn't worth it.

So now they were content to talk, as they were with us that day. They'd invited us in to sit and visit. They had many questions to share with us, and for starters, to keep to neutral, superficial ground, we shared travel experiences. It seemed that, between all of us, we'd visited and revisited every continent until we were sated with travel. Then they asked if we'd like The Tour, which meant going around both their condos and learning about all the people and places in the photos. Well, the three of them led the three of us along, quietly explaining the portraits and family photos, group pictures and foreign scenes showing one or more persons they'd known. Eventually they became so stimulated and enthused about each photo that it had the cumulative effect of leaving us further and further behind and apart. We couldn't share such memories very well, or comment on them, because among the three of them first one than another would offer exclamations and intimacies, accompanied by every sort of emotion, from outright laughter to poignant silence. We could only stand there and weakly smile. By the time we'd reached the end of the hallway and were about to enter the first bedroom, it was clear we were no longer a part of their day, so we slipped out the back door. The realtor stayed behind to explain that we had another engagement, and had to leave immediately.

Later, we ran into the realtor lady up in Waimea, where we lived. She explained that it was always that way when she brought others to visit the threesome, and she was becoming a little concerned. She'd tried unsuccessfully to get them involved in community activities, which was easy for her not only because they were good friends; her own condo was at the other end of the same building. Even when she invited them to her own place, they usually brought, not food, but a bag of their photos to share and talk about. What else is there? they'd say, except family and good friends? From time to time they went for a drive in their older model Lincoln Continental, air conditioned and cream in color, with big leather seats similarly dyed, but the lava beds all around and boring resort hotels held no interest for them. They weren't tourists and had no desire to indulge themselves in the quaint sights of nearby villages, nor to stare at the surf on the rocky shore. The beaches were too hot and even the ranchland countryside beyond the lava too bare, especially after several years of drought.

A year later we happened to run into their realtor friend at a public meeting in Waikoloa, and we told her how much we'd been impressed by the condos of the three elderly people and asked how they were doing. She wanted to bring us up to date, she said. Now and then, the subject of their things in storage had apparently come up. What to do with it all, was their puzzlement. The horrid prospect of again bringing it into their quarters was too daunting to contemplate, and the idea was dropped as quickly as it came up, time after time. Then one day, for some unknown reason, they decided to put away their photos and bring in everything from storage! What caused such a turnover? we asked, surprised at this radical change of heart for the old trio. Well, she explained, they decided they were absolutely talked out of their photo collections, and needed to busy their hands. So they hired a local trucking firm which brought all their furniture, including a piano, and over ninety boxes of books, papers, records, music and many collectibles and unloaded it all, every pound and cubic foot of everything they'd acquired over their 230 aggregate years of life. The mass of it engorged their previously empty condominiums. We were intrigued by this turn of circumstances for these curious elders, and wanted to learn more.

We asked our friend if they'd mind if we visited them again, and she said they'd remember us and to stop by anytime on our own. They loved visitors, and were now home almost all the time. So one Sunday afternoon we came down from Waimea and knocked on their door. No answer. We knocked again, and were about to give up when a voice came from inside, 'Go around to the lanai side, please, the front door is blocked!' We walked around the building and up the fairway to their lanai glass doors. What we saw shocked us.

From floor to ceiling the condo was filled with all sorts of old furniture and stacks of boxes, crates and chests. We couldn't see inside at all. There was a narrow opening at the middle, and the husband, Jared, motioned us inside. What a contrast to our earlier visit, and we could hear live music too. Making our way to the far corner, we found Rachel, his wife, playing what sounded like Mozart on a baby grand piano, on which were piled some portfolios and small boxes. Ophelia was accompanying her on the violin. As soon as they saw us, they stopped, and we made our way together into the kitchen. We all sat down on chairs and boxes as best we could. Everyone was laughing and exclaiming, as if our winsome hosts had won a national lottery or come into some great fortune. After exchanging greetings and catching up on each others' affairs, we talked about the transformation of their home. Rachel began, and it was soon abundantly clear they were anxious to share the delightful fullness of what amounted to a New Life for them.

"My dear friends, I can't tell you . . . I can't begin to tell you . . ." And she continued through tears of joy. "We have so much! Every single thing in these boxes is so precious, so full of love and excitement and . . . happiness, I never could have imagined I'd be so affected by what we've done." Jared took up her cause.

"It's been very emotional for us. There was a time back home, y'know, when we almost sold our furniture and threw out much of what we've saved. We thought life in Hawaii would be so different and carefree that we could dispense with everything else, all the junk and stuff, as we called it, except a few personal things like the photos, and start with a clean slate. How foolish we were! But then we went to a concert at the Kahilu Theatre up in Waimea, and heard the Eroica Trio. You know, those three beautiful women?" Jared smiled.

"Why, they're young enough to be our children too," added Rachel, "And that added a poignancy and passion we weren't prepared for."

"Then the intermission came," continued Ophelia, "and none of us could go out! We were all crying! We'd had a revelation, or what they call an epiphany, I guess, a religious experience. And Rachel finally said what we were all thinking. 'We must bring back all our things from storage, to live with us!'" The music of those young women, who play so beautifully together, stirred us to our bones.

"I loved the cellist. Sara's her name," said Jared.

"Oh, and Adela Penas' violin. I so wish I could play like that," chimed in Ophelia.

"Well, Erika's piano, I think, was the best of all," opined Rachel. "They play so well together, it's incredible. I love them!"

It turned out that the three of them also played as a trio, with Jared the cellist. They were strictly amateur, they insisted, but still, hearing the Eroica had galvanized them to play again together, more seriously this time. But their condos were so crowded, and there seemed to be so much unpacking to do, I wondered how they could manage to do anything at all.

"We've already started in on the bedrooms, to get stuff off the beds, and out of the bathroom. One of the tubs is full of books!" Jared admitted, laughing.

"Yes," Ophelia agreed, "And from this, all our future work will flow. There! I've waxed philosophical. You see, we're already out of that silly rut we were in last year."

They were also artists in other media, Jared in oils, and both women in watercolors. The styles and subjects they each preferred were very different. Some of their past work was pulled out of portfolios and large flat boxes, still stowed behind the breakfast nook in the kitchen, of all places. We were impressed by the quality of their work. They really had talent, all three of them. Then we were treated to another revelation. Jared and Rachel were authors! Back in Michigan they had collaborated on a series of short books on local history, after that concluding that their writing days were over. They were too old to continue, it seemed, and writing and research entailed too much work and energy. But now! Not at all, they decided. Rachel had started a journal, and Jared had ideas for a novel based on his boyhood on a farm outside Lansing. As for Ophelia, she was thinking of contributing articles to one of the island newspapers, as she'd been a reporter many years before.

The walls and mountains of boxes everywhere held all their books, manuscripts, ephemera, art supplies and art work, sheet music, phonograph records, travel souvenirs and journals, collections of relics and artifacts, and other collectibles. Over the following months their condo underwent a total transformation, this time to reflect all their many lifelong interests, their children's accomplishments and grandchildren's progress, and their new Hawaiian life together, thanks to the Eroica Trio's help in launching them into a Golden Years renaissance. Now they would live, now they would sing and play, read and write, and . . . Why not? They also set about making plans to travel to many islands throughout the Pacific, from the Philippines to the Cook Islands and New Zealand, and from Pitcairn Island to Samoa and French Polynesia. They would see it all, these island kingdoms in their new Oceanic World.

We became close friends, and their joint condos became a combination atelier and study. So much went on with them, and they became well-known in island art and literary circles. Jared published his novel, the three of them played at receptions, weddings and parties, and their art was to be found in several galleries. Thus the musical catalyst offered by the exquisite Eroica Trio had changed their very beings, their lives, and their future. They were of the new generation of Americans, those well into retirement age who choose joie de vivre over indolence and surrender, and courageously live life to the fullest, embracing it with all their enduring passions and wisdom!

THE ERRANT HEIR

This is the story often told: Once upon a time a male baby was born to parents who were the heirs to a great island estate, far out in the middle of the Pacific Ocean. This young couple, married only a year, decided to spend their second honeymoon on a long cruise, visiting North America, Great Britain and Europe. They left their baby with an aunt while they were traveling. On the way to Europe, the beautiful bride fell ill and died. A few months later, back in the U.S., her husband, also ailing, frantically tried to return home to the island kingdom to be with his baby boy. But he died in mid-Pacific and was consigned to the sea.

Thus the huge agricultural estate was left to the baby boy. It was worth many millions, and involved hundreds of thousands of acres, so the boy's aunt hired an excellent farm manager with many references to run things. Twenty years passed, and as the boy grew, he was sent away to the best schools and colleges. On his 21st birthday, which he spent at a prestigious university in America, he was informed that he could now take over the kingdom he'd inherited. To everyone's surprise and consternation, most of all for the elderly aunt and faithful farm manager, he asked them to carry on without him, because he had other plans for his future, and quite different aims in life. He became an actor, entertainer and singer, and spent his entire adult life playing on Broadway and touring the Continent in nightclubs and cabarets.

When he was ready to retire, he returned to his island kingdom. He also brought back two intimates to his huge agricultural estate in Hawaii, his male lover and his lover's mother. The three of them occupied his villa. It had been many years, since he was a young man, that the estate heir lived like this at the ranch, and this time it would be for the rest of his days. From a first, abortive marriage, he had two sons in the islands, and a granddaughter who had followed in his footsteps as an entertainer and was now on the West Coast.

The three residents did much entertaining and regular horseback riding. The heir also brought back his stage talents, and used his wealth to found a theatre for the arts, left a foundation for improving local medical and educational institutions, and performed many times on the stage of the theatre himself, with prominent guests sharing the honors. He left his two sons very little, and on his death a foundation was set up to run the ranch. His home was filled with affection and friendship, as preparations for his death and his legacy to the ranch workers and village residents legacy were finalized.

OTHER STORIES

THE JAEGER PLACE

Part 1

A pleasant, not to say intoxicating Spring day. It was the forenoon, and the only sounds around the old farm were the occasional moo of a cow or the whinnying and stomping of a horse in its stall, the bleating of ewe or lamb in nearby pasture, and the crowing of a rooster in the chicken house, about as far away. The outbuildings, sagging and no longer the color of wood, seemed to reflect the sun's warmth. They'd absorbed it first, and now radiated it, as if the wood they'd been built of seventy-five years earlier were the best storage and conductor of heat on the old farmstead.

There weren't many trees around the house and buildings, but out back, between them and the series of small lakes, ponds and swamps that formed the northern border of the farm property, there were rank Box Elder woods. Box Elder: that tree with no pattern and no grace. It just keeps reaching out like a madman.

Jim, a twelve-year-old mind in the body of a forty-year-old, stood on the back porch of the big house. He could still hear them arguing, and as usual Lola—the Black Beauty, was siding with their mother. He knew Rhea had slipped out the front door because he saw her. She was headed for her beloved vegetable garden just the other side of the road. Inside, behind them both, the uproar continued.

"Git your clothes outta here!" Lizzy cried. "I ain't got time for that, and you know it. We do wash on Mondays, and you get your things here by 8 o'clock or you're too late. You'll just hafta wait!"

"No, I ain't," blurted Heinrich, the 80-year-old father, his face reddening. "You washed Billy's and Jim's yesterday, on a Sunday! Whataya think I am, a servant? I still run this place, so you just do as I say!" Thus spoke their Daddy, who'd horsewhipped them in their youth, daughters and sons alike. His daughters' bodies, especially, still bore visible scars unto the day of their death.

'No, you don't, old timer. You don't run anything any more. Look at the girls and Jimmy. Even Billy. He takes care of Jimmy as much as Billy does him. You're the only one needs lookin' after like a child!"

"You don't mind that, Lizzy, now do you? Lettin' those boys take care of theyselves, as if they had no mother. Just like our daughters. They take care of theyselves too." He ignored Lola's presence. Up to now she'd been glaring at her father as he kept it up.

"You just stop that damn talk, Pa! Ma's been slavin' her heart out all these years, and all you can do now is run her down. You, of all people, tellin' us if we're doin' wrong by one another. You're an old dog's crap most of the time! That's right . . ." She was shouting at the top of her lungs now. " . . . an old dog's dried up crap!" What'uv you got that's worth sayin'? Say it now! Piss it out, or just plain shut up, I tell ye!"

And the mother and father kept jawin' away, helped along by the juicy, disrespectful urging of Lola, the wild one with her black-dyed hair, her big black feathered hat, and all the cosmetics. Their father was a bald, slightly pot-bellied, cane-carrying old guy, who'd long since given up on farming. Long since. He could barely make it around the place to see what was going on.

It was 1936, and the Jaeger family was just getting by. They'd never had use for electricity or radios, and kerosene lanterns would be their lighting of choice until nearly 1970, long after Jimmy, Billy, absent sister Dorothy and both parents would be gone. They'd always had a telephone, though. Oh, yes. Everybody in the family liked to listen on the party line to see what other folks were up to. Or to hear themselves cursed for the chronic eavesdroppers they were, and everyone knew them to be.

Rhea kept them in vegetables, and Heinrich or Jimmy slaughtered an animal now and then for meat, out of Rhea's sight. The animals she cared for and called pets never got killed, especially the red-polled cattle in the barn. Both Rhea and Lola were trim figured, as was their mother. They all wore old-style dresses too. Rhea looked like a peasant woman, always with bib overalls and a big kerchief around her head when outside, and stooped over. Her mother wore dark dresses and a big shawl around her shoulders. As for Lola, she dressed up as if she were going to somebody's funeral. Her hair was dyed so black it was scary. The rouge, mascara, eye shadow and pancake makeup only made her scarier. Who was she, anyway, to put on such a show, just for her family and the animals? Of course she did go to local Saturday auctions now and then, and stood out like some caricature of a mad woman. As for Dorothy, who worked in town every weekday at J.C Penney's, she dressed normal, and ever since she came of age she spent as little time as she could at the farm. When she was home on weekends, she helped her mother or Rhea, but stayed away from her parents and Lola when they started carrying on. She had bad teeth, and her cause of death would be untreated diabetes. Sometimes she brought discarded things back for Jimmy and Billy, things they asked for, or anything she thought might interest them. She worked mostly in ladies' wear.

Jimmy started down the path through the trees toward his and Billy's cottage. When he was alone he went any time of day, but if he was trundling Billy up to the house or back down in the wheelbarrow, they went at pre-dawn or at dusk, when they could see the way but no one on the road would notice them.

Jimmy liked the cottage, and preferred staying there to putting up with three women and his cranky dad in the big house. They had a cistern and hand pump in the cottage too, so they had water. There was plenty of firewood in the woods between there and along the lakeshore, and kerosene lanterns served for light. At that time the road went right by the cottage, maybe 50 yards away. The two brothers would sit on the little porch and watch wagons and vehicles go by, or kids walking and riding to the little schoolhouse a half mile south, cavorting and leaping as if they were a traveling circus.

Jimmy was a closet womanizer, just like Billy, who had to be, since women wouldn't be interested to make the acquaintance of a legless gentleman, even if he were taken places to meet them, and even if he were cleaned up and decently dressed. So they just collected things about women, and read the personal ads that bashful or brash lonely women put in those periodicals especially directed at frustrated lonely men, along with fetching photos. In that respect they were just like their three sisters, except that Dorothy had the most normal contacts in town at her job, where she had friends. Only their sister Nancy had married, way back in 1917, and she'd never returned. Her husband took her away to a ranch in Montana and they had a passel of children. That was about the time Billy lost his legs, the first year of the Great War. William was the oldest of the Lother children; he was born in 1889, so he was 47 by now.

Lola was the one who subscribed to the romance and marriage-making magazines for women. They showed men all gussied up and posing, like they were responsible gents and the world was their oyster. The women Billy and Jimmy considered seemed ready to get married, or were already married to you, or wanted you to take them out on the town, or were found in their boudoir, thoughtfully pondering marriage to you alone, and Please Come Be Mine. Most of the entries were from men and women who lived in cities and towns far away, so none of these Jaeger brothers or sisters ever really got to meet anybody. Besides, it cost money just to answer an ad, and who knew where they lived? So it had to be fantasy for all of them. Lola, Rhea and Dorothy talked about the men in the ads, and Billy and Jimmy did the same about the women in the pulp periodicals they both subscribed to, one at a time, as they could afford it.

Jimmy did covet other things though, like women's dresses and shoes, and sometimes he might dress up so as to give Billy some fun, like he was one of those women come to call. When he went to town, which was rarely, he'd always stop by Penneys and try to see Dorothy, though not for long, because he wasn't comfortable going near the ladies department, and she told him she'd rather he not do that anyway. So he'd try to let her know he was there, and she'd come over and chat for a minute. There was one curious thing Jimmy brought back from town, and that was all these little white tags with local women's names and dress sizes on them. He'd found them in the trash out back of Penney's. There must have been a hundred of them, tied up with string in little bundles so you could hold almost all of them in one hand. He took them home and showed them to Billy, who was curious at first, then gave them back.

"Why'd you bring these home, Jim? What are they anyway? Did you steal them? Dotty might be in trouble if they find out they're gone." But Jimmy told where he got them, and took them upstairs to his cot, alongside which was a growing quantity of old tins of chewing tobacco.

They kept the cottage as comfortable as they could, with two stoves stoked with wood Jimmy cut up, keeping the chill out in the cold months. When it stayed below zero, Jimmy would pull Billy on a sled up to the house, then go to sleep in his little room downstairs while Billy slept like a dog on a little pile of bedding in a corner of the living room.

Jim helped Rhea take care of the animals and fowl, but he had to do as she told him. That was one of the few times Rhea would talk, because Jimmy loved to B.S. That was his entertainment, for a feeble-minded fellow. She also felt a little more confidence with him, because he never sassed her and was fun to be around. But such a sorry bullshitter he was, with all his puns and ridiculous stories, though when it came to her pet animals and fowl, he was family too, and they treated each other as nicely as Rhea cared for her livestock.

"You want help gatherin' them eggs now?" Jimmy stood at the door of the main henhouse out back of the granary. Rhea was moving around inside, putting them in her skirt.

"You just clean out the dirt, you hear? I'll git the rest. When I'm through, you can clean it out. Don't scare my girls though. You be slow about it." But Jimmy was scared he might do it wrong, so as often as not he didn't do anything. Rhea always told him to be slow around the animals too. But he was always real careful, so why was she so worried as to keep reminding him?

"You be slow now. These are my children." She'd be in the cattle stalls, and he'd walk in.

"Just clean out the dirt when I'm through. Mind you don't get kicked. Thanks kindly, Jim, I'll be done shortly." And that was all she said, all she needed to say. They got along.

Rhea had names for all the cattle, young and old, and they were her pets: Frederick, Lawrence, Oliver, Aaron, Jedidiah for the boys, and names like Columbine, Flossy, Gertrude, Lucy, Patricia, Letitia, Lillian, Charity, Hope and Ruth for the girls. She wouldn't let her dad kill any of the cattle, only when they were too old to stand up or were near death from some disease or whatever. (Heinrich found ways of having one go down now and then.) But if Rhea found one of the old things dead in the stall or out in the pasture one morning, she'd get Jimmy and they'd dig a grave on the other side of the woods and use one of the horses to haul the deceased over there. By now her dad was so old, he didn't care any more, and just accepted her desires. More often the family ate a lot of chicken, pork and mutton. For some reason, Rhea didn't care so much if any of them were killed. Maybe because there were so many. Sheep were flock-bound, and hogs she didn't consider to be so lovable and people-like, or maybe they were all too much like some bad people, being so greedy and willing to eat anything, pushing each other around and squealing if they didn't get their way. They were given what garbage came out of the house, as well as bad vegetables from the garden. But the cattle were different; each one was like a big child, needing constant care. Twelve years later, after her Daddy died, she stopped the killing of sheep and hogs too. So they had chicken and eggs a lot after that. Or Lola would barter with neighbors for a side of beef or dressed hog, animals Rhea didn't know about. That's just the way she was. If her Ma and Pa wanted to rule the roost, along with her sister Lola, she'd side with the animals. Even some of the chickens had names, especially the roosters: Chanticleer, Royal, Pipsqueak, Ranger, Napoleon. Clara raised baby chicks too, which she'd sell along with the eggs and her vegetables in season. She had a regular little hatchery and brood pens with gas heaters.

She kept a roadside stand all summer, but her chicks had to be special ordered way in advance, like six months ahead. Her vegetables were the biggest and best around, helped along by the manure Jimmy brought out on a big stone boat by a horse. Her garden was just across the road so everybody could see them. During the Depression sometimes people would try to steal some at night. One time there was even some gunfire, of all things, all written up in the local newspaper. Heinrich told the reporter he heard people on the road and came out with a shotgun. There was an exchange of shots, but nobody was hurt. Then a car sped away. But everyone locally assumed Heinrich had embellished another of his tall tales, and the incident was probably a lot tamer than that.

They had horses too, two pairs. Heinrich didn't do much crop farming. He rented out most of his land. He did have hay and pasture for his livestock, and acreage in oats, but that was it. Heinrich named the horses: Prinz and Toni, Heinie and Fred. Ordinary, nondescript farm horses, for mowing, haying, pulling a wagon or planter, or a dead cow. Any plowing and disking he'd long since hired, in exchange for cropland use. He was beaten and worn out, an elderly man whose sons and daughters had either died, moved away, become an embarrassment, or were taking the place from him, piecemeal. And his wife. Lizzy, nee Elizabeta, was the most stubborn. She drove him nuts and put him into an early grave with all her henpecking, complaints and arguing, often over the littlest things.

Jimmy was good with horses, who responded well to him. Lola and Rhea were crackerjack fence menders. They could set or repair fence so nothing or nobody could get through. Especially along the roadsides and up against other people's land. When you drove by, you'd see sheep to the south and cattle to the east, across the road and beyond her vegetable gardens. They had no silos, which made their farm stand out.

(Was that a farm, or what is it? strangers driving by would say.) A big white house with several buildings around out back, most originally painted red, all against dark woods. They formed a sort of livestock 'village' on that side of the house. There were several piles of manure outside the buildings.

The house had been generously built and completed in the 1890s. There were four large rooms downstairs and four bedrooms upstairs, two large, two small. Lola stayed alone in one of the smaller ones, and Rhea and Dotty shared one large one, their parents the other. Jimmy had the use of the little room downstairs, but didn't use it much, because he was usually found in the cottage with Billy. It got so his daddy slept there whenever he and Lizzy were on the outs. There was very large attic space above the high second floor ceilings, with full head-clearance, and board walkways in four directions. A trapdoor in the upstairs hall led to it, using a ladder. The cellar area contained a cistern for storing rainwater, which was brought upstairs to the kitchen sink (the only one in the house) by one of those hand pumps. There was also one large room for storage of various sorts down there, accessible either by the cellar stairs or another set of stairs that opened out through a storm door onto the east porch. Also, underneath somewhere there was a wine cellar, but exactly where was apparently a family secret, perhaps known only to those who were deceased, namely Heinrich.

There were no basins or toilets on either floor. Off the kitchen end, two outhouses sat dutifully side by side (about twenty feet apart), not far from a small, chapel-like building with a cupola on top that used to be the summer kitchen, before they put an addition off the regular kitchen and enclosed it, as a handier one. There was a 2" well with a gasolene pump that was only used for livestock, because the local water was useless for drinking or bathing, being full of iron and other minerals. It tasted awful. All the piping on the farm was lead, no matter whose water it carried, from cistern or well.

Downstairs there was the kitchen on the north end, a front room, a south room with windows all around, and in the middle, a small room that had various uses over time. Heinrich and later Lizzy eventually slept there when they got too decrepit to make it up the stairs. There were four doors going outside, all save one giving onto a closed porch: the one off the kitchen went into the summer kitchen then outdoors, ditto the front porch door off one protected corner of the living room, and the main west door, which gave onto a small closed porch before opening to the farmyard. That last one was the one most used, because it was the closest to the farmyard and most of the other buildings and livestock. Last but not least, there was a door from the south room onto a little porch that was nearest the driveway, which was not closed in. So Billy could sometimes be seen out there, sitting on a pile of blankets and just watching things. If anybody came up the driveway, he'd have to get out of sight fast.

There were no bathrooms or bathtubs anywhere. One bathed using sitzbath tubs, or basins, as best one could, hauling needed water up the steep stairway, which was closed off with doors at each end, as if it barred some secret and didn't want you to get upstairs to find out more, and see the mess.

Living conditions weren't much better for the Jaegers than for their livestock. Heat was provided by wood stoves on both floors, but later oil stoves replaced them. The kitchen stove gave off heat, too. By the time the parents became aged and senile, the upstairs had become a warehouse for collectibles, junk and trash, and summer sleeping quarters for whoever wanted to go up there. That made the living quarters below easier to heat. But at this time, in 19 and 36, the upstairs was still in full use. The east side of the first floor, fronting the road, had a full, windowed porch, where on nice summer days Lizzy, Lola, Rhea, Dorothy and Jimmy could sit and watch the world go by.

Heinrich, as often as not, found some excuse to be away from the house, pottering around with old chores and doing some minor repair work. There was always something to do or lose yourself on a farm that was going to ruination. And with all the females around, it didn't take long for his patience and interest to wear thin, and he'd go off somewhere. After all, he'd lost two sons from the farm already: poor Clarence, then David when he got married, and his last two weren't of much use. Billy the full cripple and Jimmy the feeble-minded were out of the picture, being damaged goods. At least Jimmy helped and was cheery company, like any twelve-year-old would be. Dorothy stayed away as much as she could without losing her place in the family, Nancy had married out twenty years before, of course, and Lola and Rhea, although good workers and still on the farm, weren't really farmers, as their daddy saw it. Rhea was too withdrawn and Lola sometimes seemed ill herself, with all her anger and compulsiveness. Yet when threshing crews came around, they'd be out there helping, dressed in bib-overalls and swearing like troopers, the men sometimes unable to tell that they were women, after all. One thing, these two sisters were the only ones who got some of that schooling down the road, at the one-room schoolhouse. However, one time they were accused of thievery, and their father pulled them out of school. Another alienating event in the life of the Jaeger family. So here was Heinrich, eighty years old, the great patriarch gone dry, and his children had more problems than they could handle, slowly abandoning both him and Lizzy and the farm. Why, they'd stopped going to church over to Elizabeth long ago, ever since Billy was brought back without his legs. What great gifts had God visited upon them?

If company turned in to their driveway, as they sat there on the porch, with Billy at their feet and Jimmy talking big, the legless one would quickly scuttle out of sight, into the house. He didn't need any encouragement to do so. "Here come the Jacobsens! You git inside, Billy, quick!" And he'd sidle off the porch, walking on two big hands like an ape, on which he wore heavy leather gloves especially made for him by Rhea, disappearing somewhere inside, most often into that little spare room.

That spring morning, Jimmy turned and walked down the path toward the cottage, hidden from view about two hundred yards away. The trees hadn't fully leafed out, and he could just make out the lake waters farther down, shimmering in the sun. It was the time of year he and Billy liked best. They could sit outside on the dinky roofed porch that fronted the road, or even go for a row on the lake, using an old rowboat David had left behind. Billy would sit on the stern seat with a blanket or coat over his stumps while Jimmy slowly rowed. Sometimes they even fished, or shot geese. The nearest lake was the biggest, maybe forty acres, and that led to second and third, smaller "lakes," but they didn't go over there, because it meant they'd have to get out and drag the boat over a low roadbed that divided them, and Billy would never leave the boat like that, on others' land, even for a minute.

Jimmy stepped onto the cottage porch and went inside. Billy was sitting in an old upholstered chair next to the wood stove, reading personal ads in a newspaper for men with lonely hearts and empty beds.

"Some good ads in this one, Jim. You goin' to stay and help make supper?"

"I had to come down, y'know. Get away from the noise up there. Boy, that Lola's got a mean mouth. She tells Daddy off somethin' awful. Seems unholy, he bein' her own Daddy, callin' him an old dog's crap. My God . . ." At that, Billy couldn't help sniggering, which got Jimmy goin' too.

"'Old dog's crap' . . . Well now, ain't that spicy!" Bill assayed.

"Yup! Just like an old crap, y'know, like one of Rhea's cows leaves around. Oh, was she wound up, I tell you!" Jimmy was proud of himself for such sudden flashes of wit, and guffawed. When they'd stopped snickering and chuckling, Billy settled down to the business at hand.

"I got some potatoes cooked, and Rhea left some other vegetables, so we can take our pick. I'll just throw 'em into the potato water."

"I'll go kill that one rooster that's got to crowin' too much. We can eat him, as he's been singin' for his supper so much!" And he smiled as he left to go outside, over to the chicken house in back. Later they sat down in the dusk to a pretty good repast, far from the tension and muttering in the big house.

Rhea and Lola had gone upstairs to their room at the north end. Heinrich and Lizzy sat down sullenly at opposite ends of the battered and out of plumb kitchen table and silently ate what was on their plate. Rhea and Lola would have something later. Nothing was said, nothing was forgotten and nothing was forgiven. Ever since their second oldest son Clarence had died suddenly in 1910, at age 20, followed by William's disastrous experience with the World War I draft, the family spirit had deteriorated and shrunken. No family could withstand such a setback as William, the oldest, gave them, the family honor having been ruined, and ever since then he was a freak kept hidden at home all the time. Whereas the Jaegers had entertained socially in the early years, in their nice old house, since Billy's return they had hardened into a reclusive, embittered lot. And the more reclusive they became, their memories of Daddy's whippings just added to it.

Nowadays, it was a matter of day to day survival. Every time his birthday came around, Heinrich always added that he wished it were his last. Billy's main friend in the house was Rhea. The other two sisters were otherwise occupied most of the time. Jimmy and Rhea kept the animals and vegetables cared for, leaving Heinrich to hobble around the old farm buildings leaning on his cane as if he were determined to show he was still the boss, and leaving Lizzy to hold forth in the house. The outbuildings had leaky roofs and rotting members everywhere. Roofs just weren't being repaired fast enough. Manure, old bedding and rotting feed were accumulating around all the stock buildings, because Jimmy felt poisoned by the strong ammonia smell every time he tried lifting a fork-ful. So, as often as not it was left, and he walked away from the task. In any case he was always far behind, just like his Daddy, but never failing to talk it up and tell stories about every little thing, as well as their patient neighbors on the rolling southwest Minnesota farmland. As for their own relations, they'd been estranged from them for ages.

THE JAEGER PLACE

Part 2

After Nancy got away by marrying in 1917, David was next. He got off the farm by going into the army during World War I and then by getting married in 1925. Brother Clarence had left the scene first by dying at age 20, in 1910. And William might as well be considered gone by the time he returned from being a draft dodger without legs around 1918, because he was a disgrace and embarrassment to his family. They hid him and never mentioned him to others from that time forward until he died, sometime before World War II. His ultimate resting place, right on the farm, would appall those few who learned of it, long after his death.

At first Dave had stayed on the farm, having built the cottage on a parcel of the farm that was his, at the north end. He and his bride briefly stayed there, but as soon as she became pregnant, they moved into an apartment in town. Dave continued working at the local cement plant, and they raised two children. 1925 was also the year the original owner of the farm died. He was a Norwegian named Erik Jorgensen. He'd sold it to Heinrich Jaeger in 1902, then moved into town for a while until be bought another farm nearby, where he lived eight more years before moving back again, for good this time.

After Dave and his wife left, Jimmy and Billy got to spending the warmer months in the cottage, which had been abandoned by his brother. So for seven or eight months of the year they maintained housekeeping down there. The rest of the family, Heinrich, Lizzy, Dorothy, Rhea and Lola occupied the main house. It was during this period, from 1925 until Billy's death, that Jimmy and Billy made the cottage their own. In other words, about fifteen years. During that time, Billy's stumps began giving him trouble. Using his hands and those stumps to get around made it hard to stay clean. Dorothy or Jimmy brought back alcohol and cotton, but it got so he had to keep a dressing on both stumps all the time. He had leather cups covering them, but how could he ever keep all the dirt and germs out? He had leather gloves on his hands, so with every 'stride' he took, his stumps landed in the dirt and manure and ground trash, again and again. That's when he stopped walking like that, unless in the house or the non-livestock buildings, because Jimmy either lifted him into a wheelbarrow in the warmer months or pulled him on a little homemade toboggan in winter.

Either way, William more and more had to bathe and clean his stumps, which became increasingly infected and ugly, not to say disgusting, and only Jimmy would help him. In the end, Jimmy asked Dorothy to try and get some other medications in town, but they were too expensive or she couldn't get a prescription without Bill somehow going in to see a doctor, which was out of the question unless he wanted to walk! So Jim made yeast poultices with charcoal powder, or dusted charcoal powder alone over the raw flesh. He tried boiling various herbs into a fomentation and making poultices out of them, changing them every several minutes or so, until he got tired. Salt solutions or things like spirits of turpentine or hydrogen peroxide were too harsh and painful; Bill couldn't stand such radical 'medications.' Soon the cottage reeked of all these treatments, but all for naught. His stumps just wouldn't heal.

One morning after a night of little sleep, Jim and Bill sat by the pot-bellied stove. Billy was sitting on the floor, leaning against a sort of 'tipi chair' back that Jimmy had made for him. Jimmy sat in the rocker. From where they sat, neither one could look out a window. They simply enjoyed the heat from the stove, staring at calendars on the walls and glancing around the room while talking about this and that. Bill was fingering one of those romance newspapers. His stumps were uncovered and drying in the open air after one of their poultice sessions.

"I wish I knew how long this was goin' on, Jimmy."

"You mean the dressings and all, for your stumps?"

"Yeah. How long do you think I can last?"

"You lasted a long time so far. It's been twenty years now. You worried? I ain't. You're strong as an ox. Why remember ole Gus Gustafson? Cripes, he lost both arms and hung on for ages, if you'll excuse my French!" And he commenced to giggle, thinking about an armless man 'hanging on.'

"'Course I'm worried! Now cut out your kidding, Jimmy. Damnation, look at these things! They'll be the death of me yet, I have no doubt. God, that was stupid of me, to let my whole legs get frozen."

"You couldn't help it, from what you told me. Remember? You got lost and the frostbite came on. There wasn't nothin' you could do. You wuz tougher'n polar bear out there, staying away from them laws so long. Now if I had to stay out there like that. . . ! Shoot, I'd be cryin' like a baby and yellin' for Moma to come get me after an hour!"

"Jim, all your BS-in' aside, I had time to come back to town if I'd wanted, or go to that farmhouse. I could see their lights, Jimmy! It was that close."

"Well, then . . . why . . ."

"I was dead set against goin' to war, that's what! That's what kept me from goin' back. I never wanted to kill people! Why should I fight other peoples' wars and kill strangers that's never done nothin' to me? They weren't even in these United States. So I says to myself, 'Bill, you ain't no common fodder, so you can stay right here at home, come hell or high water."

"So you did, and here we are, just like we always been. We been livin' together these twenty years. Hell, life ain't been so bad for us, long's we can stay outta the house! I don't like the way they've treated you, you know that."

"Yes, Ma and Pa practically disowned me after they brought me back. You know how we all been since then."

"Yes, I know. T'warn't fair at all. Not with family." Jimmy fell into a sulk, with the corners of his often gaping mouth turned down.

"We been split up and not a family since then, Jim, and I brought it down upon us, to be honest about it. We're not even a farm any more. Daddy gave up on that, too. Then they started fightin' all the time."

"Yeah, I stay away when they're like that. But it's not all your fault, Billy. Not at all, and besides, you didn't start that cussed war." Such a gem of intelligence from Jimmy was rare, and endeared him to Billy whenever they popped up. But he wanted to continue in his self-blame game.

"It's like I brought the war right back to the farm, Jim. And none of us went to war. Well, Dave did," he added, after a pause.

"He came back home too, just like I did," said Jim. "I didn't like it either; I knew enough to come home, and thanks to Ma and the doctors, I was kept here."

"That's right, and I stayed here too. I come back from the county hospital without legs, just like they might of got shot off in the war, 'cept I didn't go to war; I got that way 'cause I 'voided it, that's the truth."

"I didn't like it either. Ma didn't want me to go; she knew I wouldn't like it. She helped me get discharged. That's when they decide they don't want you. I was glad, 'cause I didn't want to go to war neither."

'The FBIs come after me, and I flew the coop. I guess I went off my rocker, Jim. I couldn't take it any more. If I had to go, they'd have to catch me." Jim chuckled in appreciation. He always had a filial respect and awe for Billy, his older brother, for all he lost by getting his legs amputated because he hated war, or was afraid of it, and thereby lost his whole future life, and the respect of everyone, including, and maybe especially, his own family.

"You was gone quite a while, Billy; they had a time findin' you." On that memory they sat a while without talking, and the popping and crackling of the stove fire sounded good. It smelled good, too.

"Jim, I have a feeling I won't last long. I'll say it again; these stumps are rotting right off me, and they're gettin' more painful." Jimmy said nothing at first. He was thinking long and hard.

"We'll take care of you, Billy, and if they won't help you up at the house, I'll take care of you." He got up and put another couple of small pieces of wood into the stove.

"Jim?"

"Yeah? . . . What?"

"Who's goin' to remember me, once I'm gone? I've just been a burden and a shame around here, ever since I was born. I ain't amounted to nothin'" He was getting a little emotional.

"Well, it weren't your fault, Billy. Don't think that way. You're as good as any of us. It's them other people, all the high monkey-monks that wanted that war. We didn't. You're better'n them, I believe, and you sacrificed your legs too. Not many people here would be that brave, as I see it."

"Take care of me, Jim. You're the only one I can trust one hundred percent. The rest stay away and tell me to hide all the time. I ain't been off this farm since I came back in '18. It's all I know. It's my whole world, Jim. The only people I see are you and the rest of the family. I don't want to die a castoff family freak nobody wants."

"I'll take care of you, Billy. Never you fear. I'll take care of you."

As the months went by into the Fall, Jimmy became desperate. Brother Billy was in a lot of pain and needed to see a doctor. But try as he might, he not only couldn't get anyone to take him into town, the women absolutely forbad it. They left Jim to his own devices, in helping Billy. Finally, when he was in terrible pain and being eaten alive by the infected stumps, with gangrene running amok, neither he nor Jimmy could sleep. Billy rolled around on the floor of the cottage with his pants off, moaning and crying out, gritting his teeth. Jim talked with his dad, who sent him back to Billy with a case of bourbon. Billy started consuming a bottle a day. He just kept drinking it like a baby and getting thinner, and his ribs and jaw bone started caving in, like he was already a carcass in the woods. He was so haggard with a wild dirty beard and deep sunk eyes that Jimmy was afraid of him, afraid to stay close at night, when he couldn't sleep neither, what with Billy carrying on so awful. One night he slept down by the lake wrapped in horse blankets, even though it was getting colder, almost down to zero, but Billy's cries were so terrible that he decided to go to the big house, but not before leaving Billy stocked with another bottle of bourbon and stoking the stove fire as much as he could, though he knew it would go out before dawn. Jimmy quietly entered the house and aimed to sleep in the small room on the first floor, but his father was already in the cot, so he found a couple of blankets and curled up in a corner.

Then morning came, and it was five below on the porch thermometer. He headed for the cottage without eating or having anything to drink, not even a cup of coffee. He heard nothing as he approached the quaint little house. When he tried to open the door, something was jammed against it. It turned out to be Billy himself, and he was dead. The place stank of his decay and urine and shit, even at that frigid temperature. Jimmy gagged, closed the door and left. Later he came back and used a horse blanket to wrap his brother up in. He was so light, it was done in a few minutes. Once rolled up, Jimmy cut down some old clothesline and tied the bundle real tight.

He easily lifted the bundle and carried it out to the toboggan, laying it in and tying it on. Then he hauled Billy back up to the house. He stopped at the back door and went in. His parents and three sisters were at the kitchen table. His daddy looked up.

"What you want, Jim?"

"Billy's dead." Everyone looked at him now, but nobody said anything, only looked at each other.

"Where is he, Jimmy?" His Ma said.

"Right outside, on the sled."

"Well, don't leave him out there, somebody might drive in," Heinrich ordered.

"Where can I put him?"

"Dig a grave so we can bury him! What else?" his father said. Then Lola spoke up.

"He can't bury him now, Pa. Ground's too hard. Just put him in a corner on the front porch, Jim, until we figure out what to do."

"All right."

"But cover him up with a tarp or something," Heinrich added. "We don't want to see whatever it is you brought him up in. He's all covered up, ain't he?"

"Yes."

And so that's where William's remains stayed for several days. Then William's Daddy had a brainstorm. One night he got Jimmy to haul the bundle out back of one of the stock sheds, where there was an old manure pile. Heinrich followed him with a lantern. When they arrived at the appointed place, the father told him to stop, and gave orders.

"Now you just get outta here. I'll take care of it!"

"But what about. . . ?" Jess offered.

"Never you mind! Just go back to the house!"

His Daddy looked mean enough that Jimmy obeyed, after glancing at the miserable bundle on the little toboggan, as if he were seeing Billy off safely on a trip somewhere.

Heinrich set the lantern down and got a pitchfork that was leaning against the nearby shed. Digging a hole just large enough and just deep enough for the bundle, he dragged it up and dumped it into the manure hole, which was still decomposing and able to steam a little. He then covered it over in such a way as to make it look like it always had.

He stood back, assessing his handiwork, staring at the disturbed manure pile. He then stepped forward and patted it down with several whacks of the fork. He stood back again, this time dropping the fork to one side.

"Good Goddamn Riddance!" he said, under his breath, and walked away with the lantern.

It was years before he told anyone what he'd done with his son William, and no one dared say a word about it. That night a snowfall covered all traces of the interment.

THE JAEGER PLACE

Part 3

Less than five years after poor William died, Dorothy passed as well. She developed abscessed teeth and fell into a diabetic coma. That was in 1943, in the middle of the war. Then five years after that, Heinrich died, at age 92. The old man just withered unto stillness, passing away in his sleep. That left the two youngest sisters, Lola and Rhea, brother Jim and their mother to share this moribund farm for the next fifteen years, until the spring of 1963, when Jim gave up the ghost too. He died at the regional VA hospital, sixty miles west. Now only the two sisters and their mother were left, the latter by then almost 100 years old, or would have been if she hadn't died a year after her son Jimmy did. And three months after that her only surviving son, Dave, the one who married and left the farm, also died. Lola and Rhea were now on their own, and spent the next 24 years subsisting on the family's long dysfunctional, derelict family farm.

A few years after being left alone, the sisters finally brought in electricity. That was in 1969 or 70. They were probably the last farm in the county to do so. They put a few bulbs and outlets downstairs in the house, leaving the upstairs and great attic for storage only. There was a yard light, a couple of bulbs hanging in the barn and stables, and two other probable outlets, one in the chicken house and another in the little hatchery shed.

From then on, Rhea was the one who did the most of what you'd call farming. She grew her garden and took care of the stock. Lola claimed she managed things, and spoke for them both. When they'd go visiting, driving their older model pickup, gentle Rhea followed smiling while Lola talked like she was some big goddamn farmer and county councilwoman rolled into one, but she was only looking for odds and ends to buy, barter or steal for her household. Rhea was her junior accomplice.

To Rhea, who also did most of the cooking, she wasn't always kind. "You keep your damn hands off that sewing machine!" Rhea would have little to say, and she'd invariably go out to tend her garden or animals, leaving Lola to hang around inside, reading the romance magazines, turning the radio up too loud or listening quietly on the party line. They made the rounds of auctions together. Lola loved farm auctions. And though she had the money to buy machinery, her habitual M.O. was to take lesser household things away without paying for them. She wouldn't bid; she just hid. She and Rhea would hang around until the right moment came when they could load and haul away something for nothing, like a pressure cooker, a washing machine, or boxes of pots, pans and canning jars. It got so the auctioneers warned the sisters to stand back and stay away from things until they were sold. Yet Lola had ready money, and after 1994 when the farm was sold, the new owners found a large quantity of cash neatly tucked away in a place where you'd least expect to find it.

By that time, in the 1980s, the sisters were not only considered petty thieves and kleptomaniacs, but pack rats, hoarders and hermits who never threw anything out. They'd become human vermin in that sense, like squirrels, packing everything away for a dubious future. Rhea canned so much of her vegetables and fruits that, by the time the farm was abandoned and sold, scavengers found enough produce to feed a family of five for years, most of it dating back forty years or more, however. Nothing was edible, unless you dared to place your fate in the hands of the Jaeger sisters. The whole house became clogged with every kind of household and personal material, from undressed excellent lumber, boxes of old magazines, personal waste carefully wrapped and cached everywhere, including the attic, to the clothes of every member of the family, furniture of every type and description, stoves, kitchen appliances, farm records, cardboard, old-fashioned wood boxes from the early part of the century, and so on. Every available space was full to overflowing, the closed porches, the summer kitchen, and from there into the outbuildings, which were unusable because of the glut and mess of things pushed or thrown in willy-nilly. Where livestock had been, their ancient bedding and manure remained, two feet deep. The old barn was half full of decades-old hay, darkened and worthless from many roof leaks, which on a sunny day let shafts of sun in like little white rainbows. Most smaller buildings were caving in and nearly inaccessible due to jammed doors and overgrown bushes, and saplings literally barring the way. Dark, rickety stairs, slanting and failing, led to dank lofts where old horse tack, coils of rope and worn out machinery belts were found hanging over old storm windows, alongside burlap bags, pipes, and conduits or parts for machines no longer being manufactured. Only the granary and machinery shed had some structural integrity, but by 1988 they'd probably not been used as such for 40 years. Any active machinery had to be kept outside, because there was no room inside. In any case, it was gone by 1994, leaving only junk-filled outbuildings, big and small.

There was one additional oddity. At the end of the hay and large livestock barn, in what used to be horse stalls, Rhea had apparently set up little chick incubating boxes and dog pens. Yes, dog pens. She enclosed some of the stalls by hanging old blankets, curtains and ripped open burlap bags on all sides, then added a low false ceiling and boards across the front. Inside these cozy caves she added fresh straw on top of two feet of old bedding, the manure of long-deceased draft horses. Then two or three cardboard cartons were put inside, with a little door and 'loft' window cut into each. In effect, she created a little chick village, one she could watch from outside the hangings. In another couple of stalls, dogs were kept, how many or what kind isn't known. A pile of carefully folded dog food bags and old dog stool underfoot attest to that.

In the end, Rhea and Lola became the stuff of local lore and legend, along with the rest of the Jaegers. All sorts of hearsay and lore sprang up in people's minds. There'd been Heinrich and Lizzy, whose loud arguments could sometimes be heard on the neighboring farm, a quarter mile away. Heinrich had used a cane, but when out of sight of others, he didn't. He also rounded up and stole his neighbor's flock of geese, and only returned them when the neighbor came over and heard them in one of Heinrich's sheds. Another time he made the front page of the local newspaper when he was shot at, apparently by people trying to steal Rhea's beautiful vegetables at night. That was during the Depression. He returned the fire with his shotgun. There was some question if it was really about vegetables, or was he into smuggling booze from Canada. After all, one bit of lore said that 'he had business up north,' but nobody knew what it was. Maybe the alleged 'wine cellar,' located somewhere among the buildings, was a hint at what business that was, but there was no proof of it, just a lot of gossip.

Lola, the "Black Beauty," found her name on every cash register in town for bad checks, and to deny her credit and watch out she didn't shoplift. Rhea was the stooped over, smiling crone who followed Lola around, and sold her vegetables and eggs at a roadside stand in summer. And Jimmy, who'd been mentally unfit for army service and was sent home to his mother. Poor Clarence, a splendid young son, had died an untimely death of lung troubles in 1910. Dorothy was little known and died of rampant diabetes, and Nancy, who married out and was disinherited, because she kept trying to get help from her parents to pay medical bills, harassing them that way. Finally, there was William, who simply disappeared after his tragic experience in draft evasion. He'd been seen over the years, scuttling out of sight on his hands and stumps, and it was said that when he died, his remains were left on a porch until Spring. And on and on. There was no end to the gossip about the Jaeger place, that farm without silos.

Lola slept in the south room on the first floor, the one with the most windows. She kept the curtains drawn night and day, only parting them if the sun shone. She had a single bed, and her clothes were hanging on chairs, stuffed into boxes, and filled a boudoir dresser that used to be her mother's. Lola's room was the best, the prize bedroom. There was a stove in there, so she could be warmed, winter or summer.

Rhea slept on a cot out in the living room. It wasn't private, because the living room had long since been used for storage too. It was full of all kinds of furniture, including the pump organ, on which were piled all kinds of junk of a family nature. The sisters no longer liked to go to the outhouses, so they put a honey bucket in the small room, the one Heinrich and Jimmy used to sleep in. There was so much stuff piled and cluttering up the whole downstairs, including the kitchen, it seemed miraculous that they could find anything more than once.

October 12, 1984 arrived, and Rhea, the oldest by four years, had just turned eighty. They usually ate as the urge declared itself, but this day they ate breakfast together. Rhea had made some toast, oatmeal porridge and tea. Lola came in from the other room.

"I opened my curtains again. It's nice out. So how's my birthday girl? Eighty years of family progress, eh?" She grimaced with one of her sour looks, and her usual dark cosmetics allowed a synthetic smile to leak through. She was still dyeing her hair, so the combination gave her a Halloween mask. She sat and sipped the thin tea, then set it down, looking at the tea leaves in the bottom of her cup. "Feels like we're the dregs of this family," Lola mused.

"I think I'll take the dogs for a walk today. It's real nice out. I'll take them out in the south pasture this time."

"Well, you do what you want, dearie. It's your day. Y'know, I sure miss ole Jim. Sometimes it's handy having a man around, lord knows. They can lift things."

"And unscrew jars. We got food here I can't even open now."

A neighbor youth, Kent, was sometimes hired for work the two old spinsters couldn't handle, but it was surprising what they could do together. Their preference was to manage everything themselves, so they were sometimes seen by passers-by on the road, hunched together like black twins working over something and getting it done all alone.

"Kent used to like comin' over here, but he up and married too."

"Who'd he marry?"

"Mary Lee Larsen. They live over near Erhart. Her sister works at the truck stop last I heard."

"Oh, yes."

"So I don't know who we could get to come now. Maybe one of the boys down at the Chevron in Elizabeth." Lola worked the jam covered toast into her mouth.

"I don't need much help. Never have. 'Cept maybe Jimmy once in a while. But I ain't doin' all the things I used to."

They spent very little time around the other buildings now, and the house contained most of their activities. Rhea still had a little vegetable garden, but it wasn't much, and she only canned a few choice things each year. But she did keep a couple of little, short-legged terriers she got in trade. She kept them in the barn in the summer, letting them loose each morning. In the winter they slept with her in the house. Their names were Jimmy and Davey, after two of her brothers.

Lola was busy eating when quietly Rhea spoke up.

"I know what I'd really like to do today."

"What's that? Go to town?"

"No, I'd like to walk over and see William, maybe take something to put on his grave."

"What would that be, Rhea? The flowers are all gone."

"Oh, maybe a pretty vase. I found one of Ma's upstairs."

"We don't want to mark it, Rhea. We don't want anyone to find him, or know where he is."

"Oh, I know. I'll cover it. Ain't it kinda sad though, keepin' him hid where he is? Like he was never our brother to know and acknowledge? It makes me sick to think of him out where he is."

"I say let it go, Rhea. Enough of Billy and all that business. I'm so tired of it. He's long gone just like the others. We got enough to do just takin' care of ourselves. Where Billy ended up is his own choosing. Daddy took care of him and that's enough for me."

"I believe Ma would want us to keep everyone in our memory. Little Billy too."

They often talked that way about family, the house, and the farm.

"We'll have to sell one of these days, Lola. I know that."

"That's right. I've been workin' on it. There's no hurry; it's not goin' to disappear, and the longer we wait, the better price we can get."

"Yes."

"I been thinkin' we should move into town, though."

"Yes." Rhea had been dreading this for a long time. But she knew it was getting harder to manage in winter. She would miss the farm, every part of it, which she dearly loved, but for the sake of both of them, a town place would be nicer, and closer to things. Maybe she could see David's wife or even some of Nancy's children, whom they hadn't seen in so many years. Rhea would like that.

"I've talked with a realtor, and they can find a place for us, right in town. But I told them not right now, so they'll keep us in mind. It'll take time. I have to get used to the idea; you know what I mean."

"Yes, surely I do. This has always been our home. But since there's no young folks to take it, what can we do? No children or grandchildren around . . . only Dave and Nancy's children." Rhea wondered why they couldn't work out something with them, to take over the farm.

"I don't want none of them to have it! I told you that. I haven't even asked them, ever. They've only wanted our money, especially Nancy's kids. Now she's passed, they still want to know what we're doin' with the farm. They got their share a long time ago, and they know it." Rhea had nothing more to say, because it was an issue Lola had already settled in her mind.

In their early years, as young women and into middle age, they had both thought about marriage, the luck of finding some gentleman to share their lives with. But it always came down to this: 'This is our farm, and we can't bring ourselves to hand it over to some stranger, maybe a gold digger, least of all a husband.' All the Jaeger boys had died off, so that was it. Now if some rich and handsome gentleman would be willing to get married but have the farm stay in Lola and Rhea's name, that might work. They could always kick him out. But the house and buildings had become such a treasured realm and valued storehouse, in their eyes, they couldn't imagine allowing someone to come in who might redo the place as he wanted or thrown them out, no sirree. That would be the end of life as they'd always known it, almost since 1900. Just let some stranger gentleman try to do that to them?!

"Don't even think about it, Rhea, not now or never! When we're ready to leave, we'll leave. But even then, I still want to keep the place," declared Lola. We have to find takers for all this damn stuff. Antique dealers would pay plenty for some of it, I know. So we'll hang on to the farm, and take our time selling off what we got."

The difficulty of accomplishing this while living in town didn't bother her. She assumed they'd go out there with people and show them what they had. That meant the house and outbuildings would be left empty for anyone to get into, however. People don't hesitate to drive onto unoccupied property, especially an old farm with ruined buildings, and take whatever they want. It's open season. Times had changed. Lola thought she could control the farm from town, but at her age and remove, nothing was guaranteed.

So the Jaeger sisters just kept going, having their little breakfasts, messing about in the house or outbuildings among all their collectibles and abandoned farmware, keeping their oil stoves going in winter, sometimes canning a few of Rhea's vegetables and fruits (some of the old fruit trees still bore) as they became ripe in July and August, renting out the fields, etc. The livestock had all died or were sold, except the chickens, and Rhea kept on the best she could with a shrinking version of her vegetable garden. As for Billy and Jim's old cottage, it fell into ruin, just like the other outbuildings.

At last, in 1988, they decided to move into a house in town. By that time Rhea was ready too. It was a sizeable place away from the downtown, on a knoll. They brought along many boxes and pieces of furniture, for which they had to hire Kent's oldest son to haul. They moved in, drew all the shades and curtains, and never answered the door if they could avoid it. They cut a tiny square in the front door shade, as a peep hole to see who had come up the steps onto their porch. Rhea's little dogs became too much bother, and one night she fed them good and let them loose on the far side of town near David's widow's house. The elderly sisters lived there until 1996, when Lola broke her hip and had to have a leg amputated. Rhea stayed on, but she developed gangrene from putting tight bread bags around her legs full of sores.

Meanwhile the farm was being vandalized for several years by so-called 'special friends' or business acquaintances of Lola's, with or without her permission. From 1988 through 1994 it was a ripe garden for these antique and treasure hunters. When it was finally sold, the new owners had to keep discouraging them and others from continuing to ransack the place, even while they were emptying it out and remodeling. It had gotten a reputation. None of these strangers ever found where the hidden money was, but the new owners did. While they were cleaning up and moving the old furniture out, clearing space in some of the outbuildings, they just stumbled on it in the oddest place, which we're not at liberty to disclose. And so the name and reputation of the old farm finally came to an end, when a new family moved in and made it their own.

Rhea died in 1997. In the nursing home, Lola's 'special friends' would come by and help take care of her. It was while they were helping her take a bath, due to her refusal to let the nursing home staff undress her, that they found the scars from Heinrich's whippings, so long ago. It was during these visits that they also learned the details of Billy's burial. Lola just let it slip out one day, as if it weren't anything special. And yet another secret was bared, because she disclosed that her sister Dorothy had been a diabetic, and when she developed abscessed teeth nothing was done; she fell into a coma and died without any medical attention.

One day the new owner of the Jaeger farm called Lola at the nursing home. It seems he had a question about the uncured bricks and mortar between the walls of the old house, which had served as insulation, and that he was removing. All she could reply was "You're a damn fool!" and hung up. Which seemed to sum up in four words the self-image of the Jaeger family, or at least that of the one-legged surviving daughter, the "Black Beauty," who by now had ceased dyeing her hair, and wearing so much black mascara. She just sat and cussed her missing leg, and anyone who dared come within hearing, just like one of Rhea's barnyard dogs. At last, on a Spring day in the year 2001, Lola died of heart complications. And that was the end of the Jaegers, if not the end of the Jaeger legend.

THE GENEALOGICAL RESEARCHER

I'd come to this small town in southwest central Minnesota to look for some record of a lost member of the family, who used to own the farm we bought back in 1994. It was a curious and strange family, and we'd found obits and other mention and records of the parents and seven of the eight children who lived there since 1900. We were just curious to know more about them, because we'd heard so many stories and gossip that we also wanted to know some facts. The eighth child was the one unaccounted for. He was a son, Joseph by name, and the first born to them. All we knew was that he'd evaded the draft in World War I, and fled into the woods in winter, where the FBI found him with both legs so frostbitten they had to be amputated, almost at the hip. He became a cripple and stigma to his family, and they hid him and even denied his existence. He was last noted in the 1910 census. After that, there was nothing, except for all the unascribable anecdotes and hearsay, and a few of eyewitness reports. He'd apparently lived on the farm until just before World War II, and was probably buried somewhere in the woods in back of the farm.

So, idealistic and persistent me, I was determined to find more. I rented a snappy red car and drove around, trying to dig up information. I stopped at the county courthouse, the regional "Treatment Center" or mental hospital in town, the library, and finally the county museum's historical research center. I'd talked with a former neighbor, now in a nursing home, but all he could supply were more stories and hearsay.

It was early winter. The leaves had long ago left the Elm trees that lined all the streets, which reminded me of the village in upstate New York where I grew up. The ground was just dusted with a half inch of snow, and the lowering temperatures kept the streets and outdoors almost clear of pedestrians. I was alone and drove in silence, not choosing to turn on the car radio. I wanted to concentrate on the search, and believed that somewhere I would find evidence of Joseph's life. He couldn't have disappeared without a trace.

I went into the research room of the county museum, which was run by a well-organized historical society. Some elderly ladies were working on genealogy. They came there almost every day.

"I thought the missing son might have been buried on the farm property," I said to one of them. Another looked up from her work.

"Have you doused?" she asked.

"What?"

"Have you doused?"

"No." I didn't see the connection.

"You can do it. You can find bodies as well as water."

"But he disappeared over seventy years ago."

"Doesn't matter. Try dousing." I made a not too permanent mental note.

At the library, they'd had only one volume of the latest county history, and I urged them to order the other one. The historical society had a complete set, why shouldn't the library? It was still available. They were derelict if they didn't have both. So, out of my frustration, I was ordering these people around, trying to help them be better equipped to help me.

At the mental hospital, built over 110 years ago yet still in good functional condition, the interior having been renovated several times, I talked with the medical records head.

"After thirty years we give access to the records. After a hundred years, they're destroyed." She disappeared into the basement to look in the vault. There was no record of Joseph having been admitted.

I went back to the historical society's research center. He hadn't signed up for the World War I draft like his brothers either. He wasn't in cemetery records and wasn't mentioned in any of his parents' or siblings obits. Had there been a funeral? Apparently not. The neighbor I talked to had said someone else told him there was a memorial service for Joseph, but he didn't think it was true. One story said that he died in the winter and the family left his body frozen on the porch until spring, but this was the gossip of neighbors. Joseph's whole family was the object of a tenacious repertoire of gossipy stories. After Joseph shamed and condemned them all, they became very reclusive and eccentric.

Again I stopped by the county recorders office in the courthouse, to look through the death certificates for the years he might have died, in the late '30s and early '40s. The women there were welcoming, and a basket of cookies sat on the work table. Around the room sturdy metal shelving held scores of big, leather and canvas-bound volumes of birth, marriage and death certificates, going way back to the early 19th century; but I couldn't find anything on him.

Looking for this missing life, sitting alone in the recorder's office, staring at the cookies I declined to eat, I had an overwhelming sense of mortality. I thought of my own life ending some day, and perhaps I too would have a single line in one of these volumes, stating only my name. And my death certificate would probably give just the date of my death. In the old days the cause of death was given, and the coroner's name. No more. Like everything else in this age of automation and computerization, the records had been trimmed down to names and numbers.

Apparently Joseph wasn't considered to be a whole or real person, once he was returned home legless. He probably walked around like an ape, on his hands. A feeble-minded brother may have trundled him about the farm in a wheelbarrow in summer and pulled him on a sled in winter. That is, when nosy neighbors weren't around. He may have lived in an old cottage down in the woods on the farm, away from everyone, and been taken care of by that same brother, who probably buried him too. They were the only brothers surviving on the farm at that time.

In the end, I couldn't take it any more, this fruitless search for someone who'd been denied by his own family, who hid from society, and who died anonymously and ignominiously, a stigma and a pariah, a draft dodger and a freak. I left him in peace, not wanting to disturb further his troubled memory and discarded, silent remains, wherever they might be.

A DIFFICULT TIME

Fear and Anxiety are part of life experience. Fear of the unknown is my particular worry, especially to do with my health. When symptoms come along, and then worsen, especially unexpected twinges of pain, I want to know what's wrong with my body. Why is it acting up, or falling apart? Why is it feeling poorly, perhaps unhappy from neglect? Is it reacting still further to some other condition or disease that I have, or to the drugs that the doctors gave me to combat it? What is wrong? Is there any way I've been remiss, so as to bring on these symptoms?

Of course I have the full range of other dreads and phobias, like fear of precipitous heights, snakes, and dark city streets that I've never seen before. Also to some degree a fear of flying. As a boy I used to fear bullies, but now, as a full grown man, I can handle them. I do wish I could return to confront those childhood tyrants though, showing them my full adult strength and anger, as a reminder that their days of bullying are over. But, you know, I'm old enough to realize that I've really accomplished many things, and even if my jet airliner failed and put me down catastrophically, I wouldn't feel terribly deprived. The only real loss and terror would be anticipating the sudden end of everything I've ever known, and never seeing my beloved wife again, as well as places and people for whom I've retained an abiding affection and enduring memory, for whatever reasons. My anxieties are based, then, on a fear of deteriorating health and pain, life-threatening situations, the absence of familiar and reassuring surroundings, and the unknown. Not so much a fear of death itself, because that would be 'It'. I'd be appalled and paralyzed, but not afraid. Not really. What could one do, as the plane hurtles toward the earth, completely out of control? I'd just give up, close my eyes, and want It to end as quickly as possible.

I'm a homebody, and would rather not travel a whole lot. I nurture domestic habits, chores and care-giving for my hearth and home, and my loved one. Travel is interesting, once one arrives, or, if on the ground, as one is moving through fresh or foreign space, or old spaces left behind long ago. It's just the flying there, if it's necessary to fly, that bothers me. My nerves tense from the moment I walk down the gangway and cram myself into my seat in that potential group coffin!

But such ordinary fears aside, there are anxieties I have that are really unresolvable and eternal. For example, why on earth was I born to this life? I mean, what was I supposed to do, say, accomplish and pass on, before my time is up? I've never been a commercial success. Hell, I ended up a librarian. You can smirk at that, but I'm convinced that whether you're a librarian, janitor, waitress, mother, engineer or CEO, life is just as stressful for all of us. At bottom, there's no difference in degree, just in kind. Any job or relationship with others is always as much a challenge as it is a fulfillment. There are going to be as many times of struggle and loss as there are joys and blessings. For me, most of life I've stumbled around half blind, and it wasn't until I stepped off the deep end in my late 50s and was rescued by others that I began the full life, able to love unconditionally and be comfortable with myself. Or almost so, because the old times still haunt me, and from these tap roots most of my writing is derived.

We may even have relationships to places, and for some of us, these can be as affecting and troubling as any human relationship.

Both incur long memories. Let me tell a story, by way of illustrating this. A few years ago, a friend and his wife, Jan and Didi Parker, left their home on Hawaii's Big Island to go to Wisconsin, for two reasons. One was to be with their daughter and farmer son-in-law (I'll call them Patty and Tor; his full first name was Torvold) for the birth of their second child and to help care for their two-year-old, and the second was for Jan to go to the Mayo Clinic in nearby Minnesota to have his cancer evaluated. Patty and Tor's farm was in northern Wisconsin.

Jan's prostate cancer had first been diagnosed in 1993. After a radical prostatectomy (in which the whole gland is removed), six years of hormonal blockade therapy (testosterone, the male hormone, fuels the cancer) and radiation, it was coming back again with an "elevated PSA" (the test that shows how well the body is fighting the cancer; lower is better). That means that the treatments have failed and the cancer is going to spread to the bones. So they set up an appointment at Mayo. The whole trip would last about six weeks, and would occur during the son-in-law's work on his late corn harvest. The landscape would be bare, and snow flurries and maybe a blizzard or two would whiten and chill the land before they returned to Hawaii. They packed three large suitcases, flew to Los Angeles, then Chicago, then Duluth. From there they were picked up and driven the farm, located in the woodsy, rolling country of northern Wisconsin.

Hawaii is sunshine, heat and color. Color everywhere. Wisconsin in November can be cloudy and gloomy, at least where their farm was located. With the wheat and soybean harvests all in and the first snow flurries sticking on the ground, and no sun, it's a stark, bare, black and white world. The wheat and soybeans were harvested with Tor's own combine, an older Canadian Gleaner, but when he wanted to start getting his corn in, and there were 400 acres of it, the weather turned rainy. Then he began having one combine part failure after another. It just wouldn't keep going. Then the snow flurries started, and it stayed cold. His new corn dryer set-up was having mechanical problems too.

A week after they arrived in Wisconsin, while all this was going on, Jan and Didi rented a car and drove to Rochester, Minnesota, for his Mayo Clinic appointment. For the first time they found some sunny relief from the cloudy skies up north, which felt wonderful. After securing a room in a motel, they went to the Mayo Clinic, which is a maze of various hospitals and clinics in the old downtown, all connected by very nice skyways or tunnels, elevators and corridors. Parking garages were convenient and joined to this huge complex, as were some major hotels. One never had to go outside! And there were many good shops and restaurants. Jan had sent all the medical history, reports, tests and x-rays he'd had done over the past six years, and Mayo also ran a few tests, as well as verifying the original pathology as being erroneous. The "Gleason" number for the aggressiveness of his prostate cancer turned out to be 7, not 9, which is better.

On the second and last of the two days they were there, they had a consultation with the assigned doctor, the one Jan had talked to from Hawaii about two months before, when all this was arranged. The evaluation was informative and helpful, and the doctor answered in detail all the questions Jan and Didi had. The bad news was that the cancer has spread to a few places on Jan's skeleton: a small spot on one rib, the top edge of one side of his pelvis, and a spot on his backbone. But Jan was still "asymptomatic," so it was now a waiting game. However, for various reasons the doctor recommended adjusting the hormonal blockade therapy down (since it apparently wasn't working any more), to see if that might help the situation of: 1. An elevated PSA, and 2. The cancer having metastasized (spread) to the bone. So the treatment prescribed was a partial withdrawal of the hormonal blockade therapy. For all the period of this treatment, Jan had received either implants or injections every few months of Zolodex or Lupron, then taken six capsules a day of flutamide. The total effect was to block his body's production of testosterone; he was chemically castrated. So the Mayo doctor now suggested stopping the flutamide capsules, which Jan did, two days later. (He'd been so used to taking them for six years that it took a couple of days for him to make the break.) Six to eight weeks later, after they returned home, his oncologist in Hawaii would see if this change had made any difference. In the meantime, they drove back to the farm, to be re-immersed in mostly cloudy weather.

The corn harvest effort was doggedly continuing. A neighbor's cows had gotten into Tor's corn during the summer and done a lot of damage, so their owner offered to put in a couple of days' work with his own combine, in recompense. But that left over 350 acres to do. Meanwhile time was getting short, and drastic action was called for. Tor finally hired a combining crew, and after about a week they finished the job, just 12 hours before a crippling blizzard came in! All told, this was not a good corn year. But at least he got this year's corn in. There were other farmers in the area who weren't so lucky. They got snowed out.

Well, the poor guy spent a whole month working almost day and night during that period. Short on sleep, drying corn all night while he'd catch catnaps in his truck or a little heated trailer alongside the dryer (after a carpenter brother fixed the trailer door), then out on the truck and working with the combining crew all day, etc. Luckily Jan and Didi were there to help, but not exactly being spring chickens, they became worn out and stressed out themselves. Their daughter had to sleep sitting up downstairs due to nausea if she lay down. Jan and Didi helped with the two-year-old, and with the baby after she was born. Together Jan and Didi did any errands or field chauffeuring they could help with. Didi helped with the cooking.

Earlier I mentioned there were socio-cultural differences Jan and Didi encountered, between their experience and the folks in

Wisconsin. First of all, there were the long flights to Wisconsin, changing planes twice, etc. They had a room to themselves in the 100-year-old, renovated farmhouse, built before 1890, a large one, and that was great. Tor's parents' farm was a 15-minute drive away, and served as the main base for his farming. The corn dryer was on one end of their farm.

As for the neighbors and other folks who lived around there and in the nearby town, whom they eventually encountered, they were friendly enough. Well, they were nice, but they were different. You could talk about mundane, everyday things, or farm topics, but beyond that it was pretty home oriented and conservative, except that some in Tor's family had traveled abroad. Most of the family lived close to one another and their parents, which included all his brothers except one, and his sister, his uncles, aunts and cousins. In contrast to Jan and Didi's children and other kin were scattered from New Jersey to Hawaii and from Alaska to Los Angeles.

It was farm country, with a lot of social life centered in very small hamlets, small churches, and the regional town, population 9,000. There was men's work and women's work, and that set the tone for everyone. People didn't always talk readily, feeling inhibited and constrained not to talk about some things, especially the controversial, or anything that might cast aspersions on their relatives, friends and neighbors. Lots of gossip and hearsay, and that's how people's reputation was determined, whether based on actual facts or not. The older generation had the habit of keeping private matters to themselves, sometimes to their detriment if they needed help but couldn't bring themselves to ask for it except in an emergency or crisis.

Meanwhile, as a sidelight, Jan and Didi were far from home, yet wanting to begin buying, packaging and shipping Christmas gifts to their far flung children and other relatives. Once they got home in early December, there wouldn't be enough time. Accomplishing this in rural Wisconsin was a challenge, and they began thinking of their comfortable Hawaiian home, the colorful Hawaiian scenery and gentle climate.

One night Jan went to the bathroom. While sitting on the throne, he looked down and was shocked. There were big splotches of lesions, blisters and a rash across both inner thighs, and a dark, ugly infection between the pinky and next finger of his right hand. Taking off his T-shirt and looking in the mirror, he saw little red spots here and there on the inside of his arms, a few on his chest and up by his neck. What was going on?! It was an alarming and scary sight. That night he'd experienced two or three unusually intense "hot spells," one of the side effects of hormonal blockade therapy, and so he figured the rash might be due to these warm, sweaty conditions. He'd also had a benign fungal growth on his inner thighs for the years of his hormonal blockade therapy, turning the skin dark, but it hadn't bothered him.

The next morning, a Saturday, he went to the local Hospital's Emergency Room. The doctor bent over as Jan displayed the rashes and sores. "That's ringworm," he declared. "And," as he held Jan's hand and looked at the nasty dark infection between his fingers, full of pussy blisters, "That's actin-" something; Jan didn't catch the rest of it. Treatment was prescribed, and he went and bought the medicines and returned to the farm. What he had was contagious, he was told, so he must wash often and keep himself and his bedding separate from others, especially the two-year-old and baby in the household. More stress, because he didn't come to their daughter's home to spread disease among them, and now there was a newborn baby!

Three days later, his skin condition was much worse. He returned to the daytime Clinic this time. Another doctor looked, and thought it might be Impetaigo, which is also contagious.

So Jan was again urged to take all the precautions not to infect others. He and his wife carefully avoided touching each other, and slept on opposite edges of their bed. Clothes and bedding were washed and washed again, and disinfectant sprayed on anything his skin touched. But this second doctor had the honesty to confide that he was still uncertain of the diagnosis. He wanted to consult by phone with a dermatologist colleague and friend of his in Duluth, a hundred miles away, and would let Jan know his recommendations. He went home, and later that afternoon the doctor called him. Two new medicines were prescribed.

Jan and Didi tried to understand what had caused this outbreak of skin infections. There were his hot flashes from the cancer therapy, which he considered 'normal' and tolerable, and it had been two weeks since he'd stopped cold taking those flutamide capsules, after six years of taking six of them daily. Then there was another worry. A couple of days before the skin rashes and lesions appeared, Jan and Didi had explored an abandoned two-storey cottage in the woods on the farm. It hadn't been occupied in thirty or forty years, but it was filled with the personal debris of mattresses and clothes, medicine bottles and boxes, snuff boxes and newspapers, with probably mice or rat debris everywhere. Didi had gloves on and mainly just looked, but Jan got down on his knees and pawed through much of it with his bare hands. They were both concerned that he might have picked up some exotic skin disease, or worse, from all the spores and god knows what else that filthy place harbored. Jan remembered reading a news account of a janitor who'd been told to clean out an old warehouse, and had died from some rare respiratory disease he'd picked up from the dust of old mice droppings.

The medicines the dermatologist had prescribed by phone seemed to be helping, but Jan was determined to know exactly what it was he had. He called and made an appointment to see him in Duluth three days later. After disrobing, the doctor right away told Jan, "You have Erythema Multiforme, which is a general allergic reaction. It usually accompanies a body infection like strep throat, but can also be caused by being overtired and under prolonged stress. You may be more susceptible to it because of your hot flashes and clothes that are too tight. You should wear loose clothing while under treatment." Jan couldn't remember if he told the doctor about having stopped his flutamide medication after six years of being on it, but that seemed reason enough for a 'general allergic reaction' too. The visit to the abandoned cottage, the doctor assured him, wasn't related to it. And the condition wasn't contagious at all, so Jan and Didi needn't have worried about that, either.

Jan was already taking strong antibiotic pills and a weekly anti-fungal pill that the first doctor prescribed, and he continued the antibiotic and added a powerful (and very expensive) antibiotic cream topically as prescribed by the second doctor, after consulting with the dermatologist. There was also a powder that he'd mix with warm water to soak his infected hand in. All these medications had the result of getting rid of all the skin conditions. But then, a few days later he broke out in a rash around his middle, from his neck to his navel and from one armpit to the other! First he used Calomine lotion, then a Benadryl ointment to keep it from itching. After a week, when he was on the way home to Hawaii, it too went away. At last, all the symptoms were gone.

After Jan had returned to normal, he would joke of having had an allergic reaction to Wisconsin, plus being far from home and disliking the flying experience, the frustrating circumstances of Tor's corn harvest, their daughter's birthing, taking care of her little ones, the very different socio-cultural environment and the cold, colorless, sun deprived landscape. But there were medical causes as well: what they learned at the Mayo Clinic about Jan's cancer, abruptly stopping the flutamide treatment after six years, and then the confusion surrounding Jan's skin condition and how to effectively treat it. It took three doctors to solve that problem, but they succeeded. Perhaps, too, since Jan was overly sensitive and prone to anxiety about his cancer and his health, hypochondria or psychosomatic symptoms might have contributed to it.

Jan and Didi vowed to never again visit their daughter during the harvest time, and would choose instead June or July, or at least earlier in the fall. The only reason they came that late fall was because of the baby's birth, which was November, and they probably weren't planning on having more children anyway. November is probably the worst time to visit Wisconsin, at least that part of the state. Why tempt fate by plunging needlessly from light into darkness, from sun to gloom, from color to black and white, from their laid back Hawaii home life to a stressful and late harvest situation in the heartland? By the time Jan and Didi were back home, Jan's symptoms had disappeared, except that now he had a soreness in his lower intestinal tract! A local doctor said it could have been caused by the stress and anxiety he experienced in Wisconsin, and yet another antibiotic was prescribed that made it go away. Jan's body was at last free and clear once again, relatively speaking, to carry on his life as a homebody in Hawaii, wearing shorts and a T-shirt all the time and following his pet avocations: working at writing on his computer, reading, playing music on his cello, and working on their lawn and garden beds. When he woke up mornings, it seemed that a big burden had been removed from his shoulders. In every way he felt normal again, except for the cancer, of course, which he'd long ago accepted as a partner in his life, silent yet powerful, patient yet unrelenting.

THE IRRATIONALE OF THINGS

Jardine Mathewson was a peacetime student. He wasn't drafted to go to war, had high grades, and obtained his B.A. degree from an excellent small liberal arts college. From there he entered Dartmouth for graduate study. Within five years he obtained an M.A. in Philosophy, then his PhD. dissertation. He developed a theory of Being that placed the rational and logical capabilities of humans above both inherited traits and environmental influences.

He was raised by parents who led enlightened lives. Ballard Mathewson, his father, was born to a family of distinguished public servants, who had served at the cabinet and ambassadorial levels in every Republican administration since Warren Harding. His mother, nee Marie-Therese Pintot, was the great granddaughter of a famous French oil painter of the 19th century. She had studied ballet and dance, and had become a member of the Corps de Ballet of Washington, D.C., when she met her husband.

They only had the one child, Jardine. After receiving his PhD., his parents sent him to British and European universities for three years, to travel as well as pursue more graduate study. When he returned, he gained a position at Dartmouth on the faculty of liberal arts, teaching graduate courses in philosophy. After a few years, when he'd achieved tenured status, he began writing books.

The first was a re-write and expansion of his dissertation, which was published by a northeastern university press. It raised rationality and logical thought almost to the status of a religious calling. Nothing could surpass it, Jardine argued, as an arsenal of control, success, leadership and even contentment, in life as well as work. Of course, all this obsessive theorizing and sterile analysis reinforced notions of superiority and ultra-confidence in his own life ways. He attracted a debutante to be his wife, and they raised four children, perfectly, with the best schooling available. However, both Jardine and his wife had busy careers, she being an instructor in comparative linguistics, also at Dartmouth, so they hired a nanny to take care of their children much of the time.

Then one year Ballard Mathewson fell out of favor with the Eisenhower administration, and lost his ambassadorship to India. How it happened was, he took an embarrassing and unfortunate position on a policy matter of the Indian Government, and was called home. He was incensed, and let everyone know it. Most thought he'd lost control, and was finished. The truth was, he'd spoken up and given his astute personal views to the Indian media, which is completely contrary to the rules of diplomacy. He'd lost it, for some reason, and everyone was surprised and puzzled, because until then he'd been the model of professionalism in all his posts. Jardine, his son, was especially affected, because he was uncomfortable with his father's loss of control, as he saw it, and his apparently irrational conduct. It seemed to fly in the face of everything his father had learned and practiced in almost thirty years of foreign service at the highest levels.

Jardine asked for and had several discussions with his father, trying to help him understand why he'd made such a mistake. He took additional pains to analyze his entire career and record, citing his accomplishments and reminding him that he, his successful son, had learned so much at his father's knee, and had only done so well because of his example and wise mentoring. Ballard had truly been a perfect father in every way, and these admirable traits had been passed on to his son, in spades some said, by way of being critical. So, as father and son, and reaching back through previous generations, there was an unbroken line of brilliant men in education, administration and public service. And their wives, too, had been exemplary women, in the forefront of their times, proving by their actions that the distaff side could, in their way, match any of their husbands' accomplishments.

Jardine even went so far as to write a long essay analyzing his father's life and career, concluding that his unprofessional behavior in India was actually a brilliant move, bringing into the open issues that needed to be addressed by both the American and Indian Governments. Despite the embarrassing and impulsive nature of his father's 'outburst' in front of the Indian media, which used street language and name-calling, Jardine used his logic to rise above those details in order to pull his revered father out of the gutter, as it were. One day he presented the essay, which he'd had bound in half leather, to his father. It was over seventy pages in length, single-spaced and with an elegant font. His style was dense and detailed, incessant with philosophical analysis, exploring his father's every move and decision. Two days later they met again.

Ballard Mathewson, former cabinet officer and ambassador to India and other countries, earlier in his career, appeared tense and drawn. He kept a steady gaze on his well-dressed son as they shared lunch together in his father's study, brought to them by the butler. They sat in leather-bound chairs, and a fire crackled in the fireplace. It was between Thanksgiving and Christmas, and snow was on the ground. His father had just turned sixty-seven, and didn't yet know if his career as a diplomat was over or not. He was still available for service, but no inquiries, interviews or invitations had come his way from the new Administration. When lunch was finished and cleared away, the butler brought in a tray with a sherry decanter and two glasses, a box of cigars, and withdrew.

* * *

"Well father, you look well."

"Really! I thank you for that."

"Emil makes great crab sandwiches. I wish my Donald could do the same."

"How's Anne and the children?"

"Fine. We're all very busy. And I'm working on a third book."

"What happened to the other two? Still in-print?"

"Well, yes and no. One is OP, and they won't be reprinting it. The other sold a few hundred. It's really over priced. Still, I think it was worth writing. It may be a sleeper, of course."

"What was it about again? I still haven't read it, though it's been on my bedside table for a couple of years. I mean to, of course."

"Theoretical mistakes of American reform movements, looking at the socio-political basis for their growth."

"Sounds interesting. And the one you're working on now?"

"I'm looking at your line of work, father, the diplomatic service. How policies may conflict with the reality in foreign countries."

There was a long pause, and in wiping his mouth with the thick linen napkin, his father dropped it. Jardine rose as if to retrieve it.

"Just leave it!" his father commanded. He was obviously upset with something. Jardine sat back down.

"I've read over your so-called essay." He looked up and stared at his son with red-rimmed, watery eyes. He appeared much older than his years, the more so because of Jardine's opening compliment.

"Whatever possessed you to dissect me like that?"

"I thought I might be helpful at this time in your life."

"So you see yourself as my filial mentor and guardian, now that I've reached my second childhood?"

"I didn't mean it that way, father."

"Well, how did you mean it, then? I felt put down and scolded, like some obstreperous child."

"I was prompted by the incident in New Delhi, that's all."

"That doesn't concern you or your theories in the slightest! Have I ever consulted with you about it, or, for that matter, have I ever interfered with your career or book projects?"

"Well, no . . . you gave me advice, of course, but . . ."

"That incident in my own public career was really none of your goddamn business, Deeny! None whatsoever!"

"I know, father, but after all . . ."

"Stop patronizing me! I perfectly understand what I did, and why. It was long overdue."

"I know, and that's precisely why I argued in defense of your actions. I don't see why . . ."

"You were telling me things I learned long ago, son, as if I were incapable of grasping the significance and timeliness of my own actions. I made the decision to speak out as I did precisely because I believed it would be the most effective. I can't speak for those superiors who were far from the scene and poorly informed."

"But surely you'll admit you expressed yourself irrationally, father. Your statements were larded with contempt and anger. Such four-letter words are violent, full of blind emotion."

"And just what do you think life is all about, Deeny? It's the irrational that moves the world! What do you think love, hate, hope and remorse are based on, some of your so-called rational thinking and cold, mathematical logic?"

"Well, perhaps not on the instant, but underneath . . ."

"Underneath my foot! Underneath is a can of worms, a hornets' nest, and a Pandora's Box, all rolled into one, that's what!"

"But your position as ambassador, the protocols . . ."

"That's so much bullshit, my son. Pure bullshit. Do you think we talk nice when we have ambassadorial consultations, or private conversations after cabinet meetings? It's all so much groveling and grasping, trying to outmaneuver somebody else, score points, gain the high ground, get the ear of the President."

"I guess I realize that, much as I dislike the idea, but . . ."

"We're all irrational beings, Deeny, dominated and driven by our emotions, most of which are badly understood, if not ignored, especially when it comes to ourselves. We aren't aware of who we really are, on a personal level, and why we react and behave as we do. For example, do you really understand why you wrote that essay, and then presented it to me?"

"Of course, to help you, father!"

"No. Number one, you wanted to gain my approval. Number two, it was to display your superiority and dominance, the fact that you, as my son, are superceding me, and besting me at last. And it's perfectly natural for you to want to do that."

"Well . . . No, that's not it at all. Not just that!"

"You see? You're denying the irrational in your own behavior. Perhaps irrational is not quite the word. You're blind to your own psychological and emotional energy, namely your sentiments, that impelled you to analyze my life and career, do a lot of research, write that interminable, nit-picking essay, and then present it to me in such a beautifully unnecessary leather binding!"

Jardine was the one embarrassed now. The conversation was taking turns he was unprepared for. He remained silent and thoughtful as his father continued, now in a more philosophical vein.

"We're all half nuts, Deeny, if the truth were told, but we can never admit it publicly. Why do you think we order and comport our lives as we do, and dress up for daily living with so much habit, custom and decorum? Because if we didn't do that, we'd become half-mad savages again, that's why. We need our delusions of order, control and loyalty, Deeny. Some religious fanatics fall into that category, and megalomaniacal dictators. The world is full of these and always will be, I'm afraid."

"But certainly we've made progress in the West since the Enlightenment?"

"Yes and no. The Enlightenment was another form of denial, in my view, and the source of modern day delusions. For example, science and its methods are myopic and self-fulfilling. It's down side is its delusion of omniscience, of claiming to know the truth about everything, sooner or later. It claims to have the best way of looking at the world and our lives, our human condition. In terms of that, there is more truth and honesty in Van Gogh's use of color and Faulkner's use of words than all the hypotheses and theorems and experimental data you could ever bring together."

"But we can't live according to such sources of information," Jardine commented. "We need the scientific method and logic just as much."

"Of course we do. But we must never forget the origin of it all, and that's what I call the 'irrationale of life.' It's the very core of our nature as human beings. In fact, the more we are able to recognize this fact, as I see it, the more progress, as you call it, humanity will be able to achieve. When I swore like a street beggar in New Delhi, I was speaking a form of truth. Everyone listened; for a brief time I had the world in the palm of my hand. Sure it was gauche of me, outrageous and 'out of line,' as everyone pointed out, but I'm glad I said it. It's as simple as that, and not worth all the theoretical analysis you felt compelled to exercise on it."

"Yes, father."

"Listen to your inner dream and your heart, as well as others' troubles, and the world will move ahead more rationally."

"Yes, father."

And Ballard Mathewson, a temporarily unemployed diplomat, refilled their sherry glasses and proposed a toast.

"Let the good grape help us grasp all these things, my son, and never slacken our resolve!"

"Hear! Hear!"

HAZARD EVENSON

After the army, Hazard Evenson left the States to find education and travel in Europe. There was no place for him in the family business, as he saw it, and he had no head for sales and accounts receivable anyway, no matter how lucrative they might be. His father, Ruel Evenson, was a realtor and land developer, pursuing his career like a man obsessed, to the gradual detriment and eventual loss of his wife and children. Nothing mattered so much to him as a big killing in his business ventures, and everything took a back seat to that. Everything!

Since he declined to join his father's firm, Hazard assumed he was now the black sheep of the family. Actually, both his mother and his siblings, two brothers and two sisters, had also been driven away by Ruel's single-minded and rapacious career path, which Hazard sometimes likened to Sherman's scorched earth march through the Carolinas. Mrs. Evenson and the younger children were now living near her parents in Virginia, away from Mr. Evenson's stamping ground in Central New York State. It was a so-called 'trial separation,' and they were well provided for.

Throughout Europe, Hazard was impressed by the depth of history, and the relics, remains and monuments. So many languages and cultures, so much art and literature; this was his ancestral heritage, not the shallow and foreshortened one he'd known at home in the States. While he was attending the Sorbonne in Paris, he lived in a rooftop garret, barely keeping warm in winter. But he loved it. He was able to live quite nicely on the GI Bill, plus a small allowance his mother sent him every month. He lived as a French student, not as an American in France, and became quite fluent in the language. The only time he spoke English was when he stood in line at the American Express office on the Avenue de l'Opera, to pick up his mother's check. He spent his vacations in England and Scotland, and loved to collect books, scarce and rare volumes in areas of interest. In fact, when he toured the capitols of Europe as well, he made a beeline for the most venerable bookstores, and enlarged his collection, which began spilling over into the other two garrets on his floor, which were unoccupied. He'd become friends with the concierge, feting her now and then, and she only smiled when he asked if he could temporarily store his books in them. He wasn't sure what he was going to do with them all, but it felt good to have them, and he kept collecting. More and more.

Then came the day when a phone message was brought to him, "Call home at once," signed by his mother. Hazard learned that his father had been killed in a huge traffic accident in fog on the New York State Thruway near Utica. Later the attorneys contacted him, as he didn't want to leave Europe. His share of the estate would bring him millions! He was astounded. Where had all that wealth been hidden? He certainly knew that his father had been very successful, but also that he wasn't inclined to spend or share his profits. He had never traveled, but his mansion on Maple Drive near Syracuse was impressive in its ostentatiousness. It was in the classic Roman revival architecture, and only a short drive down to the Dewitt Inn, where 'Rudy' Evenson, as he was known to the regulars in the lounge, could get drunk and drown his sorrows any time he chose. Whenever he was home, that is. He'd been a miser, and had simply sat on the stocks and bonds he'd accumulated over the years, building a classic blue chip portfolio that produced a steady and substantial income.

For twenty more years, his son and heir Hazard Evenson continued his bachelor's life, attending universities and traveling, living comfortably in places like Amsterdam, Luxembourg, Paris, Vienna, Rome and London, all the time enlarging his library. He also began collecting works of art and antique furniture. His lodgings were now several rooms, most of which being occupied by his collectibles. He now began shipping some of the excess back to his father's estate in Dewitt, a suburb of Syracuse, which was being maintained by a staff of six until the return of either Mrs. Evenson or the children. Then he received word of his mother's passing, and notice from the attorneys that the estate had been left to him alone, the other children receiving large trusts. Apparently both his father and mother had admired Hazard's independent ways, and chose him from among the children to receive and take care of the family home, on condition that his siblings always be welcome to stay there. Certainly there was ample room, as the main house alone had forty four rooms.

At last, when he felt the time had come, he returned home with all his European and British accouterments to the family estate in this little village in Upstate New York. He needed to get back to his roots and home anchorage, now that the travel and expatriate urge in him had come to rest, and he was getting on in years. He'd had enough of exhibitions, conferences, retreats and conferences while abroad, and just wanted to settle down. But he wasn't finished with life, not at all, and he reached a decision. After all his years of collecting so much wonderful heritage from Britain and the Continent, featuring his large library, all of which filled the rooms of the Main House and both Guest Houses on the estate, he now felt the strong desire to write a library of books himself. He had a small cottage built down by the lake and stream that passed through the property, and this became his writer's retreat and workplace. One by one he produced works on literary, historical and philosophical subjects. In between these he began writing novels, short stories, poetry and children's books. He'd always admired L. Frank Baum, the author of the Oz books, who was born in a nearby village and wed there. Shelf after shelf filled with his own books, then bookcase upon bookcase, that lined the walls of his octagonal cottage overlooking the lake and stream, the surrounding lawns and woods. Soon the cottage was filled to overflowing with his own writing efforts. Yet his books were little noted by anyone outside his immediate family and friends. They'd all been published by a vanity press, and received little or no notice in the journals and magazines of the day. He'd churned out so much mediocre and untalented writing that it became embarrassing. Hazard Evenson became a recluse, spending every day, all day, browsing through both his main library collection, which filled three floors and balconies in the wonderful library wing of the Main House, and the collection of his own works in the cottage.

Inevitably there came a time when Hazard began ailing, despite the best available medical care. His health was going, and he was mortal after all. A question abruptly forced itself on him: what to do with both his main library collection and the collection of his own books, not to mention the family estate. The whole of it would be far too large for his local public library to handle, though they might be curious about his own writings, some of which were autobiographical and set in his home village, mentioning and describing many locals. Where could he possibly leave it all? Selling it piecemeal was out of the question; he wanted to keep it all together. Finally he decided to set up an interdisciplinary center for comprehensive learning right on his two hundred acre estate. He would leave one guest house for his brothers and sisters to use whenever they came back.

It would be a unique center for learning, this Institute. For at the core of its program and permeating its offerings and sessions, lay this principle: each participant was required to submit a twenty page autobiography on his or her philosophy of life. That is to say, self-knowledge was to be recognized as an integral, open and formal part of general learning. And these statements of self-history, self-knowledge and belief would become an acceptable and respected part of all objective and analytical deliberations at the Institute. And he would leave his millions to run it, as the Evenson Foundation for Comprehensive Learning.

When Hazard Evenson died peacefully in his sleep during an afternoon nap on his favorite chaise lounge in his cottage, bells tolled in the nearby village. Less than a year later, his estate and mansion were opened to the public, and a special open house was announced for all his neighbors and fellow residents and their families. Everyone gathered on the lawn by the cottage, right next to the modest grave of Hazard Evenson, whose dark Italian marble gravestone was flush with the ground. An elderly man stepped forward, dressed in a priest's formal robes of black, red and white, with a silver medallion of nondescript nature hanging around his neck. His beard was white, his hair overlong. The pastor turned and looked out over the crowd, which quieted down. Beyond the crowd, many others roamed throughout the mansion and grounds, and gazed up in awe at the three tiers of books in the library wing, with catwalks and ladders. The priest began speaking.

"Hazard Evenson was our child, and as an adult he pursued his dream. Now he's brought it home at last, where it has taken root and flourished, and become a living trust. For his goal was ultimate knowledge of the world, and understanding of self. More than that, he would marry these two worlds, that within us and that without. He was a hometown boy we can be proud of."

And with those words, the local high school band began playing dance melodies and other songs from Hazard Evenson's years of growing up, the 1940s and 50s, and the caterers started serving food and drink on long tables under the shade trees, and children raced pell-mell across the grass, or played with little boats down by the pond as their parents looked on.

Inside the cottage, a few curious visitors browsed among the hundreds of books Hazard had so diligently written. His desk was empty, yet one felt the presence of the author and benefactor, and admired his accomplishments. Out through the large windows, one could enjoy the view on all sides from this single room hermitage. Just outside, by the door, Hazard Evenson's remains lay in a coffin inside a sarcophagus six feet down. A toddler ran by, chasing a butterfly. Just past the cottage entrance, he stumbled and fell across the marble gravestone, giving himself a hard bump and fright. His father ran over and picked him up, saying, 'That's alright. Now be more careful. Look where you're going from now on, when chasing butterflies.' Then the father, still holding the crying child in his arms, who was calming down but still tearful, looked around and quietly added, patting his son's back, 'Now there, that's alright. Be a good son.'

LOESSEN HALL

The university professor crawled across the concrete path and under the next table. There were a lot of weeds in the greenhouse. Not big ones, just a whole lot of little ones, almost like moss. Jocelyn, the greenhouse manager, wanted all of them removed. It was a big greenhouse, built over fifty years ago, and had a heavy pipe frame and real glass panes for the roof and walls. It was summer in Seattle, and hot and humid inside, so he was wearing shorts and sweating like he would melt away. He pulled a cardboard box along with him, and after picking and scraping a quantity of the tiny weeds with a shortened hoe, he flung them in the box.

Customers walked the paths, looking over the wonderful display of potted geraniums on the many tables, red, pink and white. It was a beautiful spring Sunday at the height of the planting season, and people were dressed up. Most of them were women. He wondered if they took any notice of his tanned, muscular, sweaty body crawling around down there. The whole situation was ludicrous, and he despaired of it. Of all people, he, Dirk Loessen, a graduate of Cambridge University and come to the New World, a former tenured professor at Cornell in political science and government, having fled to the West Coast and now groveling in the chemically drenched dirt under display tables in an old greenhouse. It was absurd, and could never have happened in England. Yet he would stay, grateful for the job, and fight it out. He would teach again.

At first it had been idyllic, arriving fresh off the plane in upstate New York back in 1950, after the war, arranging to buy a small house for his young family, then teaching such subjects as Theory of the Democratic State at Cornell University. Not the most prestigious or wealthiest of the Ivy League schools, but a good one. His office and classrooms were in one of the most venerable buildings on campus, over a hundred years old. At least it felt rather familiar, similar to the atmosphere at Cambridge. He loved teaching, and his courses were always full. Not so much due to 'course content,' as we would say, but because of Dirk Loessen. He became one of the most popular professors. Students were drawn to him by his intellect, his charm, and his gentleness. One had the impression, almost the palpable awareness, as he'd expound on the political philosophy of a Hobbes or a Mill, tracing and comparing the arguments of their rationale for the perfect state, almost like storytelling—one had the feeling that Loessen's intellect was actually visible and moving, opened up wide, a kind of drama, right there before the roomful of rapt students. One listened more than one took notes, because the passion of a scholar who truly loved to teach was on display.

"Hi there! Can you come out for a while, Dirk, and help with customers? You don't have to stay there all day, you know! We miss you." It was cheerful, companionable Jocelyn, a married woman almost his own age, who was his boss. She looked down at his half naked, primitive body, shiny with sweat, kneeling on the ground at her feet.

"Cathy needs some help carrying things out to the cars," she added.

"Sure, I'll be right there."

He reached down in the box for his T-shirt, pulling it on over his head, and went outside to help. The fresh cool air felt good. He went in to the checkout counter and started helping customers haul their purchases in red wagons out to the parking lot. In this job, no matter what he was doing, he had plenty of time to think, especially when on delivery runs all over Greater Seattle and even farther out.

When he finally left Cornell, several years later, it was not by choice. He'd been called before Senator Joe McCarthy and Roy Cohn of the U.S. Senate Subcommittee on Internal Security, of the Foreign Relations Committee, in their witch hunt for "Reds," or Communists, and had refused to answer any questions. His stand was publicized, and he stood in contempt of Congress. It was true that he'd been active in socialist politics in his undergraduate days, but he declined to answer any questions about his beliefs and political associations, nor did he respond to the insinuations that he somehow might "advocate the violent overthrow" of the U.S. Government. His beliefs and associations were his own private affair, and the idea that he might be a "subversive" was absurd, in his view. Luckily, he'd taken out American citizenship as soon as he could, on arriving in the States, so the U.S. Immigration and Naturalization Service couldn't deport him.

However, conservative Cornell alumni brought pressure on the Board of Trustees and its President, and he had to resign. He moved to Manhattan with his family, and commenced teaching his specialty at Columbia, again becoming a popular and charismatic professor, with crowded lecture halls in all his courses. Twelve years later, during the height of the Vietnam War and its Anti-War Movement, he organized faculty opposition to U.S involvement in what was patently a civil war, as he saw it, and led walkouts whenever a representative of the current Administration spoke on the campus. After that, Columbia officials realized that Dirk Loessen, their most popular political science professor, had become an irritant in their midst. Complaints from alumni grew, and certain others, probably jealous faculty, pointed out that he hadn't published any articles or books. The administration reluctantly decided not to renew this adjunct professor's contract. It was then that he decided to move to the West Coast.

But try as he might, for a long time he failed to find another teaching position. So while he was applying here and there and going to interviews, mostly at small private colleges, he worked at the greenhouse-nursery, watering plants, helping with plant care, digging ditches, unloading big semis full of heavy nursery stock from California, and so on. Rather than accepting some minor college teaching job, he decided to 'take a break' with this unskilled work.

He often puzzled over his life in America, where he'd come for more freedom and less tradition. Oddly enough, in some respects at least, there was more tradition and less freedom, notably in his chosen field. Certainly the greatest 'freedom' seemed to be in the break down and fluidity of the circumstances of daily life, and in the business and consumer sectors. Religion was also an area of wide choice, and the arts and intellectual life generally, as long as one didn't go too far to the left. And in the U.S.A., 'left' really meant anything left of center, as judged by British and European political spectrums. It was basically a conservative, rather reactionary society, and liberals were actually considered to be leftists! Now here he was, relegated to a marginal if temporary situation in remote Seattle, pushing wheelbarrows and mixing soil. He chose not to apply to any of the large state universities, which were thoroughly bureaucratized and claimed to be "apolitical" in any political controversy, obviously an absurd notion.

Where to go next? He was especially interested in finding a small liberal arts college of the independent liberal kind. There were a few in the Pacific Northwest, and he applied to them all. One in particular attracted him, in Oregon. To his surprise, he was hired. He left Seattle and moved his family to rural Oregon.

He knew he'd be out of the mainstream of American education, but at his age this didn't seem to matter any more. He wanted to write. Political affairs, civic involvement and public service in the U.S. begged for analysis from a theoretical standpoint, comparing them to the classical origins and traditions of democracy. Was the United States really the most free and democratic society in the modern 'Free World'? Or were vulgar, reactionary forces pervasive? When Loessen had stuck his neck out and been active in causes he believed in, for the betterment of the country, as he conceived it, he'd been criticized and ostracized by that famous "Silent Majority" among the alumni, and been given his walking papers, time after time. It was time to write down and document his analyses and proposals, to make sure they were passed on and remembered.

Once situated in his teaching regime, he began working on writing projects. Over the next fifteen years he had four books published by university presses, none of which sold well. They were too theoretical, too intellectual, too high flown and eccentric. But there it was, down in black and white. 'That' couldn't be taken away from him. He now had time, in the relaxed and rural setting of the college, to think back. Had he done the right thing in coming to America? He missed England at times, but the local life in western Oregon was similar to his childhood county back home. As for his books, they would probably be read and remembered by a few devotees of the political arts. All would go out of print, only to be found in used bookstores. But that was alright; after all was said and done, it was teaching he loved the most.

When he was just over seventy, a Cornell alumni gathering was held in Portland. It was a grand meeting for the entire West Coast. One of his old students learned that he was living close by, and urged the organizers of the conference to invite Dirk Loessen to speak. They did, and he accepted gratefully. When he arrived, he shocked some of his former students. He had lost weight, and seemed overly subdued, not like the old Loessen. A handful of them asked him out to a luncheon. There was much conversation about his lectures, and some had even read one or two of his books. But mostly they simply wanted to thank him for being a good teacher. He was revered not so much for his ideas, but for his intellectual strength, vitality and enthusiasm. For those among Dirk Loessen's students who remembered him longest and strongest, he was affectionately held to be the 'intellectual's intellectual.'

After he'd finished his fifty minutes of remarks at the alumni meeting, in which he summarily yet concisely analyzed the current American political situation from a theoretical point of view, spicing it up with some fascinating anecdotes, he turned and sat down. The applause was immediate and deafening, and many in the audience stood to honor him. In the following months, there was a small rise in the sale of his books, then silence. A few alumni asked to visit him and his wife on their small farm near the college. His three children were all grown, two of them teachers, the third a professional musician. The Loessens would offer visitors tea, and ask how they were doing. Then topics of the day were touched upon, but not too deeply. Finally, everyone would go outside to see their few livestock, and if it was summer, their nice vegetable garden and fruit trees. The guests would leave, carrying little bags of produce as gifts, or an autographed copy of one or more of his books. Then the elderly couple would retire inside their cozy house, to sit by their fireplace, crackling with the warmth and security of the wood fire. Maggie, his wife of so many years, to whom Loessen had proposed while still at university in England, reminded him that it was almost like being back home again.

Four years later, Dirk Loessen was awarded a lifetime achievement award by the Cornell Alumni Association. He was unable to attend, due to his wife's recent death, so a videotape of the award ceremony was sent to him. Someone, sometime had also videotaped one of his early lectures, and sent a copy of that along too, from the University Archives. Further, the main lecture hall in a new government and political science building at Cornell was named after him, Loessen Hall, with a dark bronze bust of himself in the lobby. A photo of that was also included. But by the time these memorials and honors arrived, Dirk Loessen was gone. He had died in his sleep of natural causes, alone but content on his little farm in Oregon. He'd managed, after all, to achieve his American Dream. The reception he'd received at the Alumni Conference was all he needed. His intellectual enthusiasm and integrity would live on, just as he'd hoped and prayed.

PICKERING'S JOURNAL

When I found Lawrence Pickering, he was in an upscale nursing residence for independent men in Syracuse. A former executive for the old New York Central Railroad, he had retired, only to see his beloved wife die six months later of an embolism. It happened so suddenly and unexpectedly, and it never occurred to either of them that he'd be the survivor, not her. So he became a widower, forced to look at life through his eyes only.

Lawrence had no great hobbies, but he had been a lifelong reader in politics and social issues, always from the conservative point of view. So here he was in retirement, alone and with no interests other than reading. He had no real focus in life now, and wasn't getting enough exercise. His health deteriorated to the point where he had to put himself under the care of others. It was a heart condition. This he did, hence his move into a little apartment at Mansfield Arms. He was content with his new surroundings, and made himself at home.

His personal library was already impressive, and he had to have more shelving installed to accommodate its growth. His books were really taking over the place. He asked to move to a larger apartment, and six months later this was done. Pickering got along better with his neighbors there, and started becoming active in residence programs. There was a common room and library, which were open to all residents, and a book club. Naturally, he joined, and soon became its leader and host. He not only designated the books to read and led the discussion, he became the very heart of the club, its soul and conscience so to speak, because he took reading and intellectual stimulation very seriously. For example, he began reading novels for the first time since his college days, because some of the others wanted to. After a while, the book club meetings became a vehicle for his personal and intellectual growth. For all his years of being an executive, these gifts of curiosity, insight and a philosophical penchant had set him apart as an eccentric executive in the railroad's boardrooms. Yes, he knew the railroad industry in all its archaic and conservative peculiarities, but he also knew a good deal else. And it was only during coffee breaks and luncheons that his more cultured private nature expressed itself. Railroading was a lunch-bucket job, as he likened it, a nine to five salaried one that he had to shave and dress up for every day, but his interior life, the unpaid part so to speak, was his real oyster. And this was the Pickering that came out at Mansfield Arms, a home for men of independent means.

The management of the place issued a newsletter that came around once a week, mentioning activities, meetings and services of interest to residents. It was never more than a few pages in length. Quite on an impulse, Pickering asked if he could help work on it, and was promptly made managing editor. Then he had an idea. Some months before, one of the book club members had loaned him a copy of "A Writer's Diary," by Dostoyevsky, which was actually the title of a periodical the great Russian author had put out toward the end of his career. It contained solely his own thoughts and ideas on news and issues of the day. He also told stories and related anecdotes in his life, and answered letters sent in by his readers. Dostoyevsky regarded it as in the feuillton tradition, which is a melange of literary notes and articles on a variety of subjects. Every word in it was his own, and each quarterly issue contained at least a hundred pages.

Lawrence Pickering decided to turn the newsletter into the same kind of publication for Mansfield Arms. Though he encouraged others to contribute articles and news, he received very little, so he decided to make it his own. The first page or two listed announcements, an activities schedule and excursions, which was followed by "Pickering's Journal," a miscellany of writings by Pickering himself. It expanded into more and more pages, obviously becoming something much more than a residence newsletter. When the management complained of the number of pages he was adding, he offered to pay the extra cost himself. As another year went by, Pickering decided to separate from the newsletter, and launch his own periodical. At first it was distributed locally through colleges, bookstores and newsstands, with all the publishing and distribution being handled by others. Then it received flattering reviews and commentary from the media, who requested interviews. After yet another year had gone by, he found himself to be a literary light, and circulation expanded throughout the city, at all levels and in all places. This was a regional center on the coast, full of connections with foreign countries, so eventually "Pickering's Journal" established itself as a prestigious international quarterly, and grew to between eighty and a hundred pages per issue. It was hard for the critics to categorize, because there was no other periodical like it. The closest comparison made was to the "I.F. Stone Weekly," a political newsletter written and published for many years by its namesake in Washington. D.C. "Pickering's Journal" was much more ambitious and interdisciplinary, however. There simply was nothing to compare it to, except perhaps Dostoevsky's "Diary." Lawrence Pickering, the retired capitalist, was now regarded as a literary lion. He'd found a whole new life for himself, and the Journal was his voice. He was considered to be erudite and wise, a brilliant intellectual, a philosopher and mystic. Letters poured in, and he endeavored to answer every one as best he could. Many were the stimulus for additional essays.

It gradually came over him that he might be an Elder Patriarch of the Modern Age, one to whom the multitudes came to ask for advice, or simply to listen. He was invited to speak at both conservative and ecumenical or liberal churches, before social service clubs, at high school and college graduations, even university seminars, and when he would speak, everyone turned and stared, fascinated that this former railroad executive, now almost eighty years of age, could hold his juniors in thrall so easily. What was the magic? It was his confidence, his self-possession, his well organized mind and memory, and his intellectual gifts. Yes, he had graduated from a college, but not a prestigious one. In fact, if someone mentioned its name, he'd have to explain where it was located and what it was, because he'd gone so far beyond that modicum of educational experience. He was now a philosopher and religious thinker, and held forth in the library of Mansfield Arms once a month. But so many wanted to attend that the sessions were moved to the War Memorial Center in downtown Syracuse. The great minds of the country and even beyond came to him. The Mansfield Arms Seminars became a world renowned institute, all due to "Pickering's Journal," which continued to be issued once a quarter. And every word was Lawrence Pickering's.

He'd found his place at last, as a source of wisdom and direction. Critics and students alike studied the dense, single-spaced pages, in a small font, as a guide to clear thinking and imaginative analysis, worthwhile learning, and even for keys to the very significance of life itself, the metaphysics of Being. All during his working years, before age sixty-five, he'd had a successful material life, or so he thought. Now he had an entirely new life, a second one. Yet he'd had it, he knew, all along, it's just that the demands of his railroad work suppressed it. Now, approaching ninety, he fully realized that this second chance was the one he'd always wanted, and looked for.

At last there came a day when he opened his mail and found an invitation he'd only dreamed of. He was asked to speak at the upcoming Presidential inauguration. It seems the President-Elect was a loyal reader of "Pickering's Journal." Lawrence, now 94, began working on his little five minute speech.

"Life is a box of many puzzles and games. We are still children, and love to play, and to act out every possibility for joy, satisfaction and something accomplished. That is all we have, these options. We can simply survive, withstanding life and offering it only what is necessary, or we can diligently busy ourselves with honest work and good deeds, accumulating earthly rewards of every kind, or thirdly, we can turn inward, and follow the path of the writer, the philosopher, the lover and the mystic. Which shall it be, and does it matter which way we choose? The reality is that, whether we want to or not, we engage in all these choices in varying degree, depending on our nature, our personal needs and our resolve.

"This great country has found a new leader, and we must now support her. She will need and be looking for our understanding, tolerance, ideas and support. For ultimately she will be alone, just as you or I, in facing the world of old memories, daily tasks, and pressing decisions on every side that affect all of us, as well as the larger world. Let us join together and wish her success, or if not that, then. . . ."

His pen stopped suddenly, and the wizened old gentleman slumped forward. Birds outside chirped madly. Bill Hawkins, his private secretary, entered the room a half hour later and found him.

On hearing the news of Lawrence Pickering's death, the President-Elect telephoned later that evening. She asked that the draft of his remarks be sent to her, and she would try to finish it, then have a young scholar protegee of hers read it at the Inauguration. Thus "Pickering's Journal", which began as a supplement to a nursing home newsletter in a provincial American city, became part of the nation's history, and Lawrence Pickering one of its literary laureates. A dark bronze statue was commissioned, showing him thoughtfully seated at a small desk with pen in hand, and placed in a beautiful old park that was near his hometown's oldest art museum, where strollers, families, lovers, art connoisseurs, students and the curious could read the short biographical inscription on its base, which ended with these words: "All is within, Naught without."

THE MYSTICAL LIFE

When I was a boy, I was full of wonder and awe at the ways of adults. They were outsized, all-powerful, omniscient, full of surprises and secrets, wiles and extravagance, darkness and silence. One couldn't help worshiping and idolizing them, even when they claimed not to know the answer to my questions. So they were my 'once and future' gods, at least until I gained some social purchase, once I reached my own majority.

And the enlarging and broadening world! What a grand prospect, to imagine being someone important in it, at some unimaginable time in the future! Would there be room for the likes of me, or would I have to wait for the death of all my parental guides and models before my time might come? Would I really marry and have children to take care of, like them, or was I incapable of such great accomplishments?

In those childhood years, I also worshiped a doll. His name was Pumice. Actually it had no gender, but 'he' just naturally came to my lips. My playmates and siblings, all less than my nine years in age, considered Pumice a leader, master and idol. He was about 18 inches long, and had no clothes; a stuffed, cloth-bound doll with floppy arms and legs, knees and elbows that bent every which way, and a strange, inscrutable expression sewn onto his face. He had short hair, but I don't recall what color. And, I know exactly where we buried him.

This happened sixty years ago, but memory serves me well. One day we decided Pumice needed an operation. We lay him down, prepared to operate, and I made the incision in his front. It got to be L-shaped before I realized we wouldn't be able to sew him up again. Besides, the wound seemed mortal, even if we could restore him. So then we decided that Pumice had died, and must have a funeral and burial. At first we were saddened as well as alarmed that we'd no longer have Pumice to play with, but we were soon caught up in preparations for the funeral, the procession into the cemetery across the street, and the burial.

Our sitter that day was Genevieve, a large, ample young woman with big eyes, shoulder-length black hair, and a mischievous smile. She always enjoyed helping us in our fantasy play. But this one tested her limits. Our funeral procession consisted of three carts and a tricycle, with Genevieve helping lead the way. Pumice's remains, wrapped in an old towel, lay closed in a box in the lead cart, one of those wonderful wooden ones with high slatted sides that children think is the very best wagon of all. We crossed the street and followed the cemetery's curving roads through to the back. I knew there were piles of dirt to be found there, and after a brief grave side service Pumice was put to rest for the last time. As children we looked to dolls and Teddy Bears for company and support, and I think the death and disappearance of Pumice was also the death of my first childhood. From then on, I had no more truck with dolls or Teddy Bears, for sixty years at least.

I entered my later boyhood and youth. However, my love of pet animals, especially dogs, never left me. There was always the family dog, sometimes a cat. Dogs would always share my loneliness, my hurt, and my confusion; I clung to them, and included them in my play. Soon my dog and I, usually a setter, were able to cross the same cemetery to reach the railroad tracks, which I would follow across the east side of the village until I came to a high embankment. Then we arrived at the foot of a hill where a primitive dirt lane led to a defunct dairy farm on the hilltop about a half mile away, out of sight from below. It had several buildings that were gray with weathering and beginning to sink into ruin. Over the years I became a pilgrim to that old farm, where I made the acquaintance of an ancient man and woman dressed in black. Eventually a day came when they were no longer seen. There followed many years when the buildings were vacant or rented by transients, fumbling around with farming. Then a son of the old couple I'd first seen up there tried to start it up again, this time with beef cattle. But he failed too.

As a son who learned of my adoption by my stepfather by accident at age 14, I was not totally at home with myself, and was now drawn to this farm as if it were a strangely comfortable second home or hearth. In adulthood I moved around a lot, but almost every time I returned to the home village, I'd try to get up there to see if anything had changed. Then came a long period when I couldn't get back, or made such brief visits that there wasn't enough time to hike up there, or too much snow in mid-winter buried the hilltop. When I last visited the old place, almost in retirement and with my wife, the farm buildings were completely gone. I was told the neighboring state park had bought it for expansion purposes.

During pubescence I was given piano lessons and sent to watercolor painting classes at the city museum. The piano lessons gave me daily agony, and fear at recitals. So I didn't enjoy playing music myself, but I did begin collecting phonograph records, mostly of classic music. And I became an opera listener every Saturday afternoon. Then I started oil painting, and my room was turned into an artist's atelier; classical music or opera with oil painting while sunlight streamed into my two south windows, summer and winter. I couldn't get enough of it.

In college I came to worship the intellectual life. I grew into it at age 17, and later developed, at age twenty, a love and preference for the intellectual's outlook on life, always ready to peel it back and gaze deep inside. Great professors became my father-figures, trenchant thoughts and obscure words my bible. In army service, which was mandatory at the time, I was sent to Monterey for training, and made weekend devotional hikes south to the hilltops of the Los Padres National Forest, alone and contemplative. Surely these scented ravines and sunny slopes could give me guidance and offer solace, clear my mind in preparation for the future. Then our orders said we were to go to Alaska, not Europe. Everyone else in my training class groaned and wrung their hands at the prospect, but not me. I looked forward to experiencing the remoteness, the wildness and the isolation of Alaska, then a Territory, because I believed I responded to such things like an aborigine. Plant forms, the weather and simple land forms strongly impressed me, and animals had a kind of seniority. I watched and respected them all, and 'read' them for more signs as to my own nature, who I was and could be.

After the army I finally made it to Europe. I wanted to compare the heritage, history and social environment of the States to those fabled countries, each with its own language, culture, music and so on. I needed to find out if it was I who lacked something culturally or psychologically, or was it my homeland that had these deficits. In Europe and Britain I found myself in awe of their arts of living. They knew a myriad of different dimensions in life, to depths previously unknown to me, and I was left alone to take it all in. On the Continent especially, I created a new Me, and cherished all my impressions as revelations. I wasn't misguided in criticisms of my homeland after all. But I was also alienated, and came to love the expatriate life. I wanted to live in France, but circumstances forced me back home, where I eventually found meaningful work.

First I found a haven in an old antiquarian bookstore, then I became a librarian. After sampling work in a plains prison library and then a Pacific Northwest history collection, I coordinated library development and heritage research for certain western Indian tribes and then for many Alaska Native villages. While living in these remote communities, I came closer to nature as early hunters and fishermen must have known it. I learned how to live with nature, not against it. I lived in a tipi, and as a natural dwelling it was a great teacher too. Sailboats taught me similarly, to respect and learn from the winds on Seattle's inland waters. At such times I spoke little, only observed and learned, which was the ancient way.

As for Christianity and the other organized religions, I looked into them over many years, whenever I had the inclination or opportunity, but they were all too narrow and too myopic, too pretentious, presumptuous and conceited, holding that only they, each one (!), possessed the answers to life's questions. I concluded that their tenets originated in fear, guilt and human frailty, and therefore I had as much right to find my own answers, though I could also note their wisdom and psychology. After all, I was raised in a Christian environment. If I ever needed one, my default denomination has usually been Unitarian. I say 'default,' because even without such a Fellowship, I survived. Or so I believed.

Just before retirement I took up the cello, but only dallied in it, trying to teach myself. After I married for the last time, my wife and I played duets together, she on violin, and teaching me as well. I came to love ensemble play, and we formed a quartet. But I also enjoyed solo play, and found the Bach suites for cello; I was finally able to enjoy playing music. Now we have a fancy keyboard to play with, as well as a piano, which she plays, not me. I've just added a pickup and amp to my cello, so sometime I want to try improvising a base line for country, bluegrass or blues musicians, but that day may never come.

Now I decided to finish a novel I'd been working on, that centered on a boy growing up on this farm, with ancestors before him and descendants to follow. It was a fantasy biography of the boy and the farm, and his subsequent search for a missing father. Thus I married myself to the hilltop, whose spirit, character and gently rolling fields held me as the ocean does now. It was a place of longing and remembrance, and the depth of loss.

I've occasionally returned to oil painting, and am usually working on something rather impressionist, trying to reflect the reality of my aging yet still insistent vision and its interpretations. My lifelong idol among all the artists has been the incredibly honest Vincent Van Gogh, and I love the many lesser known paintings of farm scenes by the American Robert Bateman, better known as a painter of wildlife in their natural habitats, which evoke deep nostalgia for me. Unfortunately, these farm scenes are never seen in prints, because they're so valued by their private owners.

And, having come into independent income since my parents passed away, I've become a compulsive bibliophile. Always a reader of serious literature, I now collect about me all the books and writers I've always considered my companions, friends, advisors and idols. Books have a way of filling in most of the empty spaces in my apprehension and appreciation of life. From time to time I give away sub-collections from my library, but then new interests come along and it expands to fullness again, pleasing my restless mind for another short time.

Then in my sixties a crisis occurred in my life and my behavior, when I lost control. It had something to do with my adoption, how my parents and stepfather handled it, and my quest for an ideal father. I gave in to the darkness and ignorance of repressed emotions, and reached out in despair and loneliness where I shouldn't have. I 'acted out' instead of acting responsibly, which doomed me. But I didn't know where else to turn, and was increasingly drawn into a vortex of deviant criminality. After a few years of institutionalized treatment, I was transformed. Quite simply, in mystical terms I found myself, and more importantly, I found the capacity to love, something I'd never known before. My mystical quest was over. To know what the purpose of life is, I would give everything to my beloved. To know the world, apparently, one must deny its ultimate significance. To really know the meaning of life, in the end, is to realize that one can never have that answer. There is always something more, and the worst of it is, that we have been refused any ultimate, satisfying explanation.

MY IMMORTAL FRIEND

I come from a village in Central New York. While in high school, one of the most popular of my classmates experienced a terrible accident. Bob Mitchell was one of four boys. In our childhood, I used to go to his house now and then and we'd watch 8mm reels of old cartoons in his basement, in black and white and silent. Other than that, I rarely played with him. But I liked him, his brothers and his parents. They were a good family. Later Bob raised ducks in cages in the garage of a larger house they moved to, just down the street. All the Mitchell boys played on our football team, and usually one or two of the other sports teams, even though they weren't that big, and not the best of our athletes. But they had something extra to give. Each of the four of them had his own charisma and joie de vivre. Bob also possessed something extra, a great sense of humor. He could get us laughing anytime, no matter what we'd be talking about or doing. He could also be very serious, too, so often I didn't know whether to be light or heavy with him. The cues were always his.

Then one noon just a few weeks before our graduation, his sweetheart was driving him from school over to his house. They planned to get married. She drove through the only stoplight in town, and was hit broadside by a truck that ran the light. Their car was flipped over on its side and he was partially pinned inside it. When he was taken away, he couldn't feel anything from somewhere around his arms and chest on down. His girlfriend went with him in the ambulance to a hospital in the nearby city.

We all graduated and went our separate ways, except for Bob, who remained in hospital. There was nothing they could do for his paralysis, but after a year of therapy he was able to move his arms a little and breathe easier. With special devices on his hands, he was able to smoke a cigarette and even type, though very slowly. I'd sit at his bedside and talk with him whenever I came home from college on vacation. After each breath, he could speak a few words. He'd smoke a cigarette I'd light for him, suck a little from a straw in a water glass I'd extend to his mouth, and have something funny to say, usually about me. He was always curious about what I was doing currently. His intellect and wit were unimpaired, I could see that. I respected him and wished I could help him somehow, but my own plans took me away for longer and longer periods.

Meanwhile, he was busy too. Every male in the family had gone to one of the smaller Ivy League colleges, located in eastern New York State. Bob was determined to do the same, so special arrangements were made to enable him to do that without leaving his hospital bed. A special rack was set up for propping books so he could read. He'd dictate his essays and test answers, and his girlfriend Beth helped him almost every day. He'd turn pages in books using a pencil eraser fixed in his hand contrivance. So he persevered and worked until he received his B.A. degree, six years later. At the college graduation, which he attended lying propped up on a mobile ambulance stretcher, the entire audience rose and cheered when his name was called and his bed with wheels was carried up on stage. At the reception afterward he had many classmates, friends and family come over to visit him, as he sipped beer through a straw in his glass.

All this time Beth was faithful to him, which seemed remarkable. But now they both agreed she should go make a life for herself, which she did. Bob then decided to go for his law degree. He was in his second year of study when his physical systems started failing. He couldn't do it any more, try as he might, and with extra help and care from others. As he died, his bedside was attended by many, including the hospital staff and Beth, who was now married and with her second child. They were all there with him. A year later, at his class graduation from law school, he was awarded an honorary law degree.

Fate has strange and abrupt twists, and luck rides with us all. The same year Bob had his accident, in 1946, I was in the front seat of an old sedan with two of my buddies, on the outside, when it had a blowout in front of a state park entrance just east of the village. The car went off the road and I fell out, tumbling end over end right alongside a row of big concrete fenceposts. I could have struck any one of them, but I didn't. I was black and blue and in slight shock afterward, but I was alright. I could live out my life longer.

As the decades went by and I went to college, traveled to Europe, served in the army and had many jobs and repeatedly tried marriage, I would think about Bob Mitchell from time to time. If only I had his strong determination and perseverence, his holding power, his spirit and humor, I could make it, and have the good life. For I've always felt some guilt that he was deprived of a normal life instead of me, and perhaps I could have done a lot better than I have, made better use of time and opportunities, and tried harder. There's always that uneasy feeling; no, it's a certainty. Perhaps I'd have accomplished far more, if I'd been the one completely paralyzed from the neck down!

THE TRUTH MAY MAKE YOU ANGRY

Richard Smith and Mary Hollings met in the late 1920s while students at Syracuse University. He was in the school of journalism and she was in the fine arts college, majoring in piano and minoring in organ. Richard's home was Perry, New York, a venerable town in the Genesee River Valley south of Rochester. Mary's home was in Syracuse, the Hub of the Empire State. They were from very different social backgrounds, but they became sweethearts.

Richard was one of three brothers, the oldest one. Tom was the middle brother, Ralph the youngest. Their parents had settled in Perry after coming north from Pennsylvania. His father was pastor of one of the two Methodist churches in Perry, and remained there all his life. They had a modest income, so he had to work to help put himself through the university. Mary was born in Syracuse to a well-connected family. Her father, a respected surgeon at a hospital near the campus, was also active in university governance. The family lived in a comfortable, unpretentious house in the university district. Mary had two sisters, Lillian the older and Charlotte the younger. She also had an older brother, nicknamed Gus. It was a close knit family and they played music together, each one capable on some instrument or other, or with a good voice.

Lillian was the first to marry. Her husband was the scion of a wealthy local industrial family and they had two children. One night Lillian and her husband were being chauffeured from one resort to another on the St. Lawrence River up north when their boat struck the cable between a tugboat and its barge. All three drowned, leaving their two children to be raised by an uncle and a nanny in their large stone mansion, with extensive grounds around which ran a small railroad for the children and even adults to ride on. Mary's older brother married a spirited lady, his female counterpart, so to speak, who was also an early woman aviator, or aviatrix. They had one son. The youngest sister had not yet come of age.

Right after graduation, Richard and Mary decided to get married. Then Mary's mother died. As soon as possible they had a child, Richard Jr. Richard's parents had welcomed the marriage, but Mary's were lukewarm. He was from a lower social class, with no money in the family, and it was the middle of the Depression. Not long after Richard Jr. could walk, Mary's father died as well. So Mary had lost her older sister and her husband and both parents before she and Richard had been married two years. (The details around the divorce and Richard Jr.'s adoption were only learned sixty five years later.)

Richard began looking for a job, but there seemed to be no opportunities in the Syracuse area, despite all the good connections Mary's family had, which they either didn't use, or weren't utilized on Richard's behalf. Considering what happened later, it's very possible her family wasn't of any help at all. So they traveled a little farther west to Richard's home area, where he found a few meager jobs with small print shops or newspapers. After a while they continued on to Buffalo, where it was hoped friends of theirs could help Richard find a decent job. They were unsuccessful, and returned to Syracuse.

Richard's unemployment persisted and funds were running out, so he made a fateful decision. He took his ROTC commission in the U.S. Army Corps of Engineers. However, Mary declined to go with him even though, as an officer's wife, she could have. So she and little Richard Jr., and Richard's older brother Tom saw him off at the train station in Syracuse. First he was stationed in Idaho, then Louisiana, where he helped set up and manage CCC camps for unemployed young men. He regularly wrote Mary and sent her money, all the time asking her to join him with their child. However, conditions in the camps were primitive, and she would have to live in a tent and wash diapers in a pail herself, so she demurred on the option to join him. Less than a year went by when suddenly, without any warning, Mary had Richard served with divorce papers.

Since the death of their parents, older brother Gus had assumed charge of Mary's family, which was now comprised of his two surviving sisters and himself. He had been against Mary's marriage to Richard, and when Richard took the last resort in his job searching by entering the army, it was the last straw for Gus. His sister, whose photo had been on the society pages, deserved better. He urged Mary to break it off, and offered his support and leadership to do so. At the same time she was receiving Richard's letters with money for paying bills, Mary was occasionally seeing a longtime family friend, Jon Crusor, the son of another prominent local family, of her same monied and well-connected social class.

When Richard received the divorce papers and read them through, sitting in his tent in rural Louisiana, he was shocked. Mary had given no indication of being unhappy with him before then. Sure, she'd missed him, as did Richard Jr., and hoped he'd be stationed closer to home, or in better quarters, but she'd never mentioned the pressure and maneuvering she'd been contending with from her older brother, to terminate the marriage, and didn't have the nerve or heart to tell him herself what was being planned in his absence. Richard was so upset that he went on sick call for a time, then retained an attorney as well as consulted with army attorneys. This took time away from his responsibilities, and brought on a great deal of stress. His initial position, not being able to talk with Mary, or get any reply to his letters to her, was to press for custody of his son. His parents were still living, with a comfortable and good home in Perry, whereas both Mary's parents had died. Overall, he had a larger extended family to offer, for Richard Jr.'s care, than she did. But Gus, through Mary's attorney, claimed that Richard was 'incompetent,' and unfit to have custody. Richard's attorney assumed he meant 'incompatible,' or some such, because in every way possible, considering the times and his circumstances, Richard had assumed his responsibilities as husband and father as best he could. Mary flew to Reno and spent six weeks on a nice divorce dude ranch, taking her little son with her. The court gave her the divorce, but decreed that Richard was to have regular visitation with Richard Jr.

A few weeks afterward, Mary wrote Richard a letter of 'explanation.' She said that their marriage hadn't worked out because their 'lifestyles were so different.' In other words, Richard wasn't able to provide her with a lifestyle 'to which she was accustomed,' as the debutante daughter of a prominent Syracuse family. In an affectionate yet cold style, she carefully and logically typed out the rationale behind her divorce, and included a list of bills that had been paid with the money he'd sent her, while mentioning a few remaining, and thanking him for his letters and continued money support. She wished him well, and assured him that Richard Jr. was doing fine. However, some notes discovered later in her Baby Book, out of which she'd torn all pictures of Richard, showed that their son wasn't doing so well at times, and missed his Daddy. The little guy was trying to cope, as Mary's older brother imposed his authority every way he could, and they hired a nanny to fill in other parental duties and child care when they were away or otherwise occupied.

As soon as he could manage it, Richard tried to assert his visitation rights, but Gus was adamant that there be no visits by the boy's father, and proceeded to threaten Richard and his parents with compromise and ruin if he made any move to come east to see his son. He wrote Richard many long, vicious letters, warning that Richard would never be able to get another job, his parents' service in the Perry church would be thoroughly compromised if not ended, and accusing them of unsavory, dishonorable and selfish purposes in claiming to be able to care for their young grandson. The result was that Richard reluctantly decided not to try and see his son, mainly out of fear that Gus would go after his parents. And he couldn't afford a long legal battle to assert his rights.

Meanwhile, both Richard and Mary were thinking and planning remarriage. Mary decided to marry the family friend she'd been seeing, Jon Crusor, who agreed to adopt Richard Jr. The boy, less than three years old, was baptized again, in a Presbyterian church this time, his name being changed to Holden Hollings Crusor. But his Uncle Gus called him Buddy then and for the rest of his life, a possessive nickname he'd dubbed the boy with during the time Mary was going through the divorce. Mary and Jon's plan was never to tell her son about her divorce, or his adoption. The adoption papers were sealed by the New York Supreme Court, and would remain inaccessible forever.

In Louisiana, Richard met May Tully, his future second wife, in a colorful way. She had been organizing farmers all over Louisiana into coops, to get a better price for their sorghum. One rainy evening she was being driven to a distant town and her car broke down just outside the CCC camp where Richard was stationed. She and her driver came in for help, and were having something to eat in the officially closed mess hall before going to bed when Richard came storming in, dressed in rain gear, demanding in strong language that the mess hall reopen and feed his work crew.

May was immediately impressed, and they got acquainted, Richard apologizing for swearing and carrying on in the company of a lady. After several months of courtship, they decided to marry.

Both Richard and Mary remarried about a year after the divorce. Richard's new wife joined him in military quarters, while Mary gained a new family with Jon's parents, and his younger brother and sister. For the rest of her days, having lost her own parents prematurely, Mary called Jon's parents Mother and Father. Although Jon's choice of a business was insurance (after having visited Europe and trying work in a New York investment house), he tried to remain independent of his father's wealth, although it was always there to help him whenever he and Mary needed it. In the coming years Mary and Jon had two children of their own, first a daughter, then a son. There was four years difference between each of the three children.

Richard and May had a daughter born to them, who was named Mary Richard. He briefly left the army in the late 1930s, to successfully run businesses until World War II began, when he was called up. He was stationed on the West Coast, but was soon to go into action in the South Pacific. As an officer in the U.S. Army Corps of Amphibious Engineers, he participated in several landings and was once captured and briefly held by the Japanese while on a secret mission, but after a month was liberated by a commando unit brought in by nighttime submarine. At some point during this South Pacific service, he was awarded the Bronze Star. His wife and daughter waited for him in California, where May ran a small business as well.

Young Holden, ne Richard Jr., grew up through boyhood in a loving family. He was called Holdy for short, by friends and family. But his uncle still insisted on calling him Buddy, as if he'd somehow created him. His only grandparents were very kind and generous, and he especially liked his Gramma, who took him on excursions into the city. He always had playmates from the neighborhood, or his sister and brother to share activities together. In the first house they lived in, at the north end of the village, there was a 'Playplace' beyond the backyard, where he played with cars and trucks in the dirt. Beyond that was a low lying swampy area to explore, with levees and a canal, and abandoned waters of the old Erie Canal, which used to come into the village. From the time he was pre-school, the family always had a family dog, sometimes a cat. In later years such pets would give him company and solace at times of loneliness and idleness, or daydreaming, of which he was a master. After they moved a mile across town to their big, three-storey house up by the school, Holdy and friends took to playing various fantasy games during the war, like cowboys and Indians, Explorer, cops and robbers, or Gestapo interrogation, because one of his 12-year-old friends was especially good at imitating a SS officer.

Holdy had some health problems other than those of a normal child. These included stuttering, for which he was taken to a clinic, and recurring constipation, which required regular enemas. Outside his little constellation of friends, he was a shy and introverted boy, especially in school. As a result, he was vulnerable to bullying, and during recess went to little used parts of their large playground with safe playmates. Though he was close to his mother, his stepfather, like many fathers of the day, was rather remote, undemonstrative and taciturn. Still, he was home every night, weekends and vacations, and the family did almost everything together. Holdy's dad did have his masculine interests, such as fishing, hunting, tennis and bowling, but these didn't draw him away from his family unduly. His preference was to stay home and work around the house, not without grumbling good-naturedly now and then about such 'endless' chores. And since the 1920s he had taken rustic canoe fishing trips into remote Quebec in September with two or three lifelong friends, all male.

Holdy's mother encouraged his interest in the arts, as did his grandmother. He was given piano lessons, and enrolled in water color classes at the old Syracuse Museum of Fine Arts for a couple of years, from age 10 to 12. They set up their easels in the galleries, where they could hear music recitals in a small auditorium nearby. One month they were surrounded by a special traveling exhibition of the vibrant oil paintings of Vincent Van Gogh, which made a lifelong impression on Holdy.

He became interested in oil painting, and his mother helped him buy an easel, a real wooden palette, oil paints, brushes and a palette knife, and canvas boards. With her encouragement he also started buying phonograph records of classical music, playing them in his room on an old phonograph, which was soon replaced by a three-speed 'high fidelity' machine. His room on the third and top floor of the family house overlooked a park and pond to the south through two windows, so there was sunlight both winter and summer. During his boyhood he explored woods and fields and streams on the 'frontiers' of the village, mostly on foot, and early on discovered an old farm on a hilltop to the northeast a mile or so. In later years he would visit this farm regularly, and come to love it.

At fourteen, as the oldest, he felt he was capable of baby—sitting his sister and brother, but his parents wouldn't allow it yet. One day they had a sitter whom none of them liked. They gave her a hard time. Then Holdy's sister discovered her caching a bag of their canned food to steal and take home. The exasperated sitter suddenly cried out in anger, staring straight at Holdy, "Your father isn't your real father! Your father isn't your real father!" They all laughed at her outburst, but Holdy had the queasy feeling that she might be speaking some strange and exotic truth. It sounded preposterous and fantastical, yet she was so serious. And why would she say such a thing to him anyway?

That evening, when the whole family was seated at the dining room table and eating, Holdy told his parents what the sitter had said. Or perhaps it was his sister, Holdy now being apprehensive about the incident and not knowing how to bring it up. There was stunned silence and apparent distress by their parents. Holdy's mother quietly said she'd talk to Holdy the next morning, before he went to school. After breakfast, she called him into his little brother's room on the second floor. She explained that yes, he was adopted, and his stepfather wasn't his birth father. When he asked who his father was, and where he was, she briefly explained that his name was Smith, and they had divorced when Holdy was very young, after which time she remarried to his stepfather (she called him 'your father'), who totally adopted Holdy and his name was changed too. Why did you divorce him? Holdy asked. Because he abandoned us, and I never heard from him again, she replied. Then Holdy asked the obvious and painful next question: Where's Dad? Surely he should be in on this moment too, thought Holdy. But his mother explained that he had to leave for the office. And that was that; end of story, and that's all you need to know, was the implied message. Obviously neither of them wanted to talk any more about it, and she'd already forgotten details, had no idea where he was or what he was doing, etc. Holdy didn't dare ask if were still alive or not.

As his high school years began, Holdy began feeling a vague resentment toward his stepfather. Why doesn't he ever say anything to me about this? Holdy himself was afraid to talk to him about it, because he had a fear that anything this quiet and remote stepfather might say wouldn't necessarily be reassuring. So an anger slowly festered toward his stepfather, and an alienation toward everything the youth identified with him, his conservative politics, his wealthy parents and their friends, his racism, and his anti-art and anti-intellectual prejudices. As for his mother's role in the divorce, her remarriage and his own adoption, Holdy gave it little thought. In his mind, she had to be virtuous and blameless. So the family continued on, intact and stable. During World War II, for which his step-Dad was too old to serve, Holdy's parents gave their friends Farewell and Welcome Home parties, which were full of auld lang syne, and lots of drinking, smoking and music. His mother played the piano while everyone sang their old favorites. After the war his 'favorite uncle,' his mother's older brother, who had volunteered for Red Cross service in Britain, came home and announced that he was divorcing his wife and marrying a Scottish woman. His wife, who had herself served in the war effort, was stunned. She spent the rest of her days alone, set apart from the family and depressed for that, a dumped divorcee. Their son had joined the Navy, and spent the war seeing action in the Pacific; he came home safely as well.

There was one turning point Holdy always remembered. He was fifteen, and the whole family was invited to a fancy golf and country club between his hometown and the city. It was some sort of anniversary for his grandparents, perhaps his grandfather's birthday or a company reception to honor him. The youth felt completely alienated from it all, and rejected anything to do with his stepfather's privileged Republican heritage. Another overwhelming transformation Holdy experienced was to realize that, somehow, the truth about his nature included a sense of abandonment, loneliness, weakness to the point of cowardice, and guilt. Had he been 'the cause of it all,' his mother's divorce and his father's disappearance? In any case, he was the remnant. And his stepfather's silence amounted to a sullen and unspoken condemnation of his existence on the planet. So Holdy became less confident about his prospects in the world, who he was and who he might become.

In contrast to such occasional inner doubts, Holdy's home and family life were full and interesting. Every evening the whole family sat down together. They had two places in the country to go on weekends and vacations, both of them shared by the extended family as well, uncles and aunts, his grandparents, cousins, and friends of his parents. One was a fishing camp in an isolated rural setting away from the east end of Lake Ontario, without plumbing, electricity or telephone. The other was an old, family-oriented resort on the south shore of the lake. They spent most summer vacations at the lake, renting a house, and Fall and Spring weekends at the simple cottage in the woods.

Holdy's interests in the arts continued. Midway through high school he also gained a special companion with whom to share these interests, and a good deal else. They became inseparable. Lenny was a year older than Holdy, but physically was a young man compared to Holdy's boyish appearance. Lenny's parents were older than normal, and during the time Holdy knew him, since they'd lived in their first house in the village, his mother had died, then his father. After each loss, the surviving spouse remarried sooner than expected. So by the time Lenny was in high school he had parents who were not much his senior. Holdy was puzzled to note that after each original parent died, Lenny didn't seem affected at all, as though his relationship with them wasn't very deep, he wanted to forget, or was numb. So the two teenagers had much in common, which came down to a mutual need for a supporting relationship, which later included intimacy. For Lenny was gay, and introduced Holdy to such pleasures. Just before his senior year, Lenny moved away. That Fall, Holdy was physically developed enough to go out for football. Before the first game, however, he had acute appendicitis and an operation.

At 16 Holdy was told by his parents that he should choose a state college (tuition free for state residents) that would train him in a profession or vocation. He wanted veterinary school, but his mediocre grades weren't sufficient, so he chose the next closest field, agriculture. His stepfather had no patience with liberal arts or fine arts, which led nowhere and prepared one for nothing, he said. He believed, as did his own father, that a son should be trained to work. Four years later his sister would be sent to a prestigious women's liberal arts college, at great expense, undoubtedly helped by Holdy's grandparents. His younger brother went to the state forestry college, but abandoned it later for an MBA. Meanwhile, his other half sister, who grew up with Holdy's birth father and his second wife, May, was beginning education for a nursing career. Holdy's mother's younger sister married and had several children by a Catholic, which caused a temporary family crisis, and lifelong estrangement from the Elder Hollings.

Holdy began college at a small two-year ag-tech "institute" in Northern New York State. During that first winter, needing some extra cash, he bicycled out to the nearest dairy farm every Saturday to work. In those days, his school was next door to a private liberal arts college, and Holdy often walked through its halls, reading bulletin boards. A few times he attended 'public lectures' and concerts, and one lecture especially whetted his intellectual appetite, given by a well-known literary critic on some aspect of Nathaniel Hawthorne's writings. It produced goose bumps on Holdy, and he wanted to know more, much more. He did well the first year at the little ag school, but his grades fell during the second, because he had joined an ag fraternity and lived with a house full of Korean War vets several years older. They introduced him to drink and carousing, but he made it. During Spring break he decided to hitchhike to Quebec City. He went from Spring in his college town to Winter wearing only a raincoat and low shoes, at one point trudging between two highways at a fork through two feet of snow, past houses out of which people stared at him. It was his first visit to a foreign country and cultural capitol, and he was fascinated, both by the French language and what he saw.

Now he decided to apply for transfer to Cornell University's state ag college. But he was really yearning for a regular liberal arts education. He was accepted, and started there as a sophomore. As he had hoped and dreamed, Cornell proved to be an intellectually liberating experience. Even though he was an 'aggie,' he took as many liberal arts credits as he could, being warned once for taking too many, and another time for low grades. Two courses were especially memorable and beneficial, a public speaking course that helped him speak before a group with confidence, giving him understanding and control of his speech difficulties, and a course in democratic political theory, whose charismatic instructor, educated in England, was an enduring intellectual model for the rest of his life. Always interested in the religious experience, he looked at the various Christian denominations in a religious center on campus, but couldn't accept any of them. They were too narrow and doctrinaire. In the ag college, he took the required full load of courses, and the big, six credit Farm Management course took him back to the old hilltop farm outside his home town, where, in cooperation with his farmer-friend, he did a study of the farm's potential as a beef cattle enterprise in mid-20th century. It wasn't much, said his Cornell instructor, being too small, too run down, too this and too that. Holdy felt put down as much as his friend, because he'd loved the place since childhood. In the end he graduated, and because he'd had student deferment from the military draft, he had to enter the army right away, either by enlisting or being drafted. He enlisted. After Basic Training at Fort Dix he was sent to the Army Language School on the exotic Monterey Peninsula for six months one winter, for Russian language training by old emigrees. There he met other intellectually minded GIs, visited San Francisco, and spent his weekends riding a small Harley south on Route 1, to hike up into the hills of the Los Padres National Forest and spend Saturday nights sleeping alone. When he finished, on a thirty day leave he bought a large Harley and biked back east, stopping on the way at his 'favorite uncle' Gus's place in Albuquerque. During other training in Massachusetts, he spent his weekends either hanging out in Cambridge and Harvard or MIT, or hitchhiking north to hike and spend an overnight in the White Mountains.

After training they shipped him to Alaska, just outside Anchorage, where he bought an old jeep. On weekends and his short annual leave, he explored the nearby woods and hills, and in winter went downhill skiing, or cross-country skiing to photograph moose. He also attended the Unitarian Fellowship in Anchorage, where he met and became acquainted with two intriguing individuals. One was the gay pastor, whose apartment he visited one night, the other a married woman with three children who was thinking of divorcing her husband. With the latter, Holdy had long coffee talks, but never became intimate in other ways. They parted good friends, and kept in touch over the ensuing years.

After the army, he left Fort Dix and went on a two-week playgoing binge in Manhattan, before returning to his Central New York family home. He stayed there about four months, but then his grandfather sent word via his stepfather that the next time he saw him he must be wearing a coat, dress shirt and tie, shine his shoes, get a haircut, and find a regular job. After three years in the army and being told what to do and how to dress every minute of the day, he had no problem making his next decision. In the morning he called various skiers inns in New England, and found a job for the winter. Early the next day he was on his way to Northern New England in a used Plymouth coupe he'd bought.

When Holdy arrived in the small mountain town in New Hampshire, it was still Fall. The inn wasn't ready for him to start work, so he hired on at a local woodworking plant. He rented a single room with an elderly widow who was nearly deaf. During the winter he made the acquaintance of a young divorcee, but he was so obsessed with having sex while she needed his friendship and company that it was total frustration for both of them. He had a plan to travel to Europe and live on his GI Bill, but he earned so little that he couldn't save enough that first winter. In the Spring he returned home, but a month later he bought a fancy English bicycle and proceeded to ride over to Vermont to work as a waiter at a writers conference for two weeks, then attend a six-week Russian language course not far away. After that, he would bicycle south to Buzzard's Bay to visit his sister and her young family, the one he grew up with. After that brief visit, he bicycled the 365 miles back to Syracuse in 3 ½ days. He did some bicycling around his home town, and explored the countryside. By this time his other sister, in California and still unknown to him, was working as a nurse and had married. During these years, Holdy knew nothing of his birth father, where he lived or how he was doing, or even if he were still alive.

In late summer, he again drove to the ski town in northern New Hampshire. This time, the winter of 1958-59, he was determined to save every penny he could, in order to make it to Europe. He was too early for employment at the woodworking plant, so he answered an ad for help on a gentleman's apple farm outside the neighboring town, and within bicycling distance in the beautiful Fall weather. Every Saturday he went out and picked apples from this orchard of many varieties, his head up in the top of apple trees, with blue sky all around and the white-capped Presidential Range to the North. He always had lunch with the couple, the husband being the son of an American painter, William Glackens. Holdy shared with them his European travel plans. When work in town started up, he repeated the experience of the previous winter. As Spring approached, he returned home and sold the car. He finally had enough saved for travel to Europe. He booked passage on a small British freighter, the "Marengo" of the Ellerman-Wilson Line. It took 14 days to reach Scotland. When he left the ship, he had exactly $156 left, and immigration officials questioned allowing him to remain, until he told them he had relatives in Scotland. They were the family of his uncle's Scottish second wife. Holdy spent the next six months traveling all over Western Europe, as far east as Yugoslavia and Austria. He had originally planned to bicycle, but he was sold a lemon in Edinburgh, which broke down, and another lemon in Paris, ditto, and he had no more money for another. So he gave it up and started hitchhiking, walking, and taking trains. He'd arranged to write a travel column for his small hometown newspaper, and the meager pay he received from that helped pay for food, lodging at hostels, and the occasional boat or train ride. Much of the time he slept outdoors, and rarely ate in a restaurant.

In the Fall he returned to Edinburgh and began a year at the University of Edinburgh, taking Russian and Moral Philosophy. He met a fellow American, a younger woman named Kristin, and they began sharing separate garret digs at the Alexandra Hotel by the Tron Church on the Royal Mile. Their friendship lasted most of that year. In June, she was to fly home to the States, but they decided to first visit Switzerland together. After returning to Paris, they had a tearful goodbye and she left on a Pan American jet for New York. Holdy soon began a two week course in French for foreigners at the Sorbonne. His plan was to attend a French university in Provence that Fall. A week later he received a message at the American Express office to call Kristin on the West Coast.

She had stopped at Holdy's home in upstate New York before continuing on to hers on the Coast. She simply asked if he wanted to get married. This took him by surprise, because they'd never talked of marriage. He wondered to himself if perhaps his conservative parents and hers had assumed they'd had an affair and 'should' get married, and so were pressuring them to do so. She said that their parents would pay for Holdy to fly back to the States, then for both of them to return to France so he could attend the French university. Their phone conversation was awkward, and the main reason Holdy acquiesced and went through with it was because apparently she wanted to. And he looked forward to that; perhaps she'd finally had a change of heart toward his advances. So he returned to his family home, then continued on to her home, where they were married. From the very first night, however, it was evident this was not going to be a normal marriage. For nothing had changed; but perhaps in time it would. After all, they were officially husband and wife now. They'd never had any arguments; in fact, they'd rarely had intimate discussions about themselves and their future together. Perhaps this would change too, though neither of them seemed disposed to become any more interested to know the other. They were both quiet and nice that way. From her side, though she married him and would stay with him, underneath she didn't understand him at all. And beneath that was an incipient distrust. Who was this Holdy, anyway? Well, hopefully she'd find out, and he'd be more responsible in his career plans. Kristin had plans of her own, too, to finish her college education and have a career. One could surely do both: get married with kids and have a career.

They returned to France on the liner United States, still puzzled within and asking themselves why they'd gotten married. But there was never any conversation or discussion concerning their feelings and apprehensions on the matter, so things continued at a minimal level. They were friends, and that was all. They both enjoyed being in the old university town in Provence, but Holdy had difficulty being a 'French student' in a French university, and Kristin became increasingly restive with his aimless career ways. She spoke no French, only a few shopping phrases. Toward the end of his university year, she told him she wanted to go home. Reluctantly, he agreed, and as they drove to the port of Marseille to catch their ship, a new American freighter, he wept. Holdy loved France, and didn't really want to leave. This added to his misgivings over their so-called marriage. First they spent a few months in his home area, while he took a semester of Russian studies at Syracuse University, mostly at the graduate level. Kristin worked as a secretary to bring in extra money to supplement his GI Bill, which didn't go as far as it had in Europe. They stayed in family housing for veterans. Once he'd completed one semester, she said she wanted to go on to her home in Seattle. During this period they bought a Hillman convertible, and then Holdy impulsively wrote the FBI for help in finding his birth father. That is, if he was still alive. He knew that he'd been in the army, and guessed that he probably served in World War II, so it might not be too hard to locate him. In a few weeks he received a reply, giving a street address in San Diego. They packed the Hillman and headed down through the Deep South, which neither of them had seen. This was early in 1963, and they encountered segregation for the first time. Holdy had come back from Europe bearded, which had precipitated a family crisis, and it also identified him as a northerner, and a possible Communist agitator (Hirsute Fidel Castro had recently come to power in Cuba.). Their New York license plates were also a red flag, and they drew attention at restaurants and motels. From New Orleans they headed west, stopping briefly in Albuquerque to see his mother's older brother and his Scottish wife. From there they went straight to San Diego, where they'd arranged to meet his birth father, second wife and other sister for the first time.

It was an odd meeting in the parking lot of Disneyland, which was closed that day. They all went out to dinner at a deluxe Mexican restaurant, courtesy of his father. They talked a great deal, over beers. But it was also awkward. In an exchange of letters with his father before they came west, Holdy had intimated that he'd been unhappy with his stepfather, and his father intimated that he'd welcome him, and they could now start a father-son relationship. After a separation of 35 years, that was an unrealistic expectation. Also, Holdy had a closer attachment to his stepfather than he was willing to admit, when he realized that his stepfather had been his actual father, raising him to manhood, and in a comfortable and happy family home. There were many shades of gray here, and Holdy was confused as to how to go about getting closer to his birth father. He needed time, and there were a lot of questions that needed answering. At the same time, Holdy couldn't bring himself to be too prying with personal questions, pointedly about the divorce, so the result was that these things weren't talked about, only glossed over.

At their house, they briefly talked in the dining room. Richard sat at one end, his arms on the table, hands folded. His second wife stood beside him. Holdy and Kristin remained standing at the other end, as if they really didn't know what to do or say. Finally Richard asked Holdy how his adoption had affected him. 'Not at all, really,' he said, adding, 'I think it's actually made my life more interesting and challenging . . . ' And his voice trailed off. . . . 'Trying to make sense of it all, I guess.' At that, his father laid his head down on his arms, and his wife wept. Holdy felt like a fool, but was at a loss at what else to say. Some details were shared, and his wife tearfully described how they used to come watch Holdy from a distance whenever they were back east, sitting in their car. Uncovering the truth in all these matters was just beginning.

After a few days, Holdy and his wife continued on up to Seattle. They rented a small apartment right across from the statue of George Washington on the University of Washington campus, and Holdy started taking a full load of classes, in English literature this time, which annoyed Kristin. She had found a secretarial job on campus, to add money to his GI Bill checks and student loans he'd taken out. When she asked him why he'd switched from Russian studies to English literature, he said he wanted to be a writer, and this would be 'good background.' Up to that point he had only scribbled now and then, had one short story published in a student literary magazine while in Edinburgh, and produced the series of travel articles for his hometown newspaper.

Toward the end of his first quarter of studies, they moved to a better apartment. The morning of his final exams, she abruptly informed Holdy that she wanted a divorce. He was dumbfounded. They hadn't discussed anything that might be wrong, anything that should be addressed between them. Concerns had only been touched upon, as if they were like changes in the weather. Those were the dimensions of their relationship, the depth and breadth of their intimacy. When he plaintively asked her why she wanted a divorce, she said she just wanted one, and had plans to finish her own college studies. We can do that too, he said. It's too late, she replied. He left for his exams feeling numb and powerless. They'd been together for three years, and he felt he loved her and wanted to be with her. But obviously something was very wrong, maybe a lot of things, because they didn't have a real marriage. He had assumed that, over time, they would eventually evolve into man and wife. When he sat down in the exam room, he only stared uncomprehending at the sheet of questions. After ten minutes he got up and handed in the untouched exam, receiving a wide-eyed glance from the examiner, and went home. He found a note she'd left, saying that she'd moved back to her parents' house.

It was Spring. After he closed out the apartment and left the university, Kristin asked him to find a job out of town, so they could both think on what to do next. He found a job as a janitor/driver at a summer children's camp in the San Juan Islands up north. They drove up together in the Hillman, silent most of the way, and she dropped him off, driving away in tears. After she left, he felt like an exile, put away in this camp on an island, living in tipis under the trees with water all around. Holdy and Kristin hardly communicated all summer. When he came back to Seattle in the Fall, the divorce papers were ready. He moved into a small apartment, sharing it with another man, and found a job at an antiquarian bookstore downtown. Since Holdy and his ex-wife hadn't really discussed their divorce, it took him a very long time to accept that their marriage was finished. Kristin resumed her studies toward a BA degree, which eventually led her to a professional degree in the sciences, and a second marriage with children.

But Holdy felt stranded. He needed someone to talk to, by way of recovering from this blow, this failure. He'd been corresponding now and then with the older woman with three kids he'd known in Anchorage, while in the army, so he unburdened himself to her. She was now divorced and living in southern California. They warmed over their friendship, and eventually the idea of marriage came along. She was all for it, but he was uncertain. She invited him down for a visit and they went to bed, but there was no love in it. When she left the house to take the kids to some appointment or other, he stayed home. He telephoned his ex-wife, letting her know where he was and what he'd been doing, and that he missed her. He said there was nothing in this relationship he was in, and couldn't they work out their differences and try again? He told her he still loved her. Angered, embarrassed and shocked by his call, Kristin hung up.

Strangely, Holdy and the woman decided to get married. Although Holdy finally got up the nerve to tell her he thought it was too soon and unwise, as he hadn't gotten over his divorce yet, she dismissed such concerns and assured him they could make it. A couple of months later he bussed to California again, and they were married in her living room. He returned to Seattle, rented a fixer-upper house, and spent the next six months cleaning and painting it for their arrival in early summer, because she was a teacher and needed to finish out the school year. Holdy discovered there were rats in the house, and he had to mount a regular extermination campaign. One weekend while having lunch alone in the bare kitchen, a large rat came out of a hole above the hot water heater and just sat there cleaning his paws. As the school year ended in southern California, the woman either sold or rented her house and brought her household and children north, hauling a small rental trailer. Almost from the moment he looked out the front door and saw them drive up, she with her graying hair and leaning confidently out the window, but with a wan smile, he knew it was no good. They moved in, and one afternoon even played music together. Holdy was just learning to play the cello, his wife played the piano, a daughter the violin, her oldest son the flute. For a brief time, perhaps thirty minutes, they were an ensemble. She found a job as a teacher across Lake Washington, and declared that they should move over there. But that would give Holdy a long commute downtown to the bookstore, and no more bicycling, which he thoroughly enjoyed. It was clear that in this marriage, she would be in charge. Holdy would be an appendage. It was a rebound situation through and through, from start to finish.

One weekend afternoon less than three weeks after their arrival, they all went to see the movie "Lawrence of Arabia." While they were driving home, with Holdy at the wheel, they talked about the movie. His wife thought Lawrence was a homosexual, and despised him for it. Holdy said he'd read most of Lawrence's writings, and that he was an interesting historical and literary figure. He liked him for that. Always had, as a matter of fact. She then insinuated that Holdy was a homosexual himself. With the children as witnesses in the back seat (the oldest being a 17-year-old son), he suddenly and brutally hit his wife's face with the back of his hand. When they got to the house, she and the children jumped out, for a moment leaving Holdy sitting there. Then he drove away, deeply regretting what he'd done and not knowing where to go. An hour later he returned and walked into the house, beaten and depressed. He apologized as best he could. (He'd never struck any woman before, and was genuinely sorry.) With controlled anger and veiled contempt she said that they were moving across Lake Washington, and invited him along to go see their new apartment. It was big and roomy, with hardwood floors. Plenty of room for her piano, she said. She actually assumed Holdy would come along with them, and that the marriage might continue. Holdy was very quiet; he was still smarting from his outburst in the car. When they returned home, he decided to end it. He said he'd made the house for them and that he was staying. (Under Washington State law at that time, she'd be at fault in any divorce, because she'd be leaving the home he provided for her and the children.) From his point of view, it was a way to stop this charade and spare them all more damage. A day or two later he returned from work at the bookstore to find them and their furniture gone. She later filed for divorce, and they never saw or heard from each other again.

While he'd been renovating the old house, Holdy listened to a local non-commercial FM radio station. He liked their eccentric programming and now decided to answer their constant call for volunteers. He had moved out of the house, and now lived on a small boathouse on Portage Bay. Once or twice a week he'd bicycle up to their studio at the north end and fill in as engineer/announcer until midnight. Then he moved to an apartment on Capitol Hill, one of a series of moves. His sexuality was also restless and unfocused, and when he wasn't seeing a woman, he turned to bisexual associations. Always trying to gain friends or intimates, one year he arranged to buy an old VW microbus, and began to go out on excursions with the Seattle Mountaineers, an outing club. His volunteering at the radio station, bookstore work and the Mountaineers activities continued for a few years. He sold the old microbus and got a newer one, then sold that and bought a BSA motorcycle. During this period he also subscribed to the Seattle Repertory Theatre and the Seattle Symphony, and became a fan of ballet. He even spent a summer taking basic ballet lessons at the Cornish School, which gave him a new view on how one's body can respond to music, which in this case was accompanied by a live pianist. He joined a local club for French speakers, and had an affair with one of the members. At their annual masquerade ball one year, he won first prize costumed as "Death," which was a bottle of vintage French wine. He wore all black, with a top hat and cape, and his face covered with phosphorescent gray cream, his eyes black holes. He also took a class in beginning acting, and played small parts in two comedies presented by a local theatre. But his best and most memorable theatrical experiences were as walk-ons in costume for two summer productions at the old Green Lake Aquatheatre, "Midsummer's Night Dream" with the music of Mendelson, and "Peer Gynt," with the music of Grieg.

Then he decided to get into sailing. He sold his latest vehicle and arranged with a finance company to buy a thirty-foot, liveaboard ketch, which he moored in Portage Bay, and lived aboard. He sailed it to Victoria, B.C. with three friends from his old radio station, and around Puget Sound. After two years he tried to refinance it, but they refused so he had to let it go, the payments having become too burdensome for his low income. The friend who owned the moorage said he'd sell Holdy his old, auxiliary six meter sloop, and he could live on that. It was over thirty years old, but still a dream sailing machine.

It was during this time that a young woman, Maude, came to work at the bookstore. She bicycled to work too, from seven miles out! After a while they became acquainted, and Holdy began courting her. They went out on many excursions and dates, including sailing on Puget Sound. Her family, however, took a dim view of their relationship because Holdy was so much older. Eventually they accepted the two as a couple, and they decided to share an apartment on Capitol Hill. One day they were reading together and she got up. As she passed by, she gave him a resounding slap on the face. What was that for? he asked, in total surprise. I don't know; I just felt like it, she replied.

During this time, Holdy left the bookstore downtown because it was a family business and held no future for him, now that the owner's sons were growing up. He quit and took an advanced paraprofessional job at the University of Washington Libraries. After a year, Holdy decided to obtain a librarian's degree. He quit his job and started the MLS program. While working and studying there, he became supportive of the Black movements for equal transportation, equal access to education, and equal housing. He and Maude shared these so-called radical political views, and went to various meetings. Soon Maude switched to a job at the university too. They did everything together. One Autumn weekend they took a train ride to Vancouver, B.C., and a few weeks later she said she was pregnant. She now wanted to move to a larger apartment to make room for the baby, and she wanted to get married. But first Holdy must change his name to include hers, which he did. During this time there was much campus unrest. The anti-Vietnam War movement was growing, and women's liberation issues became very important for Maude. She joined a radical women's political group and went regularly to their meetings. Her strengthening feminist views started to erode their marriage. At the same time, Holdy's repressed bad feelings about himself were coming out. He was a prime civil rights activist, exercising his anger and sense of inferiority toward the Establishment and The Man, all of which served as a straw man for his stepfather and everything he represented. His low self-esteem and confused sexual orientation were also expressed in nude modeling for art classes at the university. In those days there were also various alternative 'universities' for students to take classes in subjects not dealt with satisfactorily at the UW. His wife did sketching, and when she came home one day talking about a male model, it piqued Holdy's interest, and he began modeling there too, but not in classes where his wife was enrolled. He found modeling a strangely exciting and fulfilling experience, as if thus displaying himself before strangers were some kind of legitimate intimacy or rite of passage to manhood.

After the baby came, Holden Jr., they were a happy family for about a year. His wife was now writing a radical feminist column for the student newspaper. At home, she and Holdy had more and more acrimonious discussions. Holdy tried his best to understand and support her, because he shared almost all her feminist views and looked on himself as a 'liberated husband.' But her anger was strong, as urged on by the radical women's group, and possibly due as much to a father who had abused her mother long ago, causing their separation when she was young, and a grandfather who abused her grandmother, and especially her older sister, which disrupted if not ruined almost every family gathering. Maude had grown up in her grandparents home. Grampa had fathered her as best he could, and Holdy learned that he'd been an active ILWU member and had always fought for better pay and working conditions for all workers.

Then Maude abruptly demanded a divorce; their baby was a little over a year old. This was appalling for Holdy, because it seemed like a repeat of his own experience as the son of a divorced couple, something he'd always dreaded might happen to his own child. But it wasn't to be quite that way. He moved out, and found a communal house less than a mile away. (Communes and collectives were common during the several years of the Anti-Vietnam War movement.) For six months she denied Holdy access to the baby he loved. Then, just as suddenly, she insisted he share the baby's care. From then on they shared the child's care and affection almost fifty-fifty.

Lately Holdy had become involved in the United Construction Workers, an activist, interracial group militant for equal employment opportunity for minorities. While protesting an unenforced Federal court order that was supposed to train minorities for construction, he was arrested during a sit-in on a construction site and convicted of trespassing. (The Federal order was later returned to court, and enforced on White contractors.)

The time came for Holdy to graduate with his librarian's degree. He now looked for jobs, and it took another six months for him to find one. It was far away, at Montana State Prison. He'd be representing the State Library at the Prison, providing model library services to both inmates and staff. The prospect of going to Montana upset Holdy, because it meant he would be away from his little son, now a toddler, for long periods. But he had to start working. He had student loans to pay off and child support to provide. He began work in November, driving his old VW microbus over there, crammed full of everything he owned. The following summer he was able to attend a correctional conference in Seattle, and his ex-wife agreed he could take their son back to Montana for a month. They took the train over and back. During his time in the small prison town, Holdy had made the acquaintance of a divorcee his same age, who had a little daughter about his son's age. They got along well, went out together, visited her folks in Missoula, and the subject of marriage came up. Unfortunately, she expected Holdy to adopt her Bahai faith, or she couldn't marry him. Holdy's eclectic and agnostic spiritual beliefs excluded joining any one church, except possibly a Unitarian Fellowship, which he sought out whenever it was available. So they split up as a courting couple, but remained friends.

Work at the Prison was interesting yet difficult, mainly in relations with the Warden, who exercised total control and intimidation over both staff and inmates. It had a very small prison population and staff, but it was still a challenge to work there. Holdy was kept ignorant about changes in the prison population that he should have been told about. On the other hand, he was in the advantageous position of providing contracted services from another state agency, so he felt protected and independent, much more so than his cowed and fearful fellow prison staff members.

Inevitably Holdy and the Warden had a falling out, and one afternoon he was escorted out of the Prison by one of the custody officers. He hardly had time to say his goodbyes to a few inmates who happened to be in the library when he was taken there to clear out a few personal things. While at the Prison, he had become interested in tipi culture. Many inmates were Blackfeet or Crow Indians. He ordered a large tipi for himself, and obtained permission to cut twenty-five Lodgepole Pine poles from the neighboring National Forest. He stripped and dried them over several weeks, then coated them with preservative.

With tipi and poles on the roof of his Microbus, he moved to Helena and continued working for the State Library. He pitched his tipi in the local KOA campground and lived in it. The State Library wanted him to stay on, but Holdy put being near his son as first priority. Holdy Jr. was approaching kindergarten and school age, and he wanted to share all the growing up years with him. So he resigned his good position at the State Library and returned to Seattle, taking everything with him, including his tipi, and the twenty-five tipi poles lashed onto the roof. He searched diligently for another library position, and found one in good time. It was at Tacoma Public Library in their Northwest Room. At first he arranged to pitch his tipi in the backyard of a house, so he could live in it until he earned enough to rent a small house. And when he finally made that move, he again pitched the tipi in his backyard. This traditional dwelling had taught him a great deal, and would continue to do so, and so whenever possible he installed it close-by wherever he lived.

He was hired, and found working as Northwest Heritage and History Librarian to be very satisfying. Holdy was a natural, thorough and enthusiastic student of the past in American life. He expanded the collection and made the Northwest Room attractive to patrons. He contacted local Black and Indian communities and arranged to obtain documentation of their local heritage and history. He moved into a small house, leased a new car, and at age 42 began playing soccer for a nearby club. It was the first time he'd ever played a field game, and he would continue to do so for several years, throughout the seasons, because he came to love the sport. He took training in coaching, and with his young son attended all the games of a Seattle professional soccer team.

Then a new library director was hired, a former Catholic seminarian, whose job was a total reorganization of the library, one of the oldest in the state. No longer would there be a long-tenured, degreed librarian in every subject department, guarding his or her domain. Instead, a few versatile MLS librarians would oversee (much lower paid) departmental para-professionals. Holdy actually accepted this plan, but his job was on soft, Federal money, and for some reason he feared he'd be dropped. The style of the new director was also demoralizing, because he was authoritarian and paternalistic, addressing the staff like children. Holdy's morale steadily declined until he couldn't take any more; it became a matter of his mental health. So one Friday afternoon on the eve of a holiday weekend and without notice, after almost three years of productive and fulfilling work, he quit, leaving a letter of resignation on his supervisor's desk. He never returned.

The next 3 1/2 years were among the most difficult and frustrating of his life. He lost the leased car and moved in with his former wife's grandfather, pitching his tipi next to the house. Her grandmother had died a few years earlier, so Grampa was living alone. Holdy constantly searched for another library job, but his age, just turned fifty, made it a fruitless pastime. Personnel officers who could be his son or daughter somehow couldn't conceive of hiring him, an older man, for any position, despite his varied experience, which, in passing, they also admired. The pile of resumes, job notices, application forms, and rejections got higher, until it was a few inches thick.

At one point earlier in his life, just before he turned 35, he had applied to be a U.S. Foreign Service officer. He passed the written exam, but failed the oral due to poor preparation. During the application phase, he'd had to make available a list of every address he'd ever lived for six months or more. These amounted to over thirty, up to that time, which was about one change in residence every year. He was to change residences even more often in the coming three decades.

This time he remained either unemployed or underemployed, working again for his Seattle nursery-greenhouse friends, this time for over two years. Hard pressed to meet his rent, he volunteered for a program called Home Sharing for Seniors, and lived with a partially deaf, 92-year-old gentleman for a few months. But the circumstances were too difficult and Holdy had to leave when the man started being abusive whenever his son would stay with him. Borrowing money from his parents again, he flew to an interview in Idaho, and managed to reach other interviews around the region without a car, but no job offer came. The specialization of library jobs made his varied background and experience less and less appropriate. Often someone fresh out of graduate library school, with no experience whatever in the field, was hired over him because they had the specialty training. His age and experience, which also carried field know-how, proven judgement and the stability of an older employee, counted for nothing. Or he was 'overqualified,' which is another way of saying 'too old.' His Russian language training was suspect for one rural town council member, until he explained that he'd originally received it in the U.S. Army.

Late one September night Grampa got up to do some cooking in the kitchen, while Holdy slept in the attic bedroom upstairs with his door closed. It was chilly, so Grampa turned on an old floor space heater, its cord frayed and much repaired with tape, which sat on a shag rug in the living room. When he went back to bed, he forgot to turn it off. About 5:30 in the morning, Holdy came awake. He could hear Grampa running around downstairs. Then he smelled an awful smell, like the whole world was about to explode in flames. He jumped up and opened his door, and saw a wall of opaque, acrid, yellow-gray smoke. He hastily felt his way down the stairs, at the same time yelling 'Did you call the fire department!?' After a long pause, the reply came. 'Call the fire department!' He came beneath the smoke, and glanced up as he ran through the kitchen toward the back door. There was a flickering violet light all over the ceiling. The place was about to blow out. Grampa was standing in the front door with a garden hose in his hand, spraying nowhere in particular. Holdy ran out the door in his T-shirt and shorts, to an apartment house across the street. He entered a hallway and banged on the nearest door. After a minute a startled young woman in a bathrobe opened the door. She said she'd call the fire department, and at that moment they both heard a soft boom. The heat had broken a picture window and the old house now roared with the blowout. Holdy ran back and around the other side of the house, away from the flames. He could already hear the sirens, and met Grampa in the back. He was in his pajamas and his exposed skin was pink from a flash burn, but he was still trying to light a cigar. When two firemen came up, he joked that he ought to be able to find a light somewhere around there. Grampa was taken to the hospital and Holdy went around to the front. There was his tipi, which was about to be destroyed by the heat. Taking hold of one of the main tripod poles, with all his strength he lifted the tipi up enough so it fell over on its side, away from the fire. Grampa's dog was tied to a tree close by, frantically trying to escape the heat. Holdy let him loose, then went over by the street and sat down on a mattress the firemen had pulled from the half of the house not yet consumed by the fire. A number of people had gathered, and an American Red Cross volunteer took down his name and particulars so he could receive disaster relief, which meant money for food and clothes, and once he found another place to live, his first month's rent. It was a total-loss house fire. He'd started doing occasional field recording for the non-commercial FM radio station since returning to Seattle, but his tapes and expensive portable tape recorder and other equipment had gone up in smoke.

Holdy re-pitched his tipi in the middle of Grampa's large garden, to one side of the house, and slept and ate there for the next thirty days while he looked for another place. He combed through the ruins and found only a few salvageable items. One of them was the core manuscript of a novel he would write and finish and have printed almost twenty-five years later, in retirement. He moved into a duplex located in the Black ghetto area, the Central

District or "C.D.," only a couple of blocks from where Holdy and his third wife had lived and had their baby son. He was still employed at the nursery-greenhouse, doing some landscaping for them as well, and continued bicycling across town to work. Or he'd take the bus in bad weather. He'd somehow acquired two stray Samoyed dogs, a male and female, and kept them out back with his tipi poles. He bought an old training cart, fashioned a couple of harnesses and drove his dogs around the park nearby with his son, who was now nine and playing on a youth soccer team, which Holdy coached.

But Holdy was getting desperate for a library job. He'd tried every opening over a three-year period, never landing an offer. Since returning from Montana he'd occasionally receive mailings from a self-styled Crow medicine man who now lived in Seattle. He'd been a computer programmer when younger, of all things. Holdy gave him a call. He needed advice and help in applying to the tribes for a library or research job. The elderly man took him outside to sit on a bench in the park at the center of his low income city housing. He listened to Holdy's story, then told him to write a letter introducing himself and send it to the tribes he was interested in working for. He suggested a few. Holdy went home and sent letters to three tribes, two in Montana and one in Washington State. Within two weeks he received a reply from the latter, offering him a job as heritage-researcher. He immediately accepted, borrowed money from his parents for a rental truck, packed everything inside, including his dogs and tipi setup, and headed for the southwest Washington coast. He moved so fast that, once his mail was forwarded, he found a second job offer, from one of the Montana tribes.

His new position was another one of those soft-funded, Federal jobs. His life on the small coastal reservation was primitive and simple, and the heritage work was challenging. So much had been lost. He pitched his tipi behind some trees near the shore and lived there for a year. The tipi taught him how to be comfortable, dry and warm on that wet coast. He was determined to unearth enough details about the ancestral heritage to know what life and conditions were like before the arrival of the European explorers, missionaries and American settlers, with their diseases, cross-cultural destruction and exploitative economies. He tried so hard, it reminded him of that other deferred search in his life, for the truth behind his mother's divorce, his birth father's life, and his adoption. That was his own heritage, which he hoped someday to uncover as well. He had spent ten days with his ailing father several years before, but hadn't the courage to ask him pertinent questions. In the meantime he'd died.

He spent one year with the coastal tribe, doing the best he could in working with the Heritage Committee. In his spare time he introduced soccer in the coastal communities, and established two youth soccer clubs. Then Ronald Reagan became President, and soft Federal funding for his job was cut off. He applied for a few jobs around the area and sent out resumes hither and yon, with little hope of getting anything. But then came a surprise offer from Alaska. It had to do with library development in Native villages. He again packed his things, crated his two dogs and flew north, leaving behind his old tipi for tribal use.

For three years he worked in sixteen different Native villages. Life in remote Alaska was difficult and lonely for Holdy, but he loved the wet tundra environment, the strong seasons and the Native Yupik people in their remote insular villages. Living at first in a small log cabin on the banks of the big river in the regional center (population less than 4000), he made the acquaintance of a friend, who was gay. He also found a woman friend, a widow, but in the end she drank too much. His employer was the regional community college in town, and his job was to help start small community libraries in a number of the outlying Native villages. It was to be the highest paying job he'd ever have. Each summer he went Outside, either to travel east by train with his son to visit his parents, or to vacation on the coastal reservation, where he began working on a series of heritage publications and was a player/coach on an adult soccer team. Each summer he brought his 12-dog team south, to be staked out and cared for somewhere on or near the coastal res.

He had a good life in this adopted home town in remote western Alaska, and volunteered for various community activities and projects in the town. He continued to have a small dog team, sometimes commuting to work with it in winter and exploring the trails around the village. Then funding for his job was ended by the community college, and he returned south, taking his dogs with him, including his original pair of Samoyeds. He settled on the coastal reservation again, using it as a base for his next job search. Holdy also got involved in local soccer again, and bought an old VW bug. Then he received a job offer from one of the plains tribes in Montana. He rented a truck and loaded all his possessions and the twelve dogs inside, in small kennels, and left at dawn one morning in March, towing his VW bug. In twenty-six hours he and his son, now fifteen, drove nonstop from the coastal res to the plains Indian res. They arrived through Marias Pass in a blizzard. First he stayed on a ranch outside town, then later, in the Spring, rented a house in town, which he eventually shared with an Indian woman who turned out to be an alcoholic. He soon discovered that there was no dog mushing around there, because of all the fences. Work at the tribal community college was, again, very challenging and interesting, but continuing trouble with the Indian woman decided Holdy to leave the res. He bought a large, used, red crew cab Ford pickup, dispersed all his dogs except the two Sams, and moved back to Seattle.

He rented a room in a small apartment house near the university district and found work with a lawn care and landscaping service based east of Lake Washington. Such work was getting strenuous for Holdy, who was now fifty-seven. He also began work on a book about his library work with tribes and Alaska Natives, eventually expanding it to include all the circumpolar countries. His son, who was now in his last year in high school, asked to spend that year with him, so they had adjoining rooms in the apartment house. When he decided not to do unskilled labor any more, and running into what he felt was increasing age discrimination in libraries, he returned to his nursery-greenhouse friends in north Seattle. During this year he had affairs with various women, but none of these relationships lasted because sex was all he had on his mind. Feeling badly about himself as a man, and being afraid and suspicious of women's intentions, he wasn't interested in any deeper commitment with any woman. Soon tiring of nursery-greenhouse work, he decided to sell the big pickup and return to his former home and workplace in western Alaska. At least up there the quality of life was better, no matter what kind of job he'd find. Eventually he hoped to return to libraries, but the chances of that happening seemed very slim indeed.

His gay friend was still there, and it was good to see him. In fact, the whole community welcomed him back. It was old home week for Holdy, for he loved the town as a home. He tried various jobs, and on the first one he befriended an Alaska Native woman. They eventually lived together for a year in a small house that lacked plumbing. But Holdy's personal life improved greatly, and things seemed to be going well. Then his Native girlfriend, who'd abandoned her last marriage, decided to try returning to her husband and family again, in a remote village, and she left town. Several years before she had liberated herself from an abusive home situation, traveled all around the U.S. with a young White man, then returned to Alaska, where she and Holdy met. Holdy next was hired to be manager of the small regional museum in town, which also had a gift shop. He moved in to share the apartment of his gay friend, with whom he'd long since been just friends. It was during this time that Holdy began failing morally, so to speak, and his friend asked him to leave their apartment. Then the town government decided to stop funding the popular regional museum enterprise, so Holdy was out of a job locally. But then he was notified that his parents had started disbursing their inherited wealth, and henceforth he would receive a large sum every year. Holdy's personal finances abruptly looked very promising indeed. He proceeded to rent a large log house with an option to buy in a nice section of town, where he would live alone for the next few years. He was applying for any librarian openings in town, but wasn't hired. Old story. Finally the community college hired him as a clerk and part-time Russian instructor. With his extra money, he started to enlarge his dog yard. His goal was someday to have a good dog team that everyone would admire. He then received word that he had a publisher for his book on library development in Native communities.

But something was very wrong with Holdy's life. He was depressed, lonely, and felt isolated in the community. He felt haunted by old feelings of abandonment, the inability to find love, and confused identity. He began making costly, monthly trips overnight to Anchorage, to slum along notorious Fourth Avenue, degrading himself. He was desperate for companionship and intimacy, and was reaching out in all directions, and this eventually got him into trouble with the law. He was arrested, and sentenced to serve almost four years. Included in his sentence was mandatory mental health treatment. This consumed most of his sentence, and when he returned to the street, far from his isolated village out on the tundra, he was a very changed older man, open, vulnerable, responsible and aware of his true nature as he'd never been before. The sources of his fears, anger and stress had been aired at last, and he understood and accepted who he was, and had been. Sure, he had a felony conviction on his life record, but he also had a new life, a new beginning. He was able and wanting to love someone unconditionally, and soon did so, finding personal fulfillment and peace at last.

As for his mother, birth father and stepfather, and his mother's divorce, he continued to search for the truth, and at last found it in a packet of letters sent to him by his half sister by his birth father's second marriage, with whom he'd become close by correspondence. He learned, first and foremost, that the divorce was entirely his mother's doing, and that, in effect, *she* abandoned his birth father, Richard Smith, not the reverse. Her version always maintained that he'd abandoned her, and that she never heard from him again. Also, her brother, Holdy's 'favorite' uncle, had engineered the divorce and threatened his birth father *and* his parents if he tried to visit Holdy all those years he was growing up. Another aspect of the whole affair included the fact, learned after Holdy's younger brother adopted two children, that his stepfather couldn't accept adopted children as his own. Most damning of all, however, was his mother's letter to his birth father right after she obtained her divorce. After thanking him for the letters and money he'd sent her, she took full responsibility for the divorce, then coldly wished him well.

Thus Holdy learned the truth about his beginnings, and about his birth father, who turned out to be a war hero, a good husband and a wonderful father. Unfortunately, Holdy was denied access to him, and was told lies and had much crucial information withheld by his mother. These revelations eventually elicited compassion and understanding from Holdy, toward all concerned, along with some anger toward his mother. This time, as they say in therapy, it was justifiable anger, not misplaced or irrational anger, of the kinds he used to have, before he found out the truth. So he didn't have to 'act out inappropriately' any more, to feel better. He just had to live with it in a philosophical way, and write it all down. Perhaps through that therapy and catharsis he might cleanse his soul.

THE REGISTRY

My name is Gus Grander, and yes, I was convicted of a felony in Alaska in the early 1990s. I spent some time in jail before my sentencing, then two and a half years in a correctional treatment center. I came out a changed man. This all took place when I was about 61-64 years old; I was on the verge of retirement. Fortunately, because any chances of finding a decent job were nil, I had some property and investments I could live on, as long as they lasted.

So I tried to start a new life in Anchorage when I got out on the street. I could never go back to the remote village where it all happened; I wouldn't want to go back. So I became a volunteer around town, and served with various charitable organizations like the Red Cross and Home Care for Seniors. My new life was more than okay, it was wonderful. A whole lot of emotional and ethical doors were opening for me, that's how it felt. I bought a second-hand jeep in good condition and could go anywhere, year-round. Winters I helped with the Fur Rendezvous and the Iditarod, summers I worked as a docent at the old silver mine up in Hatcher Pass, which had become a state park.

I also helped out now and then at the Pioneer Home, where I met this nice gal a little younger than me. Charlene played violin in a string quartet that came to entertain the old folks every Holiday time. Maybe I should say 'older folks,' because she was in her fifties. She was divorced and had three grown children in the Lower 48. Anyway, we hit it off and started going out. We spent more and more time together, and I moved in with her about a year later. We decided to get married the next New Years. My life was so fulfilled it didn't seem possible I was a convicted felon. I despised the old me for that, but I couldn't deny responsibility for the harm I'd done. Charlene was always there to make sure my guilt and remorse didn't overwhelm me, and of course the treatment center had taught me ways of coping, feeling better about myself, and living the good, responsible life. We'd been going to her church since we first met, and I really liked it. Once a month they invited a lay person to deliver the sermon, and after a year or so the Reverend invited me to do the honors. I couldn't believe it. Well, in a sense I could, because I'd been through the mill, down to the depths and back, and now felt I'd been blessed with a new, normal life, full of love and giving to others. It was very emotional for me. Some people say men are weak who show their gentler, loving side out in the open, or admit to a lot of sentiment about their childhood and family. Bull, I say. They're just as much a man as any Rambo with his heavy machine gun cradled in his brawny, sweaty arms, ready to kill for revenge or Christ. As a man I'm fit and strong and feel good about myself. I'd protect Charlene and care for her as long as I'm able, to my dying breath.

Then I got a notice in the mail that shook me badly. We were both upset for days. As a former offender, I had to register with the police once a year downtown. Until I die. I certainly understood people's fears about my past, because I'd broken the trust of the community, so I really had no problem about registering. But it took Charlene a while to accept my having to do it. Then another bit of news came along that was miserable, and made me angry. Actually I never got any warning notice about it; I read about it in the newspapers and heard it on TV. The registry of ex-felons and all their data, including a photo, was placed on an internet web site, accessible to anyone in the entire world. To me, in terms of my rights and my privacy, this was amazing and outrageous. Surely it must be unconstitutional? Court challenges came forward, but they'll be mired in the courts for years. Many offenders who hadn't signed up for the registry before now flatly refused to do so, and were liable to prosecution for a misdemeanor. They were placed on the registry anyway. Some parolees lost their jobs and some their housing. A few were harassed by neighbors. New parolees would have even greater difficulty finding jobs, and would have to draw unemployment and food stamps, or go on the dole. Others would beg on the streets and join the homeless, or go off into the Alaskan wilderness and try to survive. It was a lifelong sentence, long after prison time had been served. It could turn some offenders struggling just to survive into desperate men. Where could they go? They couldn't leave the state without a solid parole or transfer plan, which from Alaska is very difficult to do.

Charlene and I toughed it out. As for income, I was very fortunate. Not needing a job, I didn't have that worry. For Charlene's sake, I maintained a tiny apartment in Anchorage as my official address, where we stayed maybe once a week or so, and a post office box downtown, but we lived in her small house outside town that was away from neighbors. It was hard for anyone to reach us. My phone was unlisted and I got all my mail in Anchorage. We were getting by with some privacy.

Charlene had lived in Alaska for over twenty years, and I'd been there about ten altogether, if you count the two years I spent there while in the army many years earlier. At our age, we decided to look into moving somewhere south, and to a state that didn't have their registry on the internet. The most attractive one was Hawaii, where she had relatives. We'd visited them the past couple of winters and liked it there. They lived on Maui. I was off parole by that time, and had only six months of probation left, so I applied for the transfer. Like most states, they had a registry for ex-felons too, but it wasn't on a web site. To my surprise and delight, my transfer was granted with ease. So we made moving plans; the next summer we would go south.

We found a nice upcountry home at 2400'. Again we settled in, improving the house and adding many plants to our gardens. We picked out civic activities to participate in or support, and became active and known in those circles. Our second vehicle was my jeep, with which we explored the back roads of the island. We joined a couple of garden clubs, and the Friends of the local library. Our move had been successful, and we loved the climate most of the time, warm days with a trade wind breeze, and always cool nights. This went on for two years, with visits now and then by my wife's children from the mainland, who all knew about my past.

Then it hit us again. I'd registered with a Hawaii Probation Officer, but the conditions were more relaxed than Alaska. Again, as far as I was concerned, I had no hesitation signing up. It was mandatory anyway. I got acquainted with my P.O., and we had long talks about local history, a mutual interest. We got along fine, even after I got off probation. Then I was watching the TV news one evening when I was knocked down again. It was announced that the state had established a website for the registry. I couldn't believe it. Again, all my pertinent data was there, including our address and my photo. We were very upset and dismayed, and a little afraid. There were only eleven offenders like me in our zip code, which is a very small number. This public stigmatization was following me everywhere. Would I ever be free of this surveillance and public exposure, in this case before the whole world, not just local residents? I knew I had ceased being a threat to anyone, ever since I left the treatment center five years earlier. The next year I made our phone number 'unlisted.'

Well, we put up with it again, and we have for almost twenty years now. I'm almost 90 and my wife just turned 80, but I'm still on the state registry, and on the website. And I still send in an updated registration form every six months. We are both ailing, and in fragile health. No one's bothered us over the years, and we get along fine in the community and with our neighbors, some of whom know about my past, of course.

But I've always resented what I believe is the unconstitutionality of these internet websites, with worldwide access, for those who've committed crimes, have been released and are trying to lead normal lives. It just doesn't seem fair, and maybe it's an ominous trend, registering more and more classes of people that way. If it's considered within the constitution, why not register those who sell drugs, especially to children? Why not those offenders with lifelong records of assault? How about deadbeat dads, and those guilty of any Federal crime? Why not websites for convicted drunk drivers, especially those who've killed or injured others? Eventually, as the usefulness of the internet grows, we'll see more such information on these websites, just as for a long time now we've been able to find out 'anything about anybody' through investigative services on the internet. I'd say our so-called privacy and individual rights are eventually going right out the window. And Big Brother is going to be right at home with us.

I get to thinking about this trend, and I can honestly say that I'm glad I won't be living much longer. Perhaps my generation is the first to be recorded and watched by a worldwide surveillance network, and I'll be glad to see an end to it. Once I'm dead, they won't have me to kick around any more, as Nixon once said. I'll be left alone at last. No more people trying to sell me things I don't want, either. For each of you, too, in not too many years, there may be a 'personal doom' like mine, because something you did or said in the past or something about you, who you are, will trip you up, and you'll be nailed, stigmatized and crippled in your life effort. You'll have an ID and dossier with worldwide access. It's already known what your credit, finances, debt record, driving record, military and work record, marital history, age and ethnicity are, and our Social Security numbers already serve as a national ID. So we're well on our way down the road toward international control of everyone in the 'civilized world.' Mark my words. If I were young and strong enough, I'd be tempted to head for the Third World, go into the wilderness and subsist on as little as possible, and disappear. That alternative might be good for one more generation, before Progress and its authority catches up with you there, too. A Personal Doom. Think about it. It's not so far fetched when you consider the directions that automation, computerization, electronic data banks and internet technology are headed. Everyone will have an electronic dossier, and anyone will be able to access it.

TWO CHARACTERS FROM THE NOVEL "THE CROOKED WAY HOME"

1. Arthur

The setting was a July morning in the Lafayette sitting room on their hilltop farm outside Fayetteville, New York. Arthur slowly moved in his old fashioned rocking chair, smoking a pipe, now and then gazing out the window over the fields. His legs were crossed, he wore an old leather vest over a work shirt with the sleeves rolled up, and baggy denim pants. His feet were white-stockinged, as we'd left our boots and shoes on the outer porch. A light rain was falling, which is why he was able to take time out from cultivating his corn to talk. We could see his horses in a small paddock next to the barn. I'd come from the Fayetteville Ledger-Courier to interview him, and after a half hour we were relaxing with coffee that Marthe brought in. He was in an expansive mood. I'd just asked him when he found out he was an orphan.

"Aunt Maudy told me when I was real little. 'Your Mommy and Daddy left you here with me,' she said, 'because they had to leave and had no time or care to take you with them. They went far out west somewheres, but I don't know where. When Curtis, your Daddy, got out of jail,' she said, 'he couldn't find any jobs around, or only lousy ones, so they both decided to go west. He was going to change his name and they'd start over. It was as simple as that, and there's no way you're going to find them, not in a whole month of Sundays. So don't you even try, Punkin.' That's what she called me. 'We're your Mommy and Daddy now, and we'll just love you to death.'

"And they did, as long as they lived. I was real young then, when my parents left me, probably one or two years old, so I don't remember anything. In some ways I wish they'd never told me I was an orphan. It's as if the world didn't want me, or nobody had time to raise me and teach me all they knew. But Maudy and Bob did, and I'm glad they kept me. What my Daddy went to jail for, I wouldn't find out for a long time. He wasn't in for very long, so I was told, but in and out is sometimes more than enough. It was for him, apparently. I think it broke him and my mother. His neighbors around Sylvan Beach, where I grew up, never let him forget it though, what he'd done. Nobody trusted him or would hire him. All he did was pass a few bad checks.

"That was ages ago. Here I am fifty years old, talking to you like this, to no account at all! Those days are way long gone. But you know, I remember them, my real parents, Maudy and Bob, the ones that raised me, very clearly; I can still see them. But I wish they'd never told me I was left behind. That was much later, of course, when I was old enough to understand. That's when I left home and headed south to start my own life. I was just fourteen, but big for my age. I told them, I don't want to live here any more; I want my own place. And they understood, They knew exactly what I was saying, and they knew I could take care of myself. 'Course I didn't get any farther than Fayetteville, only thirty miles away, but that was far enough. Sylvan Beach raised me, all the good people there, and I still go back and see them. It's got some of the best fishing around, you know. Oh yes! And boating. Onieda

Lake is popular with folks from Syracuse to Utica. They all go up there. I still go fishing myself, when I have time. And I visit people, too. They all know me. I took care of my folks as they got older, when I was able to. Even brought them down to the farm a couple of times. But they were real old by then, when they didn't care what they heard or what they saw. Everything was changed, and they had nothing to do with it. That's what they kept saying. I guess that's how some old people think. But I'm glad I brought them down. They could see I found a home for myself and was happy. I was needed here, and it's my place too, along with Marthe. We've made it so, even if we're both orphans, both adopted. You didn't know that? Oh yes. I think that's what brought us together in the first place.

"But I'm getting ahead of myself. You see, when I first came this way, young as I was, I didn't know which end was up, where to turn or what to say. I'd go to a storekeeper or a factory manager, a farmer or the town hall down here in the village; I'd just stand there, my mouth hangin' open like a dumbbell, I'm lookin' for work, I'd say. They'd look me over and every time they'd say, You're too young, Sonny. What're you down here for? You should be home helpin' your Mommy and Daddy. But I knew they didn't need help, and would bless me no matter what I did, as long as I respected their good name, which was Benedict. I found out my new name when I was old enough and was starting school. Your name's Arthur Benedict, they said, and that's what I always told people, at least until I came here. But I knew it wasn't my real name, so I always had in mind to have my own name and my own place someday, when I could look down on the world and say, This is who I am, and this is my home, where I'll stay until I die. And it's been that way ever since, especially since Marthe came here with Junior. It's our home together now.

"Anyway, at first I couldn't find any jobs worth shoot, and one day I was walking around down below, and I seen these buildings up here on the hill. Well now, I says to myself, there's a farm right close by I haven't seen before, so I scouted around and found a way up. I just walked in like a perfect stranger, except, you know, it was like I'd come home. The Lafayettes were needing help, and I turned out to be just the ticket. They had a son almost my age, and we hit it off. So I helped the old man every way I could. That's C.J.; C.J. and Sissie. Gus was their son, and even though I was a little older, we became like twin brothers.

"After a while the Lafayettes became my family, and I never used the name Benedict again. It wasn't really mine anyway, to tell the truth, and since my true Mom and Dad left me to grow up on my own, I just decided to take the name Lafayette. Why not? It's my life now, and I'll make of it what I will. I've got me a farm and a good woman, and we're raising Junior too. That's Marthe's boy, from her first marriage with the Captain. She moved up here long after I got here, a grass widow with her little son, and we naturally hit it off. It just seemed perfect for the both of us, as time went on. All we wanted was a good home for ourselves and Junior, and C.J. and Sissie like as turned over the whole place to us.

"But over the years I've always gone back to Sylvan Beach, like I said. Not just to visit but to learn more about my blood parents, and what I heard wasn't always good to hear. My Dad wasn't able to make it in anything worth while, and then he and my mother had me. And maybe that was the last straw for him. They had to go west. Maude was her cousin, so they turned me over to her and Bob. All I know is, they took me in and raised me. What more could a kid ask for? Then when they passed away, I kept going back there, trying to learn more, and doin' a little fishin'. So I got some roots in Sylvan Beach, too.

"So I settled down here, and that's it. This is my home, Marthe's and my home. I came first, then she came along. Her first husband, the Captain, was C.J.'s stepson, you know, and he just took off once they were married and he got her pregnant. Just like that! Never did figure him out. He never even saw his son. Just left Marthe high and dry. She's still hasn't gotten over it. This place originally belonged to Sissie's family, the James, and she inherited it. Then she married C.J. and they moved up here. Gus, the one we call the Captain, was her son by a previous marriage, but she divorced him. Anyway Marthe came up, and we were like a team. It's like we'd been waiting for each other all our lives! It seemed so natural to be together, and we been that way ever since.

"You know, you're the first person I ever told this to, and I don't want you to repeat it. Not for the paper anyway. No. I know, these antique faires we been putting on attract a lot of attention, but I don't want no credit for that, neither. There's no need to even mention such things about me. It's all Marthe's show, and I'm just her friend and partner. Look at it this way: We put on these faires, and I'm just helping out; I'm here. It's all her doing, and she does it for all the family, her son, his dead father, C.J. and Sissie, and everyone who comes up here. I'm not that way; I'm just here to take care of the farm and her, that's all. I'm her husband and caretaker up here, doing what I feel is right. Yes, of course I help out with the faires, but I don't want my name mentioned, Okay? No. I'm just here, and leave it like that, if you don't mind.

"Now if you want to talk about the farm and what I've done with it, that's another matter. I don't usually talk to reporters about this, but in your case I'll make an exception, since you're local. I've turned this farm into a place with a history and a heritage. It's not just any farm, it's Every Farm, from the beginning to now. That's how I see it. The rocks, the soil, the trees, the buildings, the landscape and the ruins out there, in the woods and under our feet, all the blood spilt, everything. You know how in Europe they claim to be a thousand years old? That's how old Paris is anyway, so I've been told. Well, I've never been there but I know how they talk when they come here, like we've got no history at all. That's what I mean. We do have a history, just as long and as deep as theirs, maybe longer. And it's all here, right within our fences and woods. So I've spent my life digging it out, doing the research, writing it down, to try and pass it on. I call it the Heritage of Place, and this I'm proud of. I'll stand on it and defend it to my dying day.

"In a nutshell, this farm means everything to me. You know, when Marthe first came here, she couldn't figure me out. What are you doing here, Arthur? she'd say. You could do so much better somewhere else. I knew that, but I chose to stay here. There comes a time in your life when you need to stand for something, and to be remembered for that, and for me this farm is it. Someday it will mean something to everyone, and they'll learn from it. So that's my goal, to create something up here that will be meaningful and lasting not only for Marthe and me, and her son, but show respect for Sissie and C.J. too, and everybody before us who ever had anything to do with this hilltop. Do you see what I'm saying? Yes, it's as simple as that. Someday people will come up here and say, So that's how it was. Now I know a little more clearly who I am, and where I come from. That's what they'll say, and I'll be glad, smiling in my grave, right over there, in that little cemetery plot in the woods, where C.J. and Sissie are both buried, and Bless'em both."

*   *   *

Naturally I didn't include much of this in my piece on the farm, but just getting to know him gave a certain depth and sensitivity to it, and I showed him the draft of it for comment or correction. He didn't have any.

2. The Captain

The Seattle Post-Intelligencer was interested in Captain Lafayette because of his sponsorship of various artistic groups, and allowing his own mansion to be used for activities in the arts. As a cub reporter originally from Central New York State, the City Editor picked me to interview him. He figured we'd have some things in common. Actually I was originally from the west side of Syracuse, near Camillus, so I really knew little about Fayetteville, his home town. However, I'd been to a couple of the big antique faires they used to have on their hilltop farm, which is where he was raised. After showing me around the old green wood-frame mansion and its two wings, which was filled with all kinds of stuff he'd collected, including a lot of old furniture and art work of every description, he invited me upstairs to his cubby-hole office at the top of the main part of the house. He sat in his swivel chair by a rolltop desk, pointing out a small love seat opposite where I could sit comfortably. For some reason he had dressed up for my interview, so he had on a black, double-breasted officer's outfit with brass buttons. His shoes appeared freshly shined. He was bearded, and his hair was neatly combed. His was a salt and pepper beard, and he cut a quite distinguished figure, in total contrast to the messy surroundings of his office. His whole house resembled an abandoned warehouse or museum, as a matter of fact. Anyway, we'd been talking about women, and he mentioned that he had a wife and child back east. I was surprised by what he said next.

"There was nothing to it, really. Her name was Marthe. She obviously believed she could get me to swallow my pride and anger and stay home, up there on the farm, forget all the abuse by my stepfather and settle down on that worthless place with my parents, just because she got pregnant. I'd made up my mind long before that I wanted no part of it. But you know the pressure a young man feels to do what his family want him to do. Yes, I was her husband; I agreed to that. And I fathered her child. But that doesn't mean I can be someone I'm not. I could never settle down the way she wanted me to. First of all I didn't trust her. She seemed to know exactly what she wanted; I didn't. So we went through the charade of our courtship and marriage. I knew it was shaky all along, but I went along with it. The last thing I wanted was to be a farmer, and the very last thing I wanted was to settle down on my father's farm. You know, women like Marthe think they can change a man just by getting pregnant by him and then hauling him in. She was single-minded that way. She loved the farm and my mother's family and would do anything to stay there, assuming all along that I'd forget about the past and become like her. In a backhanded way, getting her pregnant was my way of saying, 'Sure, I'll go back to the hilltop with you, but in the shape of our baby, no more. And you can have it all; I want no part of it.'

"Why did I move out to Seattle? To get away from her and my folks, to be honest. At the same time, of course, I wanted a home of my own. I joined the merchant marine so I could travel, and visit places all over the world. Well, I've ended up staying mostly on the Pacific, but that's alright. It's different, sometimes exotic, and between going to sea and enjoying my mansion, which is a pretty big one, as you can see, I keep busy enough most of the time. I moved in here not long after I arrived in Seattle and started to make a life for myself, without other people or family interfering. And it's worked out okay. I've always liked Queen Anne Hill, and I'm close to the center here on the south side.

"I love Seattle and the Pacific Northwest, just as much as she wanted to stay on the farm. So there we were, and there's never been any possibility in my mind that I'd ever go back there again, and she knows it. But she keeps hinting that I'll eventually come back. No way! Now as it turns out, I know I've had problems that she was blind to, so she's lucky. She thought she could cure me of anything that might be bothering me, that I didn't want to talk about, but I know she's wrong. She doesn't know me at all and never could. I can't seem to ever be really satisfied with my life, no matter where I am or what I'm doing. "That's just the way I am. That's a given, and nothing will ever change me. There are bad feelings inside me that just won't quit, and believe me, I've tried every shrink I could afford. So I've put everything into this place, actually a former mansion, with two wings. I have a lot of interests, I travel, and the Townsends are the best caretakers and friends a fellow like me could ask for. So I hang on the best I can. Why drag her and the kid into it? I know it may sound selfish and irresponsible, but on the whole I think I've saved her another kind of grief. Sure, she'd like me to come running back there and be a regular husband and father, but to me it would be like asking me to dig my own grave. I can't do it.

"But I'm getting ahead of myself. Let me go back, to before I ever met Marthe. C.J., the old man who raised me, wasn't my real father. No, it was some guy named Ragland. But apparently he took off and left my mother and me. Why, I don't know. I know nothing about him, and for all I know he could have been a bum or a hero. My mother never filled in the details, so I've had to concoct some kind of father in my mind, and I haven't done a good job of it. In fact, I haven't even tried. Not seriously. So I suppose I should have accepted the story that he was a bad guy, someone I should despise and forget about. But to tell the truth, I haven't been able to do that. He's still around, in my memory, and keeps bothering me, because I have to wonder: What went on back then, between my mother and him? Why did he run off, leaving my mother to fend for herself, though she came from the wealthy James family. So she marries C.J., a one time farmer and cripple, a bitter ex-soldier. You know, that bastard may have lost a leg in the war, but he thought he could win his war with me! I think after he came back he just fell into my mother's arms and said 'To hell with it! And I'll make that son of hers work for everything I've lost.' And that's how it felt, you know? He seemed so frustrated and angry with himself, not being able to do so many things any more, that he drove Arthur and me like a team of horses bringing in hay ahead of rain. Only thing is, he favored Arthur and couldn't stand me. At least that's the way it felt. He never let me forget that I wasn't his own, and that my real Dad didn't want me! That really hurt. Then Lewis came along, his own child now, and things got really bad. But then my mother got sick and tired of his carrying on with me and couldn't take it any more. She farmed out little Lewis to cousins over to Phoenix, you know, north of Syracuse near Three Rivers? Then she laid down the law to C.J. Oh, that made me feel good! Only thing is, C.J. and I started getting into real fights when I got big enough, 'cept he hit the bottle out in the stable when he was in those moods and couldn't harm a flea, but it was still miserable being around him. You know, he used to razz and cuff me all the time when I was younger. His favorite was a hard cuff across the back of my head. Really hard! He liked to surprise me that way. And his mouth was filthy at such times. Well, there came a time when I was ready for him. When I got strong enough and mad enough, I shoved him away so hard he could hardly get up. I just stood over him and threatened him. I would have loved to work him over, but what's the use with a miserable drunk? I couldn't stand him. But even after Mom warned him to lay off, he still kept it up, but only when she wasn't around, you understand. Then we reached the point where he knew I wanted to beat the shit out of him so bad I could taste it, and suddenly he laid off. And I didn't care any more either. Sure I stayed there a few more years, until I finished school, but I was through. I was the one swearing now. Every time I spoke to him, everything he stood for was trash. 'Course around Mom I treated him good, but he knew what was behind my smile! I'm sure she knew something was rotten between us, but because we never talked about it any more, she never let on. I think she gave up too.

"I'll never forget the day I told him me and Lewis were leaving, and wanted nothing to do with the farm. Oh boy, I could see he was hurt, and hurt bad. And the funny thing is, I think he actually expected me to take over the farm, and me and Arthur would run it. Well, he had another think comin', I'll say, and that's the end of that. I couldn't wait to get outta there. The happiest day of my life was when I walked off that hill for the last time, with Marthe on my arm. She was already pregnant. And that last time, y'know, I never even looked at C.J. I just gave Mom a peck on the cheek and we left. One thing, I knew I got her pregnant the other time we were there, down in the woods off the hill. I just knew it. I thought to myself, Let this kid try to make something of it, if he wants to, 'cause I can't make head nor tail of it. If he wants it, let him take it. C.J. and Mom will be gone, and he can have a free hand. Marthe and I will probably be gone too, and Arthur, but that won't matter. Good old Arthur, he was our hired man from way back. Now there's a guy would help you any way he could. He's one guy I was sorry to leave behind.

"What do you want to know about Seattle for? I already told you enough, and besides, anything more is none of your damn business! This is my life out here, and I can do whatever I want. Okay, I know, I don't mean to be hostile, it's just that Marthe keeps asking what I'm doing and I get tired of it. I write her once in a while, sure, but I don't want to hear her constantly whining about us getting together. I ignore her. But it bothers me that she keeps after me, keeps after me, on and on, like she won't ever quit. Get on with your life, I say. What's the point? Do I have to spell it out for her a hundred times? I'm never going back. Never! Everything I have is out here, period. But you know, I'd be the first to admit that things haven't worked out very well for me, either. Here I am, essentially alone, and Marthe pines away and my boy's getting older, and Lord knows what shit they're feeding him about me. To hear Marthe, you'd think we were still married and I was a saint. Crazy! And I've been gone almost fifteen years now. I used to send her money now and then, but she doesn't need it since Mom's folks left her everything. She's flush. She's really come into the Mother Lode now. And that's okay.

"Let me tell you something. I wish I didn't hate that farm and everything C.J. stood for. I miss a real home like that, with a wife and kids. Out here, you know, I've tried to do the same, but nothing sticks. I've had more girl friends than I can count, but they come and go. No, truth is, I come and go. I just can't settle down with a woman forever. I don't trust them. I mean I don't trust myself with them. Any woman is better and smarter than a man, doncha know? God damn it! They got their marbles together, no matter what you do. Me? I'm a born bachelor. But I do love Alice. Yeah, good old Alice. I can see her anytime I want. She lives on the west side of Queen Anne, so it's a hop and a skip over to her place. We've had a lot of good times together, but we'll never talk marriage! Why should we? We're happy just like we are; at least I am. She's been through the mill too, y'know. Her daughter went off and left her, and she hardly ever hears from her, so we have some things like that in common. She's alone and I'm alone. We get along good because we don't make demands or expect anything else. We're friends. I stay at her place now and then, but we don't interfere in each other's lives. Another way to put it, I guess, is that we're both independent and easily dissatisfied, if that makes any sense. I don't want us to be tied down like other couples. We're not looking at any permanent future together, in other words. Whenever I come by, she's always glad to see me. We talk a little, visit a while, I pet her cats and do any heavy work she has, and that's it. Sometimes we go for a walk or I take her shopping or on errands, and that's it. No more than that. I don't want any more! 'Cause if we got into a Marthe thing, I'd leave her. I'm sure I would. And she knows that. In fact, I have, more than once. So we keep on that way, and the only thing I expect of her is that she see me whenever I come by. And that's enough.

"Of course, sometimes Alice lets on that she'd maybe like me to move in with her, at least for a while, but I've got my own place, right around the corner. We're only a half mile apart. If she wants to come stay at my place, fine. She could come now and then, y'know. That would be alright with me. But we both feel the same way; we're afraid to leave the homes we've made for ourselves. She collects books and reads all the time, I travel and collect a whole lot of stuff. I used to take her out to eat a lot, but she'd get sick from the food in some of the restaurants I'd take her to. I love foreign food. I eat it all the time in my travels. But she's got a touchy stomach. Anything other than all-American food she reacts to. So we stopped doing that. I stop by her place and she'll have something simple for me, along with some tea and cookies. And that's it. To be honest, that's enough. She doesn't drink, and I don't drink when I go see her.

"As for my job, it's just a job. I like the merchant marine, and as an officer I have some privileges and job security. I'm good at math, and always liked navigation and communication. At sea, I'm the one who knows where we are, and what's going on in the world. I have some authority, some special knowledge and skills everybody needs. But beyond that, it's just a job. I guess I'll stick it out until retirement, but you never know. Maybe I'll quit early. I've got enough stuff in this mansion to keep me going into old age! I also sponsor a lot of community activities here, as you know. It's too big a place for just me and the Townsends to rattle around in. Besides, I need the company, even if I can't count a single real friend among them. Sometimes I rent some rooms or even the other wing to an art school or dance academy, and help out myself if I'm home. But someday I want to have the place to myself, after the Townsends retire up north.

"I don't know. Sometimes I'm sitting up here in my office, and I wonder what the hell I'm doing, what have I done with my life. What's it amounted to, anyway? Ever get that feeling? I get it all the time now. Well, at least I can always go over and see Alice. She can cheer me up in a minute. As long as she's around I've got a life."

* * *

There was so much that was personal in our first talk that I found it embarrassing. He wanted to talk. So I had to come back for the material I was looking for. By that time he realized what I wanted and was very helpful and charming about it. The rest I got from library research and other interviews.

ANY REGRETS?

When I was in college, a half century ago, "Books in Print" was contained within two manageable volumes, one for access by author and title, the other by subject. It is now several volumes. As someone has said, it seems everyone needs to write a book these days. But the appalling additional fact is that it's now possible for almost anyone to do so! Electronic vanity presses such as Xlibris and others will publish anything not libelous for only a few hundred dollars, and you may see your book in both paperback and hardbound forms, listed and described by electronic booksellers on the World Wide Web. To have one's own book published so easily is to become immortal for only a modest sum. It used to be that only the gifted could be remembered that way, and the rest of us had to settle for photographs, correspondence, portraits, diaries, or business and public records to document our lives, as long as these were saved and preserved, and survived.

In response to this exponential growth of publishing services for the common man and woman, the 'writers group' has proliferated throughout the United States. There must be hundreds of thousands of them now, perhaps millions, not just in Meccas for writers and artists like San Francisco, New York, Boston, Chicago, Seattle or New Orleans, but everywhere, in the smallest town in the most remote corners of the country, even on cruise ships.

Over the years I've been in many, in a variety of locations and circumstances, some good, some discouraging, some controlling, some that simply became stagnant. Writers groups are found any time three people desiring to improve their writing as a craft get together and share their efforts. (One has to be a coordinator.) Creative writing courses at all levels tend to spawn writers groups. In looking at this phenomenon, I've been surprised to note that I've been in far more writers group situations than I realized. In remembering and reviewing each one, I've picked out the best and worst, the helpful and unhelpful features of each.

There are all kinds of reasons for writing: therapeutic, storytelling, to earn money, to put down one's thoughts for future reference, report to others, or stimulate their intellects, or hopefully to become famous. For some, writing is a serious calling, a vocation, something one feels compelled to do, for whatever reason, to feel good about oneself and one's life, even to find and preserve one's mental health. Writing can also serve as a form of revenge, or justification of one's life efforts, if other ways of contributing to the common weal have failed, been ignored or frustrated, perhaps arbitrarily squelched by others.

The first writers group I ever attended was in a provincial city in the north, where we met in its central, palatial public library. We sat around a huge, square, beautifully varnished table, and there must have been twenty in attendance. These sessions were run by a woman who, as it turned out, offered her editing services for a fee. There was no reading of one's work, only the talks of guest speakers, usually published, who fielded questions afterward. I was put off by the whole thing, and stopped going.

The second one, in the same city, was much more interesting. It's meetings were held in a private apartment, and began on a weekday evening around nine or ten o'clock. Usually six to eight people attended. It consisted entirely of active, mostly young writers reading their own material and receiving feedback on the spot. There were some remarkable individuals in this group, and I looked forward to it. As often happens in writers groups, a couple of people tended to dominate and offer more comment, in this case the apartment dwellers, but on the whole I received a lot of help and stimulation. Not having a car at the time, the late hours made it difficult for me to attend. But whenever I wanted to air my writing laundry, so to speak, in a supportive setting, the others were good listeners. I was offered rides home by fellow attendees, and a few of us met privately on the side, exchanging stories and poetry between our regular meetings. It was a congenial, positive and intimate gathering of amateur writers, mostly in their twenties and early thirties. I was by far the oldest, being in my fifties. Another reason I liked these meetings was for the intimacy, informality and ready humor. At moments the atmosphere seemed almost clandestine and diabolical, as if we were a coven of magicians and sorcerers, conjuring up new worlds and old selves simultaneously, being freed for the first time.

The third group was also formed in the same city, a couple of years later. The first floor of a long vacant, never used small apartment building was converted into a ramshackle coffee house and meetings rooms on the first floor, with cheap apartments above for students and artists. They invited groups of any kind to meet in the rooms downstairs. This writers group was older, and a few had been published in the literary journals or newspapers; one had written a children's book which was still in print. When I first attended, a former journalist was presenting chapters from a mystery novel he was working on. He'd bring in photocopies for the ten or twelve members to take home, receiving comment the following week, or sometimes on the spot. This was a more serious group, and the sessions resembled business meetings, with some us bringing our work in large envelopes, attache cases or on clipboards. On the whole it was a fair, open and mature gathering, and no one person dominated it. They were very careful about letting that happen. The only intimidating feature was the attitude of one of the coordinators. He referred to our meetings as 'chop sessions,' where we were all supposed to chop and tear apart every piece of writing offered. Thankfully, more considerate heads prevailed, and the criticism was almost always warranted, fair, and encouraging. The ex-journalist later had his mystery published, and it became the first of a series based on his main character, a state police detective in remote Alaska.

Other writers groups I attended took place in small towns on one of the Hawaiian islands, where we moved several years ago. It was actually one group, but kept moving around. We first met in the waiting room of a local business that provided various kinds of alternative therapies, which one of our members owned. This one was coordinated by people into New Age kinds of impressionistic and mystical writing, combined with music and forms of relaxation therapy, but other genres of writing were heard too. The atmosphere was more romantic and less critical, and praise was lavished on everyone's attempts at writing, no matter how faulted. It was not a group to my liking, and I dropped out.

Later, the more serious of us started weekly meetings in the small coffee shop of a major bookstore chain on the island. One would think this might be an ideal setting, but it wasn't. Too much noise from the public address system, and when the holiday season approached we were asked to leave, so their customers could use the shop that one evening every two weeks when we met there. We looked around for another venue, and agreed to meet in a large coffee shop around one table, but the setting just wasn't suitable for our needs, and besides, one young man always brought a fat briefcase full of drafts of a huge non-fiction writing project he insisted on getting help with every time, so the rest of us felt shunted aside. Finally various members of the preceding groups on the same side of the island met in a cluttered used bookstore just down the coast. It was a long drive for me, but initially it seemed promising. Six or seven of us sat around one oblong table squeezed into the middle of the stacks, and coffee or tea was available, sometimes a little pastry. We all bought books there, after our meetings, so it was a compatible situation for the young male proprietor. However, this group soon developed three detracting elements that eventually drove me and a husband and wife team away. They were trying to collaborate on children's books, he being the writer, she the artist. The first bad feature was that the same people attended all the time. Secondly, a couple of people came only to criticize, which they did readily and mercilessly, sometimes with ridicule, yet never or rarely offered their own writing for review. And third, someone entered the group with an outside agenda. She had a writing class of her own, and at first I liked her contribution, except that her critical and analytical comments on each piece were rather long-winded. She was grandstanding, dominating the group, trying to impress and recruit us for her class that way. After a while her voice was about all we were hearing, to the detriment of others who wanted to present their writing efforts, so the combined impact of all the above made me cease attending. She never offered any writing of her own, by the way.

The most recent and best group I attended was a spin off from a night class in creative writing at our local alternative high school, one of its adult education classes. Those of us who wanted more met with the instructor in a private home where coffee, soda pop, tea, wine and cookies were offered. The setting was very comfortable and relaxed. Although the same half dozen local amateur writers attended (myself and the instructor being the only ones who'd had things published), it was the instructor himself who became the strongest feature and influence in our meetings.

He always picked the best chair in the room, slowly and thoughtfully priming his mind with a glass of vintage white wine, and proceeded to hold our attention and respect for the next two hours as he commented, along with the rest of us, on someone's writing, copies having been distributed at the previous biweekly meeting. Stan was well learned in literature, and had a philosophical side. He was an astute critic, but always encouraging. He had his own writing he was working on, and toward the end of our sessions, brought a short story for us to review and comment on.

I should add that the private home where we met was my own. I offered it to Stan and the group. I did this for selfish reasons, which I will explain. How often have I felt like an expatriate in my own country, in some out of the way place, born at the wrong time, an oddball, not of my country's way in commerce and popular culture. Only in places like San Francisco, New York or New Orleans, or certain provincial enclaves, might one feel at home as an artist and writer. In recent decades, since the 1960s, the atmosphere has slowly been transforming, and we find many more cities and towns willing to tolerate the more Bohemian among the general population. The excesses of the Red Scare in the fifties, civil rights protests, the anti-Vietnam War movement, the women's movement and accompanying sexual revolution, all have helped shake up the Establishment's conservative hold on our mores, allowing more freedom of expression, or at least a sense that more freedom is out there.

Being an amateur writer of an earlier generation with a preference for rural and remote places, and not a denizen of the academic world, I've missed always having intellectual friends and contacts around. In the early 1960s, after spending a few years in the army, I worked in a skiers' inn in northern New England, then fled to Europe and Britain, partly to prove to myself that I wasn't insane in the American dreamland! Later I lived on Indian reservations and worked in a prison. At last, a lifetime later, and having retired to our homey place on Hawaii, we could invite guests like Stan and the group. It felt good to do so, to provide a comfortable home environment and atmosphere to talk over our literary interests. To be intellectually alive, in other words.

Eventually Stan became burned out with us, and wanted a break from meeting with the same group of local amateurs all the time. Apparently he'd been meeting with this same spinoff group for years, before we'd ever moved to Hawaii. So for a short time I felt privileged that I was able to host the group, and have no regrets that it ended. Well, yes, I do, and I'd do it again in a minute, but such occasions are rare and precious. Where can one find artists, writers and musicians who are willing to share their search for the Muse? Perhaps I do have one other regret, that I was a late bloomer and haven't been gifted enough to rise above the amateur level. My mind is there, primed and full of the desire and a calling, in the deeper sense, but I started too late and was too confused, had too many personal problems. I couldn't get a clear grasp of any art, least of all my writing. That's one durable regret I've always had, and can never surmount. End of confession.

GOOD WORKS

For a lifetime, Rev. Stuart Harbison ministered to his suburban congregation. He was popular, available day or night, and gave all his energy to his vocation. Truly, others looked on him as a man gifted, able and willing to give selflessly in service of the Lord and His Church. He must feel entirely fulfilled in his pastoral work, they concluded, needing little support from others save the usual friendly assistance from dutiful members of his flock, who were usually the older ones, or had thriving families whose children populated the Sunday school classes.

He'd always believed that surely a pastor had found the most blessed life anyone could find. To help others live a full and meaningful life out in the world, what greater reward could one have? At the same time, his home life was not so perfect. He was married to a woman who simply couldn't share his deep calling. Dorothy Harbison went through the motions of being a pastor's wife as best she could, but her heart wasn't always in it. As a result, over time their marriage became, to some degree, an accommodation, not to say an estrangement. They had separate rooms, and beyond companionship and serving the ministry, little was shared. It was a cool home life they maintained, though friends and others could hardly tell. Yet companionship has a great deal to offer those who preserve it faithfully, as the Harbisons did.

Then a schism began appearing in the congregation, because Rev. Harbison had decided that the church needed to do more to recognize the special needs of older single women, widows and widowers, pregnant teen mothers and the like. So he formed a committee of the more liberal parishioners to see what could be done. He also let it be known that perhaps it was time to declare an 'open congregation,' and to invite minorities and even the gay community to participate. Surely everyone would eventually benefit from such a welcoming church policy, once the initial difficulties were overcome.

He did his best to introduce these new policies in a gentle and Christian way to the whole congregation, but to his surprise and frustration, almost half resisted the proposed changes, some by an icy reserve and silence, some by open criticism at trustees meetings, and others by withholding their tithes or simply leaving the church. Word soon reached the diocese of such protest and dissatisfaction, and he was called on the carpet.

Rev. Harbison was praised for his diligent work for the Lord and the Church, and it was pointed out that he hadn't had a real vacation or rest in many years. The Bishop offered him a choice. Either take a long leave of absence, or retreat, to reconsider his service to the Church and find peace, say three months, or take on another assignment that he had in mind. The Diocese needed another interim pastor, one who would be available to stand in for other pastors who were on vacation, ill, or otherwise indisposed. It would amount to an itinerant position, traveling around the county and ministering to any congregation temporarily lacking a shepherd. All these 'satellite' churches were within commuting distance of his home, so he and Mrs. Harbison wouldn't have to move. After considering the possibilities and talking it over with Dorothy, Stuart decided to accept this interim position. He'd been in the Church long enough to know that conservative policies would prevail for the foreseeable future, and it was really futile and suicidal to introduce, let alone insist on such changes that he knew, in his heart, had to come eventually. He wanted the Church to become pro-active, but the Bishop had made it clear that his whole approach was clearly unwarranted and unwanted, and at worst disruptive and dangerously premature. People, even good Christians, needed time to change their view of the world and others unlike them. Church supporters and loyal tithe givers wanted things left just as they'd always known them.

He began commuting from home to spend a Sunday or two or three, and a day or two besides, to chair meetings and meet parishioners at each new parish. At first Mrs. Harbison went along, but she tired of the constant change and not knowing anybody, and in the end stayed home, minding their flower gardens. Stuart was always glad to return home to her company, because the next stint might well draw him to the other end of the county. And so it went. He'd wanted change and he got it, but not the kind he felt was long overdue. This interim work began to dissipate and break down his life's vocation, a kind of sentence or punishment that the Bishop had imposed.

After two years of this regimen—for he chose to stay an itinerant pastor, Rev. Harbison decided on a new approach. Since he was here today and gone tomorrow, so to speak, before all his temporary congregations, before the whole diocese, in fact, he would occasionally mention his more liberal views of the Church's prospective role in his sermons and at meetings of local church trustees. Not abruptly or shrilly, but slowly and carefully, calmly, as if it were the most natural thing in the world, and always allowing for the expected disagreement and counter argument. In this unobtrusive way he planted seeds in the ears of those church members who were receptive, whether consciously or subconsciously. After all, each family who attended services or Sunday School had young members, and he knew a higher percentage of them would welcome a more liberal or liberated

Church. It was a slow process, but in this way he felt he was genuinely contributing to the Church's growth. Put another way, he believed he was facilitating its response to the modern and more progressive, more inclusive needs of a community coming closer together. As Rev. Harbison saw it, the days of exclusivity and bigotry were declining at last. And in a strange way, he felt a personal empathy toward the excluded. His status and experience in the Church, not to mention his marriage, suggested this parallel in such liaisons.

Over time, the ideas Rev. Harbison patiently cultivated throughout the diocese took on a life of their own. Times were indeed changing, as were the attitudes in the congregations he visited. Meanwhile his retirement was near and he needed an easier row to hoe, preferably on his home turf. He asked to be returned to his old congregation once more. At the same time, diocesan policies were about to shift, and at last the concept of 'welcoming congregations' actually came to pass. All the good Reverend's work of two decades was vindicated. When the old Bishop retired, conferences were held to choose the next one, and Rev. Harbison's name came up. After all, it had to be recognized that he'd shown the way. But Mrs. Harbison was ailing, so when a delegation approached him to see if he might accept nomination to the Bishopric, he had to decline, due to Dorothy's health problems and his own advanced age, which had just passed seventy.

Instead, he chose to return to his original congregation. Under the new, liberating policies, it was a great satisfaction to see that its composition had totally changed, and for the better. But at first he and Mrs. Harbison only recognized a few of the elderly, and those newcomers they befriended seemed from entirely different social and cultural backgrounds. The community itself had changed and grown as well. Had the Reverend and Mrs. Harbison become relics from a different era? Stuart and Dorothy had no extra money for travel, so they had to stay put. Between the two of them, there had been little in the way of social life except church-related activities, which had now multiplied and become very demanding. At their age, they had little time or energy for anything else, not even gardening. Their household took on a tired silence and gloom that seemed unfair and puzzling to Stuart. Dorothy was seeing doctors more often, and he never could get quite enough sleep. They had served the surrounding communities all their working life, yet felt abandoned and ignored by the passing parade of modern life.

Finally Rev. Harbison told the diocese he wanted to retire completely, and let a new young pastor take over, though he and his wife would stay in town. They settled into the routine of a retired cleric, and Stuart toyed with ideas for writing a book. Once in a while he was asked to give a sermon, but these occasions were so rare that he despaired of them as much as he was grateful for the invitations. When he looked out over the pews, everyone had become a kind of stranger. He even seemed a newcomer himself. He no longer recognized where he was or who he was. The old days were gone, and he was a has-been in the annals of local Church history, a footnote and listed name in the diocesan records. Granted, he'd been asked to be nominated to be Bishop, but that grand opportunity had come too late.

Then Dorothy took a profound turn for the worse, and lay dying. This was a shock for Stuart, and the trauma of Dorothy dying and the prospect of him, the survivor, living alone was a hard realization, for Dorothy had cared for Stuart all their adult lives. So much had been cherished, even as so much had been missed. And there was an added poignancy, undoubtedly a common one for any bereaved, in that they hadn't reached out to each other enough, over their lifetime together. At her funeral, fewer of the congregation from the church attended than one might have expected, because most of their old friends and supporters were gone, either died or moved away. When he returned home afterward, the silence of their house was deafening. Stuart slowly ascended the creaking stairs and entered her bedroom. He dropped to his knees and leaned his elbows on her bed. The house remained quiet except for his baritone voice, muffled in her bedclothes, intoning a prayer:

> 'Blessed Jesus, I beg you to help me understand the meaning of this life . . . What have I done, and what have I accomplished in thy name? The end has come for my dear wife Dotty. My house is empty, and my career has ended. Should I stay here until I die, and am buried alongside her, or leave and spend my last years somewhere else? Please help me . . . give me guidance and strength . . . '

Every day for a week Rev. Harbison beseeched the Lord Jesus Christ to help him decide what to do next, but he couldn't discern any answer or hint. In his heart, he wanted to do so many things: travel and see the world (except he couldn't afford it), perhaps look for another partner in marriage, continue to help others through local charities, find another church in this or a neighboring diocese, or write a book about his faith and philosophy of service. On and on his prospective life choices lay before him, but they were either too limitless, too broad and diverse, or too exotic. No two of them seemed to fit into his mind together.

One summer afternoon he was sitting on the porch, gently rocking in the large glider he and Dorothy used to share, she knitting, he reading a newspaper. Suddenly he was aware of company beside him, enjoying the day. At first it seemed like some divine presence, then the feelings of affection and peace reminded him of Dorothy. What was happening to him? What was he experiencing?! Who had come to him? It was then that he realized it was his own sense of fulfillment, of good works and long service, with Dorothy's help, to Jesus Christ and the Church.

That same week he made inquiries at a nearby abbey in the neighboring state. He went over for an interview, and was accepted as an adjunct fellow, a servant of the Lord ready to come home. At last he would have time to enjoy the simple things, breathe grace and thankfulness, share his strong faith, and continue work in the Church. For the monastery brethren were only cloistered part of the time, so engaged were they in various enterprises, along with charitable work and a hostel, including extensive gardens, craft shops, and a small vineyard, even travel in support of missions abroad.

Stuart held a large moving sale, sold the furniture and house, gathered a few mementoes and clothes in a well-worn suitcase and readied to leave. He visited Dorothy's grave more than once, leaving a large spray of wild flowers. As he drove off in his old car, he smiled mightily through his tears, and pulled over to let the emotions come forth. With all these memories, he would have a full life in retirement, with God at his side.

DONNA

Joe Goldsmith was on his eighth year of prostate center. Since it had been detected, that is. He was only fifty five, so he was an early victim. He'd known he'd probably get it, because his father and all his paternal uncles had, and died from it. Still, after surgery to remove the heavily infected gland, then hormonal therapy when the cancer returned, plus some judicious radiation, he was a survivor. He was able to maintain a fairly normal lifestyle, and continued working in the West Seattle Branch of the Seattle Public Library, commuting by bicycle. Of average height and weight and clean shaven, he kept in shape through his bicycling, and his hair was still brown and just beginning to thin on top. But he was usually tired after work, and went straight home after picking up a few groceries or fresh bread. Joe loved his work, and was loathe to cut back to part-time or quit altogether. His retirement pension would be reduced, and what would he do with his time? Lie around and sleep, watch TV, take his medicine, mope and brood? No way. So he kept at it, checking in books and tapes, setting up the day's newspapers in their wooden rack, answering reference questions and showing people, especially kids, how to use the library.

Joe's home was a small apartment near everything, which also meant near the noise of traffic coming up the hill from Seattle, across Harbor Island and the bay. Full of books he'd collected over the years, his apartment was truly about all he had, along with a nice three-speed bicycle, which he also used to go on errands and get some exercise. For other transportation he utilized Seattle's excellent bus system. He used to have a dog, but Ralph, a cocker spaniel, had been put to sleep a few years before due to some kind of internal blockage. And Joe didn't feel up to taking on another one, so he gave up pets. Cats weren't his preference. Evenings he stayed home alone reading, listening to the TV news or some PBS dramatic or cultural program, pottering around the kitchen, culling out some of his books to sell, or napping. It wasn't a very exciting life, most of the time.

He'd been married or affianced five times, but none of them had stuck. It had become Joe's revolving door of life, these in and out relationships with women. And he'd been 'serious' with every one of them, or so went his versions. But for some reason his women always decided against staying with him, so he'd be left alone again to ponder his lack of success. He was good at the Don Juan part, able to attract and seduce a woman almost any time he wanted to, but for the rest, he was at sixes and sevens, totally inept. His paramour would stare at him. 'What do you want, Joe?' Or, 'Do you love me or don't you?' Or, 'I hardly know you, after all the time we've been together.' And so on. Joe was left with a lengthening row of question marks after his name, and had no idea how to remedy the situation.

From time to time he answered personal ads in the lonely hearts newspapers he picked up at the checkout counters and from sidewalk dispensers. That was one way he met some of his lady friends. He likened it to shopping at the supermarket, but much more chancy! It was easier to pick a raspberry banana yoghurt from among ten or fifteen different yoghurts in the dairy case, because to select a few women to contact from among a hundred delectable and intriguing ads was a dismal game of blind roulette. Still, he had what it took. Luckily, his surgery hadn't impacted his sexual potency, and the hormonal therapy (masking over his testosterone) hadn't affected his libido at all. In fact, he was willing and able to exhaust himself in love-making, which unfortunately turned off some women, who complained that he kept falling asleep on them. But he did so because of the 'edge' he felt, regarding his mortality. 'Seize the time,' he thought, and 'It's now or perhaps never again.'

As for the rest of Joe in any love affair, he was impotence personified. They always saw through him, always seeming to know himself better than he did, always came to distrust him. Eventually they'd hold back, then back off, then bid him Good-bye, Joe, and Good Luck. 'Take care,' was the usual parting phrase. So he'd continue to work the ads, circling the ones to call up, writing phone numbers larger in the margin so he could read them by the phone, as his eyesight wasn't what it used to be. But he'd also go through periods of lassitude and disinterest, especially after a couple of successive failures, when he didn't contact anyone, stayed off the phone, didn't buy those newspapers, and threw out whatever ads he'd accumulated.

One ad had been especially productive, however. A divorced doctor in West Seattle held pot luck dinner parties for six, three men and three women, in his home. They were really nice occasions, with candlelight and China table settings on a white linen tablecloth. Semi-formal dress was the code, so one dressed up a little. The doctor supplied the wine, and the guests, selected by him from the many respondents to his ad, supplied the food. The three men had the pick of three women, and vice versa, and Joe could almost always find someone to follow up with each time. Couples seemed to pair up like that, always one or two per dinner, which was held once a month. Joe became a regular, with the approval of the doctor, who was a rather lascivious guy, and over the course of that year Joe went to bed with four women. That seemed to be the clear aim of these liaisons, to go to bed and 'get it on.' But there was always the yearning too, to find a soul mate. Once in a great while this came close to happening, but usually it was a case of remaining good friends for a week or so, then drifting apart. Joe got tired of this merry-go-round and stopped going.

Then he answered an ad that surprised him. Right away she asked him to come visit her in her apartment, instead of the usual meeting over coffee somewhere 'neutral.' Her name was Donna. He found her address, which was up a staircase over some stores in the center of a shopping area. Her place was one of a half dozen apartments in the small building, against the wall of which electric trolley cables and wires were fastened, and neon commercial lighting garishly colored the world outside her curtained windows at night. He knocked on her door.

She was huge, and later told him she weighed over three hundred pounds. At first he was put off, and felt like apologizing and saying he could only stay for a few minutes, it was too far from his place, he had to go to work early, etc., anything to put an end to it. But she seemed nice enough, so he stayed and made himself at home. Or rather, she made him feel at home. She had a quiet yet cheerful smile, a warm manner, and offered him wine and snacks. She was divorced, she explained, and originally came from Wisconsin, where she had three grown children and an ex-husband, who was ailing. He was sick with something serious, though she supplied few details. So Donna was another divorcee to Joe, lonely and open to free love. With most of his women he always had inhibitions, because he didn't want to offend a prospective conquest. But this Donna was different. She was genuinely interested to know him, and drew him out on every aspect of his life, including those he'd carefully kept hidden from others.

They talked about every sordid, depraved and loner indulgence he'd ever used to fill out his life, and how unsatisfactory it had all been. They even acted out some of his most intimate and outrageous fantasies. From Joe's point of view, in terms of a relationship, it was a dream come true. Here was a woman he could tell and show anything to! He even went so far as to find out how life was with her and what she liked, so it wasn't just one-way. However, she usually demurred showing him her preferences, only listening to his. He gave her something special and she countenanced him in every way. Whatever he said he liked to do, she encouraged him to show and tell, which he did.

As for sex, yes, they had sex too. Only she never took off her gown-like dress, and it didn't last long. It couldn't, because it was difficult due to her bulk. Obviously, it wasn't sex that kept them together. It was the companionship and other kinds of intimacy that they shared so completely. Always before any sexual intimacies, they sat down to a veritable feast supper, with enough food for four or five very hungry men. There was so much food of every kind on her groaning table, as nicely set as if they were newly married, with ironed and folded cloth napkins and always the two candles, that Joe was embarrassed to take relatively small helpings. No matter; Donna smiled and made him feel utterly at home.

This went on for several months, pretty steadily. Their trysts took on the semblance of a courtship, except that they never went out, and always met at her place. She was too embarrassed to go out with him, and only went to work as an assistant accountant at the bank right around the corner. A market across the street supplied her food. But as for going anyplace else, she had a car, but rarely used it because of its age. Joe actually found that he was getting serious about Donna, not to get married, you understand, but just to stay with her and keep their friendship and companionship going. As for Donna, she had other ties in her life, mainly to her family, and especially to her ex-husband, at it turned out.

One evening Donna broke the news. Her ex-husband and the father of her children was seriously ill, and needed her care. She was reluctantly returning to Wisconsin, and her children, all of whom lived nearby. It was a necessary decision, but one that Joe readily understood. Not that he liked it, but he understood. In fact, as he looked back, he sort of expected this might happen. She liked Joe very much, but there were priorities in her life, and he sadly recognized this assertion of them by Donna. She'd kept him up to date on her family's doings, after all, but without ever intimating that she might actually leave Seattle and move back to Wisconsin to take care of her ex-husband, husband, or whoever he was. So to Joe, the whole situation seemed a little far fetched. Didn't she and Joe have something going too, something of value and worth preserving? Well, he had to admit to himself that their relationship wasn't even beginning to approach that of Donna's with her family, and especially with her ex, who now appeared to be her de facto husband, the man she still loved.

So Joe and Donna parted, and soon after she left Seattle. Weeks later he received a letter, then a while later another. She was staying in Wisconsin for good, and her family needed her. Her ex-husband or husband was improving a little, but had relapses. Joe realized it was over, and reverted to his loner ways again. He went out less, and slept more. Then his oncologist said it was time to start chemotherapy. His energy and well-being deteriorated, and after switching to part-time at the library for a year or so, he finally quit. Later on Joe moved to a nursing home, and as an afterthought, so he wouldn't lose her entirely, Joe sent Donna a card telling her of the move, with his new address. One day several months later he received a letter from Donna. Her husband had died, and she asked how he was doing. It was full of affection and care, thanking him for the wonderful times they spent together. She couldn't leave Wisconsin, she said, and knew Joe would understand, and he would always be in her thoughts. Unfortunately, Joe didn't have the strength or will to answer her letter, which, for the rest of his days, he kept carefully hidden close by, either under his pillow or in the drawer of his bedside table.

After Joe died, the nursing home director, mistakenly thinking Donna was his next of kin, sent his few personal effects to her, including her letter. When she received the brown paper bundle tied with string, she opened it and read the director's letter with tears in her eyes. Now she had two men to mourn, the one who fathered and helped raised her children and whom she loved for that, and the man who had warmed her heart while she was alone in Seattle. When she opened her old letter, she found four words laboriously scrawled at the bottom: "Dearest Donna My Love."

THE ULTIMATE CLICK

These days, life with a computer screen in front of me morning and night is supposed to bring me closer and closer to what I need, what I want. Or so they tell me. One morning at predawn I awakened in the midst of a dream and immediately got up to write down what I experienced.

'I'm sitting at my computer. On a map of the United States, I clicked on my home state and it filled the screen. Clicked on the name of my hometown and a street map of it filled the screen, with every building and house shown by a little dark square. Clicked on this one tiny square over here and a familiar house filled the screen. Clicked on the front door and an interior view filled the screen, obviously the attic. Clicked on an old steamer trunk in the shadowy background and it filled the screen. Clicked on the lid and the open trunk could be viewed. Clicked on a cardboard box in one corner, on top of its homely contents, and it filled the screen. Clicked on the box again, and it opened, showing bundles of letters. Clicked on one bundle and the screen showed many letters spread before me. Clicked on one letter and the front of the envelope filled the screen; it was addressed to me, from my stepfather. Clicked on the first page, and I could read the letter, scrolling down. I did so; I read. Then I stopped. I clicked on the full-screen icon, so certain lines would fill the screen, holding my full attention. I read them carefully, word for word, in his inimitable handwriting, broad yet sharp, slanting to the right. Yes, it was true. There it was, in his own words. My stepfather, long dead, really did love me, despite himself. He loved and cared for me; he really did, despite everything. He loved me . . . '

THE PORTRAIT

A third book that made the New York Times Best Seller List! His most recent was based on a trip they'd made on the Trans Mongolian Railroad several years before. It was a long time between successes, and Bernie's sixty-second birthday was nigh. Now here they were, Bernard Renfrew and his wife Melanie, strolling again in Moscow as if they owned the place, luxuriously bedded in the Golden Lion Swiss Diamond Hotel. They took taxis everywhere and expense was not a consideration.

However, Melanie had tired of all the high class touring, personal guides and exclusive dining. She wanted to walk the streets, too, and meet everyday Russians. So one morning after breakfast in the dining room (instead of having breakfast brought to their deluxe suite), they went downstairs to the lobby and walked hand in hand out through the elaborate revolving doors, waiving aside the cabbies' invitations to drive them "anywhere, anywhere at all," always for a stiff price in the newly capitalistic Russia of 2001.

They went to the corner and crossed over Smolenskaya to the famous Arbat, that pedestrian mall that begins alongside the gothic foreign ministry, built in Stalin's time along with six other look-a-likes around Moscow. The Arbat was historically the street on which to see and be seen, full of society folk and nobility showing off their carriages and livery, their finery, and their well-placed guests and friends. Now it was full of restaurants, vendors, street musicians and stage theatres, lining both sides. Artists displayed their work for sale, and portrait artists offered to do "lightning" likenesses for a small fee.

Melanie took Bernie's hand and led him along. She had an idea for his birthday present, namely to sit for one of these half-hour portraits on the Arbat. It would be fun, and a nice souvenir of their trip. She thought her husband deserved one, and even he'd mentioned wishing he could have some kind of portrait done some day.

For Bernie was into longevity, reincarnation and his overall legacy, how he'd be remembered. His books were his main effort, but his thoughts also roamed over other questions. Have I lived a worthwhile life? Will people remember me, and for how long? Will my books be reprinted, and remain available to someone wanting them, 100 or 500 years in the future?

He was certainly realistic enough to realize that his so-called best sellers wouldn't last. That was the most ephemeral kind of publishing, such titles usually being forgotten within ten years or so, at the most. So anything else he could leave behind that said who he was, and showed that he had existed, was worthwhile, wasn't it?

They found a portrait artist whose style they liked, just as he was finishing up with another customer. Bernie was invited to sit down, facing the artist, who wore dark clothes and a bill hat, and had his own chair. At first Bernie directed his gaze at the artist, at a point between and just above his eyes. But the artist motioned for him to look past his left shoulder. So Bernie fixed his gaze on a storefront decal, twenty yards behind the artist. And he kept it there for the next 35-40 minutes. Observers came and went, looking first at Bernie, then at the portrait, which was being done with an oil-based ink of some kind, with a variety of brushes, very precise and delicate, very versatile and adaptable in the results. At times he couldn't see the storefront decal because of the standees, but he could imagine where it was, whether beyond a woman's bosom or a man's jacket, or over the top of a child's head, and kept staring fixedly ahead. He hardly moved. Melanie took a few photos of the event, moving around, and in between times she strolled the Arbat nearby. Observers usually stood briefly and watched, so that once in a while Bernie heard a comment, usually unintelligible, or fragments of stray conversation that he couldn't follow.

At last the artist signaled that he was done. "Awesome!" one of those watching remarked. There were other murmurs of approval. Bernie leaned forward and looked at the artist's work. It was an amazing likeness, even he had to admit that. The artist must have been impressed too, because after Melanie paid him the twenty dollars, he asked to take a photo of him sitting beside the finished portrait. Another observer offered a compliment directly to Bernie, who murmured "Thanks . . ." The artist removed the sketch from his easel board, rolled it up and put a rubber band around it, and Bernie and Melanie began walking back to the hotel. So now, for the first time in his life Bernie had a portrait of himself, not just another photo. It was really an excellent job, quite remarkable in fact, a really sensitively done, true portrait of Melanie's Bernie.

For the remainder of their Russian visit, the portrait was forgotten, rolled up like a scroll in Bernie's airline carry-on bag. But when they returned home to their Central Park West apartment in New York, Melanie insisted they immediately go and have it nicely framed behind glass. She also had plans for it to be hung in a prominent place in their home. At first she declared, quite without consulting Bernie, that it should be in their entrance hall, opposite a large mirror. But Bernie said Absolutely No! so she found another nice spot in their palatial living room, overlooking the park. No, no, said Bernie, I don't want people to see it every time they come visiting. So they finally settled on a corner of their bedroom, where only if one stood in the center of the room could it be seen. And it was comforting for Bernie to know that very few of their guests would ever be in a position to do that. He was satisfied on that point, at least.

For he was bothered by his portrait in other ways. It was too composed, too calm, too fixed. Must he now compare himself to it for the rest of his days, and would it become a standard or idealization of who he was, or, worse yet, the 'gray eminence' of who he might have been, had he striven harder in his life efforts? In sum, the likeness seemed so perfect that he actually felt embarrassed to acknowledge it as his own.

He thought back on the wandering path his life had taken, all the missed opportunities, the lack of resolve at times, when he wanted to give up, and a recurring sense of failure when he felt inadequate to challenges that he should have taken in stride. What would the Portrait Guy say of all this? What was he saying? For at moments he seemed to declare 'This is who you might have been, and who you are not . . . '

Melanie was concerned with Bernie's obsession with the portrait, and they kept talking about it. He even half-seriously suggested they cover it with a curtain of gauze, so its stare would be muted. Melanie thought he was joking, but Bernie wasn't; she might like his portrait, but he was quite uncomfortable with it. Finally it got to the point where they both agreed he should seek counseling, because it had become an issue with them. An appointment was made with a psychologist, a Dr. Mapsley, and to Melanie's surprise Bernie insisted on taking the portrait along with them. It was a matter between Bernie and Portrait Guy, and they both must go into counseling!

The psychologist was surprised to learn that Bernie wanted what he called a 'joint session,' between him and his portrait, with the PhD. sitting in a moderating position between the two. Melanie asked if Bernie wanted her to sit in, to which he replied, 'No! This is a matter between him and me!' He carried the portrait into the inner office, and Dr. Mapsley stepped forward.

"Carl Mapsley, Mr. Renfrew. How are you?"

"Fine."

"So, how should we get started? Is that the portrait?"

"Yes."

"How shall we begin, then?"

"I'd like to set the portrait in a chair between us, so we can both see it."

"Alright." And he brought another chair over and placed it beside Bernie's chair.

"No, I want it opposite me, please, and so we can both see it." Dr. Mapsley placed the portrait on the third chair directly opposite Bernie's chair, about ten feet away. The psychologist then drew his chair up to a point between them.

"Now," stated the doctor, "What seems to be the problem?"

Bernie nodded toward the Portrait Guy. "He's the problem."

"How so? Don't you like it? Seems like an excellent likeness. Very well done."

"That's the whole point, doctor. It's too good. I'm having a hard time with it."

"Oh?"

"I mean, how can I possibly live up to this image of myself! It's too much!"

"And how is it 'too much'? Can you be more specific?"

"He's too perfect, too composed and calm, too confident. I can't take it."

"Meaning. . . ?"

"If that's me, it's unnatural and false. And pretentious."

"But he looks just like you! It's really an excellent likeness."

"Not really. That's not the real me. It's who someone thinks I look like, or should be, and how others see me. I wish he could show the flaws and scars that I feel, or had a twisted mouth, one eye looking strangely, some warts or something. Anything abnormal that would hint at the truth about me."

"In other words, you resent his apparent peace and composure, and his seeming perfection."

They both studied the Portrait Guy's unchanging visage, which seemed to mock all Bernie's complaints. Then the doctor spoke.

"Mr. Renfrew, may I make a suggestion?" He went to his desk and pulled out a black marking pen, and offered it to Bernie.

"Why don't you put a black moustache, a big black handlebar moustache on him? Just make it on the glass." And he handed Bernie the pen.

Bernie smiled nervously. "Why?" he asked. "What would that do?"

"Just try it," invited the doctor. "Bring him down a peg or two!"

Bernie laughed, abruptly rose and went over, and carefully placed a beautiful black moustache with outlandish handlebars right across the still composure of his portrait!

"Wonderful!" exclaimed the doctor. "Now give him a pair of thick horn-rimmed glasses. Yes, that's it!"

Very quickly the Portrait Guy lost all of the pretensions Bernie had ascribed to him. He was now a laughing stock, and Bernie was delighted. He thanked Dr. Mapsley, took the portrait under his arm and joined Melanie in the outer office. He was grinning like an ape and chuckling to himself.

"Look Melanie! I've put him in his place!"

"But Bernie, dear, you've ruined it!"

"No I haven't! I can take it off or put it on, turn him to the wall or simply enjoy his good side, whatever I want. He's mine now, and I can make him any way I want."

"Whatever you say, dear. I'm sure he won't mind if you have a little fun at his expense!" She was relieved, and exchanged a grateful smile and wink with Dr. Mapsley

"I sure hope not, because that's the way it's going to be."

And Bernie and Melanie strode happily arm in arm down the corridor to the elevator, laughing and chuckling all the while.

"OCTAVE LANSING'S CHILDHOOD HOME"

It was a mystery, but one we were interested to learn about, and wanted to see. In our rural part of New York state there are few historical or literary sites that are designated as such, probably because communities usually aren't aware of them, or don't bother to publicize or otherwise take advantage of them once they're discovered. You take the case of Octave Lansing, supposedly an American author from the late 19th century who apparently wrote serialized romances and published a few books of poems, but who was best known for his novel, "The Grace of Our Elms," about rural life in the Genessee River Valley and the little towns thereabouts, like Perry, Avon, West Rush and Garbut. We were living in Rochester at the time, and heard about this literary site, located in a place called East Shale, through a bulletin board notice in our branch library. We made plans to go there the next nice weekend that summer.

Wending our way south, we at last found the little county road that led to East Shale. It wasn't much, but we expected to be surprised at how much this little hamlet had been transformed, to honor the memory and works and life of this Octave Lansing! Maybe we'd learn a little more about local literary history. And such is our inborn American entrepreneurial spirit that it must also bring some income into what would ordinarily remain a lazy backwater, a derelict shadow of town life left over from the 19th century. East Shale still seemed to be a moribund village of less than a thousand population, clinging to the bottom of a narrow valley, with a main street that was about six blocks long and full of old brick buildings with only partially occupied store fronts, including an abandoned textile mill and a leaky, moss covered dam across the creek that flowed parallel to the town's core. First we stopped by the Octave Lansing Visitor's Center to find out more information about him, and perhaps to purchase some of his writings, or biographical and critical materials about him. We've always been interested in learning about authors who've described life in our region, even if they're minor and uncelebrated, and long since forgotten. They had something to say, possibly a vision of local life from long ago, and you can learn more about your roots from such writers.

The small building by the falls was staffed by a couple of older ladies, and they showed us a room in the back that served as a sort of pocket museum on Lansing's early life in East Shale. There were photos displayed all about, some early furniture, cooking utensils and old clothing, and a wicker perambulator, that presumably once carried the little Octave, but we didn't see any copies of his writings. We asked if any of his work was still in print, and were told that there were plans to do so, but as yet none was available. If we'd leave our name and address, we'd be notified when they were. We then left and looked around town, and found the old house that was Lansing's childhood home. Curious to learn more, we stopped at the local library and asked to see any holdings of Lansing's books. There were a few, but none were available at that time, according to the part-time librarian, an older man with a full beard. We decided to draw him out on the subject of Octave Lansing.

"Well, he grew up here, y'know, but moved to Syracuse when he came of age. His parents weren't the kind to settle down here. They moved around."

"So what did his father do?"

"He was a mechanic at the textile mill, as I understand it, but he didn't last long. The times were hard and they had to move on." Our informer seemed uncomfortable with all our questions.

"Where did he write his novel, in Syracuse? We can't find it in the catalog, by the way."

"Oh it's checked out all the time. It's out of print, and people here take it home a lot. Almost impossible to get a copy in hand any more."

"Well, you must have non-circulating copies?"

The old man smiled and fidgeted, apparently searching for some kind of explanation that would satisfy us. I was puzzled by his seeming discomfort with our full and natural curiosity regarding their hometown celebrity. He even seemed amused at our persistence.

"The novel does exist, doesn't it?" I asked, "Where could we find a copy to look at?"

"Oh, it exists alright, but you'll have to go to the State Library in Albany to see a copy. We have a limited number of copies in town and local residents have priority. There's always a waiting list."

"Well, that's certainly odd, because we came down from Rochester to learn more about him, maybe buy some copies of his writings, but you say there's nothing available, not even to look at here?"

"Not right now; maybe later. If you leave your name at the Visitor's Center, they can probably help you."

"We've already done that." I was getting frustrated and impatient. We'd come all the way to East Shale, which wasn't easy to find, and had drawn a blank. Who was this Octave Lansing, anyway? Where were his writings, and his novel? Did he ever write one at all, I began to wonder.

We ate in a nice local restaurant and cruised around town, and bought some colorful homemade aprons and a burl doorstop that my wife wanted. I found some old farming magazines in an antique store that caught my collector's fancy. East Shale was a charming place that summer day, but we had little to show for our quest for the regional author "Octave Lansing," not to mention some sign of his writings and other literary accomplishments. Annoyed at getting what I was beginning to suspect was a runaround, I was determined to somehow find out more, and told my wife I was going to the one bar in town and talk to anyone who might clear up this mystery. The sign outside said simply, "Bar," and I opened the creaking door and stepped in.

No one greeted me as I entered, and when I called out 'Hello?' A middle-aged man with a large potbelly came out from the back.

"Can I help you?" he offered.

"Yeah, I'll have a Miller's, if you have it."

"All I have is Carlings Black Label."

"That's fine." Carlings was a long time brew of our region. As he popped open the bottle and placed it and a glass on the bar, I opened with a question that was intriguing me.

"We're visiting from Rochester. What can you tell us about your hometown author, Octave Lansing? We're having trouble finding any evidence of his writings and books."

The barkeep said nothing at first, then smiled. "You say you're just visiting?" he asked.

"Yes, we came down for the day to learn more about him. We saw a notice in our local library. But where the hell is he? We can't find any of his writings around here at all."

"Well, if you want to know the truth, there isn't much to tell about him." And he started chuckling to himself. "Y'see, about five years ago a few of us decided the town needed something new. We'd heard about these towns like Chittenango, Talcottville, Pleasantville and Sag Harbor, even Albion up west of Rochester, that had famous authors living there at some time or other, and how that brings in the visitors. Well, we had no famous authors or anybody like that in our history, so we decided to create Octave Lansing. Actually there is a sort of novel called "The Grace of Our Elms," but it was never published. That's why you can't find it. Well, technically speaking it was published, but not in the usual way. It's kind of complicated, but I'll try to explain, if you have the time."

"Sure, go ahead." and I slid onto one of the bar stools.

"Back in the 1880s, a group of women here in East Shale decided they wanted to start a subscription library, which turned out to be our first library, but they needed to raise some funds. They decided to collect reminiscences from the founding family elders who were still around, about the early history of these parts. Well, they accumulated quite a lot of material, but didn't know what to do with it, y'know, by way of increasing subscriptions and raising the needed money. At that time, our newspaper publisher, Oscar Lansing, offered to publish it in serial form in his *Chili-*

Shale Bulletin Dispatch, which he did, giving a percentage of newspaper sales toward the ladies' library. And as the series appeared, that created more support too. So we got our library, but as for "The Grace of Our Elms," it never reached a publisher in book form. To tell the truth, it was never intended to. It's full of local lore and gossip about prominent local families. Everybody around here reads it eventually, but it's in loose-leaf form, like a big spiral notebook, and several copies were made, but as far a 'Octave Lansing' is concerned, that's just a concoction to bring in visitors. I don't think anybody outside East Shale would be interested in "The Grace of Our Elms.""

"But why have 'Octave Lansing' around at all?" I asked.

"Well, that was Randy Lansing's idea. He's Oscar's great great grandson, and runs the paper now. He didn't want his dad's actual full name used, since he was behind the first publication of the series, so he made up the first name of Octave, don't ask me how or why. He's an odd duck. It's just a gimmick to bring people down here, and most people think it's ridiculous. Randy sees himself as an idea man around here. Now we have to keep explaining and backfilling and covering his 'Octave Lansing' concoction. 'Octave Lansing's' childhood home is actually Randy's house."

"The librarian seems to be having fun with it. He told me a song and dance about Octave working at the textile mill and then moving to Syracuse." The barkeep laughed.

"But this is supposed to be his "childhood home," not where he lived as an adult! Ed should get his facts straight!"

"Ed?"

"Ed Lewellen. That's the librarian's name. Also one of the oldest families around here. He likes to josh with visitors, especially when it comes to 'Octave Lansing.'" I was fascinated to hear this additional information, and protested to the bartender.

"I think people would be very interested to see that book, "The Grace of Our Elms." It sounds like a local classic."

"It is, but it's also our own. The descendants of the women who put it together don't want to get involved with 'Octave Lansing', and don't want to see their family names become a tourist souvenir either. So we're just leaving it like that. Take it or leave it, we say."

Well, I returned to the car and told my wife what I'd learned. She scolded me for taking so long, but she'd been doing crossword puzzles she brought with her, and even had time for a nap. She agreed that homespun novel or memoir or whatever it was probably deserved better treatment and regard by the locals, but what can you do? There it was, parlayed by a few local boosters into a nonexistent hometown author and fictitious celebrity. They were having fun at our expense! Yet the idea brought people into town now and then, picking up the economy a little. The entrepreneurial spirit was alive and well in East Shale, and the legacy of the oldtime families was remembered, respected and left intact. We would have to be satisfied with their illusory and silly image of 'Octave Lansing,' and fill in the rest for ourselves! We also decided to visit East Shale regularly in the future and get to know some locals better, especially the nice librarian, in the hope that some day, we might just be lucky enough to get our hands on a copy of "The Grace of Our Elms"!

PROFESSOR AND MRS. THOMAS BANDY

Thomas Bandy taught students at a Kansas university for over thirty five years. His main course for graduate students was the History of International Organizations, which was required for those under his tutelage. Other courses he taught were inconsequential or elective for undergraduates, and he had the reputation of being a very boring lecturer. Still, he managed to survive, and the university press published the one book he came up with, which was entitled "A History of International Organizations," and which became the textbook and main reference for his graduate seminars.

Students called him "Stone Face," because his facial expression rarely altered and his close-cropped light brown hair always stayed perfectly groomed, no matter what shenanigans his students perpetrated in his classes. His face was a flat, seamless, pale visage, as if he were two steps from the grave. In lecturing, his gentle twang shifted to and fro without emotion, usually putting a few students to sleep. Yet he knew his subject, and was respected for that. He wasn't a popular lecturer, and had severe standards that he applied to one and all, regardless of the consequences, whether a student was the son of a prominent alumnus or a popular and key football player.

Eventually he was forced into an early retirement by a combination of alumni pressure and a change in administration that wanted to bring in younger and foreign faculty, which would broaden the department's international offerings. Besides, Thomas Bandy hadn't published anything in twenty years, and was too inflexible in his relations with other programs at the university. He had to be pressured to serve on faculty committees, and rarely contributed to discussions that were pivotal for the faculty senate's important role in revamping and modernizing the university's curriculum and admissions policies.

This relegation to retirement proved to be a boon to Thomas Bandy and his wife, Deirdre, who was so plain and quiet as to be in his shadow all the time. Still, she was a loving wife, and they thoroughly enjoyed each other's company. In retirement now, they planned to do a great deal of traveling, something they'd never had time or occasion to do before. They would go to the far corners of the earth and visit the sites of all those ancient civilizations they'd only dreamed or read about over their lifetime.

And so they began, flying or sailing around the world to immerse themselves in India, China, Greece, Meso-America, Iraq, and the Andean civilizations of South America. For years they traveled, rarely spending more than two or three months at home in Kansas between times. Eventually Mrs. Bandy developed arthritis in her hips, and had increasing difficulty keeping up with her husband. She carried a cane and folding chair combination, so she had support in walking and could sit down whenever she became too tired. Her husband began scolding her for being slow in following the tour groups they joined.

"We're lagging behind, dear, we'll have to move along." At this point in his life, Thomas Bandy, former professor and now inveterate traveler, had little patience with the infirmities of others, even those of his faithful wife. So far he was blessed with relatively normal health and energy, and was rather smug about it.

But Deirdre couldn't do it any more without much pain, because she was heavier, and the effort to keep up caused her to sweat and labor uncomfortably, especially in warm climes. Then there came a time when she stayed home while he tried traveling alone once or twice, but that was unsatisfactory for both of them, and they ceased traveling altogether. Now they preferred to stay at home, with their rich travel memories and shelves of albums full of thousands of photographs from around the world. What to do now, confined as they were at home, without children or grandchildren?

They lived in an ample brick house in the university district, but had lost touch with all their old university friends. Some had died, others had moved on, or had retired to places like Florida, Arizona and Hawaii. They wondered what to do with their remaining years. Mrs. Bandy was now a semi-invalid, and required some help from Thomas to get around, make meals, keep up with housekeeping and so on. He wasn't in the best of shape himself any more, either, because his heart was starting to fail, leaving him much weaker than he'd ever been, which was ironic, because in appearance he continued to seem in good health. Eventually, however, his luck ran out, too. He hated to think of being considered physically feeble and senile by others, but that's precisely what happened. His hearing was fading, his speech became slurred, and finally his facial features began sagging and his eyes watered incessantly. His frozen and pale facial expression of many years was finally thawing and collapsing, revealing an irritable, frustrated and self-absorbed Professor Thomas Bandy, long retired and idle. Meanwhile Deirdre stayed pretty much at the same level, and actually became stronger and more capable than her husband, relatively speaking.

They evacuated the second floor of their house, setting up a bedroom in their old dining room downstairs. A ramp was built alongside the front steps, and there came a time when neither of them could drive, so Thomas couldn't leave the house except in a wheel chair, as helped by a neighbor boy. They signed up for regular van service to the market, had hot meals brought to the house once a day, and now and then took the van down to the local senior center when something festive was going on. Thomas had completely lost touch with the university community, as it seemed to have dispensed with him.

One day, there was a knock at the door. Deirdre opened it after a minute or so, just in time to catch a young man almost out to the sidewalk, thinking no one was at home. He was invited in, and they both joined Professor Bandy in their sitting room. The visitor's name was Randy Abelard, he was a third year student at the university, and he had an old copy of "A History of International Organizations." He'd stopped by to ask the professor to autograph it for him.

"Well," said Mr. Bandy, "It's very flattering of you to seek me out. I never thought anyone would remember me." He was quite moved, and became emotional. The medication he'd been taking had the side effect of bringing his emotions out in the open. Deirdre took over for him.

"We've been out of circulation for so long, it's really nice of you to take the trouble to pay us a visit. How did you find us?"

"Oh, Professor Bandy's still listed in the faculty directory, you know, along with all the other retired and emeritus faculty. My instructor in International Relations told me about his book, which I found in "Puss 'n Books," the used book store, and he suggested I come over. Hope you don't mind." Thomas had composed himself, and took over again.

"Well, Randy, it's certainly good of you to go to all this trouble. Deirdre, find a pen for me, will you, and I'll sign it. We don't want to hold him up with our talk."

Randy handed him the book, and Professor Bandy laboriously scrawled his name across the title page.

"There! Is that alright?" Bandy asked.

"Yes, and thanks. We're collecting books written by all faculty members, you know, and getting their autographs whenever we can find them."

"And what will you do with them?" Deirdre queried, suddenly curious.

"Well, the administration's arranging for a display of them in the foyer of the new library. They have display cases that are being set up for it. After that they'll be put in a special collections room in the library."

"Really! We've heard about the new library, but we haven't seen it." Deirdre confessed.

"Would you like to ?" Randy asked.

"Oh yes, but it's so awkward, and we don't know the best time to go there." she added. It was such a monumental chore for them to do anything outside the house.

Randy arranged for them to come down when the display of faculty books was officially opened. There was quite a crowd, and all the university big wigs were there. With Randy's help, Thomas and Deirdre sat near the front of the arranged seating, to hear better. Sure enough, there was a copy of "A History of International Organizations," prominently displayed near the middle of what seemed like hundreds of faculty titles published since the founding of the university. As the speakers stood up and introduced the display, expanding on these faculty contributions, it turned out that Professor Bandy was the oldest faculty author present at the ceremonies, and he was asked to say a few words. Randy took hold of the wheelchair and rolled Professor Bandy up alongside the podium, where a microphone was lowered for his use. Deirdre was so pleased and proud, she pulled a handkerchief from her purse and dabbed her eyes.

"Thank you," began Thomas, in a low, gravelly voice, laden with emotion. "I'm pleased to be here, but I'm not sure what to say. We've been away from the university for so long, did a lot of traveling for a while, and now don't get out much. I'm really at a loss for words; what can I say? It's good to be back, and thanks again."

And he began to weep, his voice breaking when he tried to continue. Randy quickly came to his aid, Deirdre stood up shakily to help, and he was brought back to his place in the audience. The President of the Faculty Senate returned to the podium.

"We all want you to know, Professor Bandy, that we appreciate your many years of lecturing to our undergrads, and your guidance of graduate students. Welcome back!" And with that, a large bouquet of varicolored roses and Baby's Breath was brought to him by a smiling woman staff member.

When they were back home that evening, sitting watching TV together on the couch after a modest supper, Thomas took Deirdre's hand in his and kissed it. She leaned against him, and they both were smiling, through tearing eyes. This was better than any of their far flung travels, his book, his counseling of so many grad students, or his many years of devoted classroom teaching at the university. To still be with Deirdre, this was his supreme good fortune and happiness.

ON SPEAKING UP

At various times during our tour of Russia with an Elderhostel group, certain individuals became prominent, for no particular reason except that some odd or chance circumstance brought them to the fore. One had bad legs and was always last, so we watched over him. Another spoke Russian quite fluently and was always going off by himself, searching for Russians to talk to. Another became our group spokesperson at formal banquets, not because he knew Russian, but because he looked distinguished and could speak extemporaneously and with polish given any pretext. Overall, our group was comprised of retired people, married couples, a few pairs of women, one pair of men who were lifelong friends, and a brother/sister pair. It was this last couple that interested me.

The brother was a recent student of Russian, and let everyone know it, though his fluency was of the beginning student's kind. He knew tourist vocabulary, but his grammar and syntax were very limited, not to mention his familiarity with idioms. Still, he tried on every occasion to improve his use of the language, impressing his sister as well as the rest of us, even though Russians usually had difficulty understanding his needs.

One day at supper we happened to sit at a large round table for eight that included the brother/sister pair, one of our guides, and some of the more sophisticated of our group. As usual, a table conversation began, and then to our collective surprise the brother, whom I'll call Terry, decided to become our table's M.C. for the duration of the meal. He had obviously done some basic reading in Russian history and politics, but so had the rest of us. At any rate he proceeded to parade forth some of these salient and hackneyed facts, much to the boredom and embarrassment of the group. His whole tack was banal as well as self-serving. He was obviously trying his best to impress the group, and failing spectacularly. The more he rattled on and gesticulated, as if regaling us with some kind of intellectual prowess, the more uncomfortable we all became. No one took him up in his forced conversation, and we bowed our heads lower over our supper, busily eating. Finally he told an incredibly lame and puerile joke about the "pearly gates,", and the silence afterward was leaden. No one laughed, and every face was a blank. He became the object of our pity. To be polite and to save him a little, one of the ladies commented briefly on his remarks, and Terry seemed justified and affirmed. Rising to the occasion, he proposed a toast to our Elderhostel tour, which was nearing its end, and mercifully one of the more learned men at table, an experienced traveler and retired psychoanalyst, saved the moment with some generous comments of his own that nicely and generously graced the pathetic display that had gone before.

Throughout the meal I found my own memories being jogged by similar recollections, just as uncomfortable and embarrassing as those wretched moments Terry had endured at our table that evening. I remembered my early years of mortification back in grade and high school, when I was terrified to have to go to the front of the room and give an oral book report, or even to reply to a teacher from my seat. Later, in the colleges and universities I attended, preparing to be a teacher, I took every public speaking course I could. I slowly learned to control my stammering, taking deep breaths and pauses to compose myself, measuring my speech that way, which slowly gave me confidence. I began seeking out more opportunities to build on these new found skills. I joined clubs that I knew had occasion for public speaking. I was a civil rights activist for several years, in the 1960s and early 70s, and found occasion to address large meetings and rallies, even to make street harangues during militant anti-war demonstrations. Through deliberate exercise of my diaphragm and abdominal muscles, I was now able and willing to deliver speeches in an auditorium, a noisy meeting or a dining room full of chatting guests, without any electronic amplification. I was able to project my voice to the farthest corner and highest balcony, just like an oldtime orator, accompanied by dramatic gestures and body movement. Such a skill inflated my ego and swelled my head, tempting the demagogue and poseur in me, making me a public man, as well as feeding my own private demons as a fearless public speaker! Eventually that shy and fearful schoolboy had become a formidable voice, able to dominate any gathering, any audience. And my lectures as a professor became dynamic and popular. After I retired from teaching, though, I really had few opportunities to use it.

Then in middle-age I became interested in amateur theatre, and took a basic acting course. I learned how to refine my voice control still further, but in more subtle and intimate ways, and to suppress most of my self-consciousness in expressing a character's particular emotion as asked for by my acting coach. My fling at theatre was brief and inconsequential, however, for acting is a different art altogether, to which I was unsuited by nature. But it made me more sensitive to how we express ourselves on a smaller, more intimate scale, and I enjoyed the confidence gained in understanding the challenges any actor must experience.

With these musings of my own, I could readily understand and commiserate, if that's the right word, with our friend Terry's situation, what he was trying and hoping to do at our table that evening. In thoughtfulness I wished him well, and we later became friends, as I'd also been a student of the Russian language all my life. This pilgrimage of ours to Mother Russia offered both of us many opportunities to try out our language skills. But as far as telling jokes, I assured him that I could never do that, because long before any punch line I always dissolved in laughter at the peaking humor of it, to the point of choking and tears and emotional helplessness. So he had me there, with his little "pearly gates" joke, which really wasn't that bad!

AUNT ELSIE DONE WRONG
By "Gus" Van Ness

Before I tell you about my Aunt Elsie, let me speak generally. The main event for her was when her husband of twenty-odd years, my Uncle Gene, dumped her in a gratuitous postwar divorce. For purposes of perspective and a broader view, my account warrants a renewed appreciation of the times we've lived in. Our family, which lost no one in World War II, was forced, in the aftermath, to accept this one open wound inflicted on the home front.

I think it's a fair statement that the predominant social history of the United States during the 20th century can be summed up by the disintegration of the family. Contributing to it were five major wars, the vote granted women, followed by gains in legal control over their own affairs, the 1930s Depression, and after World War II, the rise of the youth and drug cults, the minority civil rights struggle and its advances, and the birth control Pill. Women's status became steadily more independent through all these changes, if they so chose, because their life options grew steadily in number, fullness, and equality to those of men. Divorces increased to one half of marriages, and the latter institution became very shaky and less formal. The overall effect of all the above on American society and culture included a fragmentation and ephemeralization of life, and often a trivialization of the relationships between individual men and women, less patience in pursuing them, and sexual promiscuity, both in the old and young. Finally, economic as well as social intercourse was intensified toward the end of the century by automation, computerization (including internet communications), the deregulation and expansion of corporate dominance, and an increasing globalization of the marketplace and financial networks. The introduction of television at the mid-century mark brought a daily, two-dimensional stream of sensational news, dream and fantasy stimuli to viewers, especially the young. As for us older folks, television, compared to radio's few stations (AM only) during the 1940s, became a bullying and domineering, merciless and shameless 'media' presence in our homes.

When one weighs in all these strong influences, it's a wonder that 'normal' life has continued as it has. Of course, not all Americans and their families, and especially women, have experienced the impact of every one of the above factors, but we've all been touched by them in some way. In more conservative small town life and the circumscribed lives of certain ethnic communities, and especially in rural areas and on farms, the old values and roles for men and women have lasted longer and been less affected. Having described the Big Picture, as we used to say, I now turn to Aunt Elsie.

Although, when I think of examples of lives close to me that have been twisted and transformed over the years, several family members come to mind, Aunt Elsie's divorce is among the most memorable. And it's one I've wanted to explore for a long time, because of the ambivalent and compromising nature of her experience, and because I admired her so in my youth, before she had her fall.

One afternoon back in the 1960s I decided to find out how she was doing. I was now living in Seattle, and making visits back home every couple of years. I knocked on the side door of an old house in the lakeside town of Melrose Park, at the north end of Otisco Lake in upstate New York. It was located away from the town center by a mile, without a lake view. I'd been told where she was now living, and wanted to see how she was faring since the divorce over fifteen years earlier. It was an initiative I had taken on my own, because she was now 'not family,' in the eyes of her ex-husband's, namely my mother's family, yet she'd been one of my favorite and dynamic adult relatives as I was growing up. Not that she wasn't visited and invited to Van Ness and Lambert gatherings now and then, but the situation must have been an estrangement for her.

The old-style, solid white door without see-through windows finally opened, and there she was. I recognized her, but barely, because she had changed so. She greeted me, her long lost nephew, while still using the diminutive by which only she and her ex-husband, Uncle Gene, had ever addressed me. I'd spent most of the intervening time away from the home grounds while so much was going on in the family: the deaths of beloved elders, births, graduations, and marriages. Later, I learned what role Uncle Gene had really played in my own life story, while I was yet a toddler. So she and I had things in common now: she'd been separated from our family since her divorce, and I'd deliberately distanced myself from them, for reasons that amount to the other point of this memoir, how I've been affected by my mother's divorce and second marriage to my stepfather, as urged and engineered by Uncle Gene.

She was alone and invited me in. She was thin and subdued, and as I looked around, I was struck by the darkened and cluttered look of her modest apartment. Our conversation seemed forced, and I felt inhibited in not pressing questions on her, and she, for her part, talked only pleasantries, asked how I was doing, and how everyone was. It seemed pained, and I hadn't the heart to say how I really felt. I excused myself soon enough and left, feeling a renewed anger toward Uncle Gene. I had other cousins in Melrose Park, the family of my mother's younger sister, Lucile and her husband Jim Lambert, and found out more from them. Aunt Elsie had found a job in downtown Auburn as a bookkeeper, but more importantly, the Lamberts had not excluded her, and to them she was still family.

During World War II, all three members of Aunt Elsie's small, nuclear family served our country. Uncle Gene volunteered to be a Red Cross Field Director, and was sent to England. Son Jim joined the navy, and served in the Pacific. And Aunt Elsie joined the WACS (Womens Army Corps) and served Stateside, keeping the home fires burning, so to speak, while coordinating correspondence between the three of them, which went halfway around the world. They were far apart for the Duration of the war.

When it ended, Uncle Gene came home to Aunt Elsie, but with a tragic announcement that devastated her, as well as the rest of the family. He wanted a divorce, because while in England he'd met a divorced Scottish woman with two young sons and they'd decided to get married. What could Aunt Elsie do, or say? She was being unceremoniously discarded, and Uncle Gene would have his way. Their son Jim was angry and fed up with his father, but what could he do? Uncle Gene's old habit of getting what he wanted no matter what harm he brought to others was still in place. Our own family was shocked by his decision, and for a long time hardly knew what status to give beloved Aunt Elsie, now that she was done and cast off by my mother's older brother. Uncle Gene returned to England and brought back his new wife. They briefly visited family and friends in Central New York, then moved to Phoenix in the Southwest, where he started what became a very popular family restaurant on the north side. Later, son Jim, who'd married, also moved to Phoenix, probably at the insistent invitation of his father, and started a landscaping business.

How had she felt after her husband said he wanted a divorce? Probably rejected, hurt, angry and thoroughly mortified. What did she have left? There was undoubtedly a money and property settlement, and then she was on her own. Perhaps there was a blessing too, in time, of being free at last of Uncle Gene's selfish ways. She'd kept them together during the war as best she could, but after all it wasn't what he wanted. He wanted out, and perhaps their pre-war relationship had been rather stormy at times. They both had strong personalities. Despite the wartime letters she shunted back and forth, which were received infrequently and at long intervals, with encouragement and reassurance on her part from the 'family center' at Stateside, it had all failed, and was phoney. Uncle Gene had turned away from her, probably from the day he left to serve the Red Cross in England.

So Aunt Elsie fell into eclipse, and, in personal terms, assumed the guise of a cast off and spare soul. She rarely visited us and we saw her less often at family gatherings, because she'd changed as well as aged. I had lost the cheerful, vigorous aunt with the rollicking laugh that I knew and loved as a boy and youth. Before she met Uncle Gene, and while he was courting her, my mother told me she'd been a barnstorming aviatrix in the 1920s, and a very independent young woman. I remember being shown her old leather flying goggles and cap in our attic. I was impressed!

If the Lamberts and their kids did take Aunt Elsie into their fold, was this alienating to my mother, who, ever since she re-married into the wealthy James family of my stepfather and thereby acquired a new Mother and Father (my stepfather's parents, after her own parents died during the Depression years), had become the Gatekeeper and Guardian of both the Van Ness and James family reputations? Apparently not. And did the Lamberts drift apart from us for that reason, because my mother preferred to keep us ignorant of Lambert family doings, so we'd stay separate and uninformed about each other? No, and this untoward assumption originated mostly from my own biased point of view. But from what I know of her tendency in later years, of not keeping us informed of the existence and doings of other relatives in the region, I wouldn't be surprised if she lacked interest in sending me off to go visiting, for she preferred that I stay with her during those rare summer weeks I was back home. Of course, for so many years I was absent too much from our family's home turf that I'm no judge of how things were with everyone, the family relations and such. But few stopped by to see my parents in their cozy country retirement home, after they'd sold the big house we children grew up in, one reason being that my stepfather had come to dislike visiting or being visited. He was a stay-at-home and just wanted to be left alone to potter around the house. Eventually I'd ask where this or that cousin, aunt or uncle were now, and would be minimally told by mother. Surprisingly, most of them lived less than a half hour away, yet it was like pulling teeth to learn their address or phone number. By that time my parents were too cloistered and infirm to enjoy hosting many visitors, whether family or not. And when someone did stop by, they hardly knew how to respond or what to say. They been 'out of the loop' for a long time, and were rather diffident toward the larger life of the younger generation, whose life plans sometimes surprised and confused them.

But my mother and Uncle Gene, her older brother, were always very close, and not only because he became head of their family after their oldest sister and both parents died just before and during the Depression. He was aggressively instrumental in her divorce from my natural father, as I've said, and sent many threatening letters to him and his parents, warning him not to exercise the visitation rights he'd obtained during her completely unexpected divorce action, which shocked and dismayed my dad. He'd entered the job market during the Depression, and was the son of a humble Methodist minister in a little Genesee River Valley town, so when he couldn't find a decent job after college graduation, Uncle Gene decided that he wasn't good enough for my mother's well-connected Van Ness clan. (As a young woman, she'd been a society debutante.) Eventually, and without help from my mother's family, he took his college ROTC commission and was sent to Montana and Mississippi to set up CCC camps for the unemployed. My mother, with me, a babe in arms, declined to join him, and a year later hit him with divorce papers, despite money and letters he regularly sent, pleading with her to come join him. Her grounds were that their "lifestyles were too different." Uncle Gene would have his way again, accompanied by my mother's discriminating preference, to protect her social position as a Van Ness.

After that day, when I visited Aunt Elsie out in pleasant Melrose Park, I never saw her again, except once. My first wife and I were in France, where I was using my GI Bill from army service to attend a French university, and we arranged to meet her coming off a Swedish cruise ship at Ville Franche. Our visit was very brief, less than an hour, and though she was alone on the cruise, she seemed busy and well occupied. Was she able to make a life for herself in Melrose Park and Auburn back home, with her job, the Lamberts' family doings and a circle of friends? Did her son Jim return for occasional visits from Phoenix and Santa Barbara, where he later moved after his divorce, to get away from his father's interfering ways? Undoubtedly. Did she go on more cruises? I wondered about such things a lot, because I felt a growing resentment at how she'd been treated by Uncle Gene, which, from my point of view, was just another of his lifelong, bullying actions.

When Aunt Elsie's health began deteriorating and she could no longer work or get out much, her son Jim brought her to the West Coast to live with him. For those remaining peaceful years on the California coast, I'm sure mother and son shared bitter recollections of her husband, Jim's father. I know Jim had come to despise the man. Correspondence between the two of them and our families back east diminished to naught during her remaining time. She died in Santa Barbara and was buried there. Afterward, my own son took the trouble to go visit Jim, at my urging. He was my teenage idol during and just after the war, and I felt it would be good if they could meet. I think behind my invitation was also a desire to ally myself with Aunt Elsie and Jim one more time, and to draw more distance and anger toward Uncle Gene. A number of years after that, I was told that Jim died of cancer.

Earlier, about the same time I visited Aunt Elsie in Melrose Park in the '60s, I had had an exchange of letters with Uncle Gene. As a civil rights activist all through those years, I remembered what I conceived as his exploitative treatment of Chicano workers in his Phoenix restaurant, where I had worked in my 16th summer. I wrote him a very critical letter condemning his employee policies, and received a defensive and righteous response. Years later, when I heard that he was dying, I wrote again, this time an adulatory letter thanking him for being a good uncle! After he died, his Scottish wife wrote to thank me, because it helped put him at ease in his last days. But I expressed my feelings out of ignorance and misinformation at the time, and it was twenty years later before I learned his true and more complete story, how additionally manipulative and cruel he had been toward my biological father and his Methodist pastoring parents. So should I embrace compassion, and not blame him for things he obviously felt were right to do at the time, and that he meant no harm? I could do that, but at the same time he did do irreparable harm, and he'll always be a part of an array of family-based angers that lingers in my mind.

And so the dispersal of family graves continued: Jim and his mother in Santa Barbara, Uncle Gene and his Scottish wife in Phoenix, Aunt Lucile and my stepfather and mother in Central New York, along with my stepfather's parents, who were my sole grandparents, my own natural father and his wife in a military cemetery in the high desert above Palm Springs, his own parents in Albion, New York, and my own future grave in Hawaii, where I live.

Despite these frustrations and lifelong, troubling memories, which came out later in both anti-social behavior on my part and mandatory institutional therapy that clarified and released my demons, I was content and well cared for in my childhood and youth, and simply stuffed any uncomfortable emotions from teenage on. But I obviously noted well our peculiar family panorama of avoidance, cover-ups and secrecy. Sure, there were all the gifts of life to be experienced, and they were, by me and everyone else. Life goes on, by hook or crook. The Depression and various wars were survived, and everyone carried on as best they could, but increasingly without much extended family stability around us, and hindered by estrangement, dislocation, and broken roots. The silence in the resulting fragmentary households comprised a seed bed for future troubles and recurring heartaches, and a yearning for the oldtime heritage of ancestral family life. The American Dream of individual success and personal fulfillment continues, and we've been a part of it.

THE CHASM, THAT PRIMORDIAL MUD

The one dream image that kept recurring to Vincent was as bizarre and inexplicable as it was persistent. There was this growing sink hole in front of him as he stood on the edge, with a system of dilapidated pipes, yellowish in color, visible amongst all the melting, softening mud below. The earth itself seemed to be losing all shape and stability. And beyond, far to the north of the Arctic slope where he stood, sat the Arctic Ocean itself, icy cold and waiting for the time to come south and drown the chasm. For the void before him was expanding and deepening enormously, by miles across and to his right and left. It always appeared like that, as if alive.

He ordered another beer, his seventh of the morning, and toyed with his glass on the sticky table of dark, venerable wood. After six months of work at Prudhoe Bay up on the Slope, he'd needed another break from the isolation of the oil fields. He'd begun to hallucinate again, and his dreams included other images, just as unnerving. Herds of caribou swarming past him all day and night, grunting and grazing, about to carry him away once they forced him to mount one of their kind; a boar grizzly engulfing his head in its maw and shaking him like a doll, then dragging him off somewhere, yet he felt no pain because he went limp, and welcomed the warmth of his big wet tongue; a great eagle swooping down and hooking his talons into his parka and taking him aloft, to a nest high in the mountains to the south, to be fed tasty carrion like the other eaglets; being borne along on the frigid current of an arctic creek on the back of spawning salmon, crowded so close together that he barely got wet, their twisted snouts and reddening bodies mocking his fear of drowning or worse.

Whence came all these strange imaginings and fates? But the one of the geothermal chasm and deadly pipes down there, that was the most indelible! He couldn't erase the image from his mind: those rickety pipes, now working, now leaning, breaking apart and collapsing, the shiny soft mud all around them, always lowering; the scene wouldn't stop melting and moving, unsettling his world with the nightmare of it.

And yet, every time, he was always standing on a solid brink, a hard shelf of safe if appalling observation. The world out in front of him, the earth's surface away to the north, across the endless tundra, that's what was collapsing, not where he was. Vincent was the witness, the one in contemplation. This gave him a thread of assurance, as he sat there with such reveries, and when his friend Toby finally returned from the toilet, having just vomited all over a commode in the men's room, he actually seemed as composed and thoughtful as a stone sober judge.

The Sourdough Bar and Grill on 4th Avenue in Anchorage had always been their place of refuge and recovery from months on the Slope. They'd hang out for days in the 24 hour place, until they could stand it no longer, then fly back north again to Dead Horse. Toby slipped into the booth and lay his head on his arms. Vincent stared past him out onto the street, seeing nothing much through the doubling, tripling vision of his eyes. Both had reached the limit of 'arctic exploration' and the epitome of 'oil extraction,' and were exhausted. They were no longer human, no longer their own man. They'd become near savages on the loose, stumbling about.

What a change from their early days up there, when they'd eagerly sought work on the Slope, with its high pay, the best accommodations, and generous, periodic leave. Both were inveterate readers, and took full advantage of their off-duty hours to go through the boxes of books each had brought with them to Prudhoe. There, through both summers and winters (there wasn't much of a Spring or Fall), but especially the six-month long darkness of winter, they read and read. Then the two of them got acquainted one night in the company library, and from that point on something strange began happening. Instead of isolating to read alone in their rooms, Vincent and Toby began sharing ideas and dreams. Especially dreams. They even agreed to write down their dream descriptions by keeping a pen and notebook at their bedside, and the next time they met, to recount them to each other for interpretation.

Toby's dreams were about sexual conquests and orgies with women, which contrasted totally with his reading fare, which was in science and mathematics. Vincent's dreams were so strange and haunting as to be equally obsessive and compelling, but in the direction of darkness, the unknown, phobias and the occult. The one thing that additionally brought them together in a common bond was their periodic trips to Anchorage for R & R, and to frequent the strip go-go joints and wild topless bars along 4th Avenue. Not that they had any fraternization with these ladies of the night. No. It was the drinking to oblivion that drove them that way. The naked women dancing around them seemed more sacred than obscene, and any depraved ideas they kept to themselves, mouthing them as the alcohol-induced nether thoughts of Hell.

And in the end, one winter night of 20 below, when both of them wandered down by Cook Inlet and stepped out gingerly onto the shore ice at low tide, which makes dark caverns sixteen feet beneath the crust, they went too far and for too long, repeatedly falling, eventually breaking through into the tidal void, unseen and unheard, their remains never to be found, having become stranded and drowned and entombed in the tidal mud down there, as the flood returned, somewhere south of Anchorage's noisy streets and bright lights, farther still from their demons on the North Slope.

910.4
Hills

Hills, Gordon H.

Cruise Ship Tales and Notes

65,971

JAN 0 2 2011	DATE DUE	

DISCARD

Goff-Nelson Memorial Library
Tupper Lake, NY 12986

Printed in the United States
5018